Theory and history of historiography. Translated from the Italian by Douglas Ainslie

Benedetto Croce

THEORY & HISTORY OF HISTORIOGRAPHY

TRANSLATED FROM THE ITALIAN OF

BENEDETTO CROCE

BY

DOUGLAS AINSLIE

B.A. OXON M.R.A.S.

LONDON

GEORGE G. HARRAP & CO. LTD.

2 & 3 PORTSMOUTH STREET KINGSWAY W.C.

AND AT SYDNEY

First published May 1921

Printed at THE BALLANTYNE PRESS
SPOTTISWOODE, BALLANTYNE & CO. LTD.
Colchester, London & Eton, England

PHILOSOPHY OF THE SPIRIT

IV

THEORY & HISTORY OF HISTORIOGRAPHY

PREFACE

TO THE FIRST ITALIAN EDITION

ALMOST all the writings which compose the present treatise were printed in the proceedings of Italian academies and in Italian reviews between 1912 and 1913. Since they formed part of a general scheme, their collection in book form presented no difficulties. This volume has appeared in German under the title *Zur Theorie und Geschichte der Historiographie* (Tubingen, Mohr, 1915).

On publishing in book form in Italian, I made a few slight alterations here and there and added three brief essays, placed as an appendix to the first part.

The description of the volume as forming the fourth of my *Philosophy of the Spirit* requires some explanation; for it does not really form a new systematic part of the philosophy, and is rather to be looked upon as a deepening and amplification of the theory of historiography, already outlined in certain chapters of the second part, namely the *Logic*. But the problem of historical comprehension is that toward which pointed all my investigations as to the modes of the spirit, their distinction and unity, their truly concrete life, which is development and history, and as to historical thought, which is the self-consciousness of this life. In a certain sense, therefore, this resumption of the treatment of historiography on the completion of the wide circle, this drawing forth of it from the limits of the first treatment of the subject, was the most natural conclusion that could be given to the whole work. The character of ' conclusion ' both explains and justifies the literary form of this last volume, which is more compressed and less didactic than that of the previous volumes.

B. C.

NAPLES: *May* 1916

TRANSLATOR'S NOTE

THE author himself explains the precise connexion of the present work with the other three volumes of the *Philosophy of the Spirit*, to which it now forms the conclusion.

I had not contemplated translating this treatise, when engaged upon the others, for the reason that it was not in existence in its present form, and an external parallel to its position as the last, the late comer of the four masterpieces, is to be found in the fact of its publication by another firm than that which produced the preceding volumes. This diversity in unity will, I am convinced, by no means act as a bar to the dissemination of the original thought contained in its pages, none of which will, I trust, escape the diligent reader through the close meshes of the translation.

The volume is similar in format to the *Logic*, the *Philosophy of the Practical*, and the *Æsthetic*. The last is now out of print, but will reappear translated by me from the definitive fourth Italian edition, greatly exceeding in bulk the previous editions.

The present translation is from the second Italian edition, published in 1919. In this the author made some slight verbal corrections and a few small additions. I have, as always, followed the text with the closest respect.

D. A.

THE ATHENÆUM, LONDON
November 1920

CONTENTS

PART I

THEORY OF HISTORIOGRAPHY

PAGE

I. History and Chronicle 11

II. Pseudo-Histories 27

III. History as History of the Universal. Criticism of 'Universal History' 51

IV. Ideal Genesis and Dissolution of the 'Philosophy of History' 64

V. The Positivity of History 83

VI. The Humanity of History 94

VII. Choice and Periodization 108

VIII. Distinction (Special Histories) and Division 117

IX. The 'History of Nature' and History 128

APPENDICES

I. Attested Evidence 136

II. Analogy and Anomaly of Special Histories 141

III. Philosophy and Methodology 151

PART II

CONCERNING THE HISTORY OF HISTORIOGRAPHY

I. Preliminary Questions 165

II. Græco-Roman Historiography 181

III. Medieval Historiography 200

		PAGE
IV.	The Historiography of the Renaissance	224
V.	The Historiography of the Enlightenment	243
VI.	The Historiography of Romanticism	264
VII.	The Historiography of Positivism	289
VIII.	The New Historiography. Conclusion	309
	Index of Names	315

PART I

THEORY OF HISTORIOGRAPHY

I

HISTORY AND CHRONICLE

I

'CONTEMPORARY history' is wont to be called the history of a passage of time, looked upon as a most recent past, whether it be that of the last fifty years, a decade, a year, a month, a day, or indeed of the last hour or of the last minute. But if we think and speak rigorously, the term 'contemporaneous' can be applied only to that history which comes into being immediately after the act which is being accomplished, as consciousness of that act: it is, for instance, the history that I make of myself while I am in the act of composing these pages; it is the thought of my composition, linked of necessity to the work of composition. 'Contemporary' would be well employed in this case, just because this, like every act of the spirit, is outside time (of the first and after) and is formed 'at the same time' as the act to which it is linked, and from which it is distinguished by means of a distinction not chronological but ideal. 'Non-contemporary history,' 'past history,' would, on the other hand, be that which finds itself in the presence of a history already formed, and which thus comes into being as a criticism of that history, whether it be thousands of years or hardly an hour old.

But if we look more closely, we perceive that this history already formed, which is called or which we would like to call 'non-contemporary' or 'past' history, if it really is history, that is to say, if it mean something and is not an empty echo, is also *contemporary*, and does not in any way differ from the other. As in the former case, the condition of its existence is that the deed of which the history is told must vibrate in the soul of the historian, or (to employ the expression of professed historians) that the documents are before the historian and that they are intelligible. That a narrative or a series of narratives of the fact is united and mingled with it merely means that the fact has proved more rich, not that it has lost its quality of being present: what were narratives or judgments before are now themselves facts, 'documents' to be interpreted and judged. History is never constructed from narratives, but always from documents, or from narratives that have been reduced to documents and treated as such. Thus if contemporary history springs straight from life, so too does that history which is called non-contemporary, for it is evident that only an interest in the life of the present can move one to investigate past fact. Therefore this past fact does not answer to a past interest, but to a present interest, in so far as it is unified with an interest of the present life. This has been said again and again in a hundred ways by historians in their empirical formulas, and constitutes the reason, if not the deeper content, of the success of the very trite saying that history is *magister vitæ*.

I have recalled these forms of historical technique in order to remove the aspect of paradox from the proposition that 'every true history is contemporary history.' But the justice of this proposition is easily confirmed and copiously and perspicuously exemplified in the reality of historiographical work, provided always that we do not fall into the error of taking the works of the historians all together, or certain groups of them confusedly, and of applying them to an abstract man or to ourselves considered abstractly, and of then asking what present interest leads to the writing or reading of such histories: for instance, what is the present interest of the history which recounts the Peloponnesian or the Mithradatic War, of the events connected with Mexican art, or with Arabic philosophy. For me at the present moment they are without interest, and therefore for me at this present moment those histories are not histories, but at the most simply titles of historical works. They have been or will be histories in those that have thought or will think them, and in me too when I have thought or shall think them, re-elaborating them according to my spiritual needs. If, on the other hand, we limit ourselves to real history, to the history that one really thinks in the act of thinking, it will be easily seen that this is perfectly identical with the most personal and contemporary of histories. When the development of the culture of my historical moment presents to me (it would be superfluous and perhaps also inexact to add to myself as an individual) the problem of Greek civilization or of Platonic philosophy or of a particular mode of Attic manners, that problem is related to my being in the same way as the history of a bit of business in which I am engaged, or of a love affair in which I am indulging, or of a danger that threatens me. I examine it with the same anxiety and am troubled with the same sense of unhappiness until I have succeeded in solving it. Hellenic life is on that occasion present in me; it solicits, it attracts and torments me, in the same way as the appearance of the adversary, of the loved one, or of the beloved son for whom one trembles. Thus too it happens or has happened or will happen in the case of the Mithradatic War, of Mexican art, and of all the other things that I have mentioned above by way of example.

Having laid it down that contemporaneity is not the characteristic of a class of histories (as is held with good reason in empirical classifications), but an intrinsic characteristic of every history, we must conceive the relation of history to life as that of *unity*; certainly not in the sense of abstract identity, but of synthetic unity, which implies both the distinction and the unity of the terms. Thus to talk of a history of which the documents are lacking would appear to be as extravagant as to talk of the existence of something as to which it is also affirmed that it is without one of the essential conditions of existence. A history without relation to the document would be an unverifiable history; and since the reality of history lies in this verifiability, and the narrative in which it is given concrete form is historical narrative only in so far as it is a *critical exposition* of the document (intuition and reflection, consciousness and auto-consciousness, etc.), a history of that sort, being without meaning and without truth, would be inexistent as history. How could a history of painting be composed by one who had not seen and enjoyed the works of which he proposed to describe the genesis critically? And how far could anyone understand the works in question who was without the artistic experience assumed by the narrator? How could there be a history of philosophy without the works or at least fragments of the works of the philosophers? How could there be a history of a sentiment or of a custom, for example that of Christian humility or of knightly chivalry, without the capacity for living again, or rather without an actual living again of these particular states of the individual soul?

On the other hand, once the indissoluble link between life and thought in history has been effected, the doubts that have been expressed as to the *certainty* and the *utility* of history disappear altogether in a moment. How could that which is a *present* producing of our spirit ever be *uncertain*? How could that knowledge be *useless* which solves a problem that has come forth from the bosom of *life*?

II

But can the link between document and narrative, between life and history, ever be broken? An affirmative answer to this has been given when referring to those histories of which the documents have been lost, or, to put the case in a more general and fundamental manner, those histories whose documents are no longer alive in the human spirit. And this has also been implied when saying that we all of us in turn find ourselves thus placed with respect to this or that part of history. The history of Hellenic painting is in great part a history without documents for us, as are all histories of peoples concerning whom one does not know exactly where they lived, the thoughts and feelings that they experienced, or the individual appearance of the works that they accomplished; those literatures and philosophies, too, as to which we do not know their theses, or even when we possess these and are able to read them through, yet fail to grasp their intimate spirit, either owing to the lack of complementary knowledge or because of our obstinate temperamental reluctance, or owing to our momentary distraction.

If, in these cases, when that connexion is broken, we can no longer call what remains history (because history was nothing but that connexion), and it can henceforth only be called history in the sense that we call a man the corpse of a man, what remains is not for that reason nothing (not even the corpse is really nothing). Were it nothing, it would be the same as saying that the connexion is indissoluble, because nothingness is never effectual. And if it be not nothing, if it be something, what is narrative without the document?

A history of Hellenic painting, according to the accounts that have been handed down or have been constructed by the learned of our times, when closely inspected, resolves itself into a series of names of painters (Apollodorus, Polygnotus, Zeuxis, Apelles, etc.), surrounded with biographical anecdotes, and into a series of subjects for painting (the burning of Troy, the contest of the Amazons, the battle of Marathon, Achilles, Calumny, etc.), of which certain particulars are given in the descriptions that have reached us; or a graduated series, going from praise to blame, of these painters and their works, together with names, anecdotes, subjects, judgments, arranged more or less chronologically. But the names of painters separated from the direct knowledge of their works are empty names; the anecdotes are empty, as are the descriptions of subjects, the judgment of approval or of disapproval, and the chronological arrangement, because merely arithmetical and lacking real development; and the reason why we do not realize it in thought is that the elements which should constitute it are wanting. If those verbal forms possess any significance, we owe it to what little we know of antique paintings from fragments, from secondary works that have come down to us in copies, or in analogous works in the other arts, or in poetry. With the exception, however, of that little, the history of Hellenic art is, as such, a tissue of empty words.

We can, if we like, say that it is 'empty of determinate content,' because we do not deny that when we pronounce the name of a painter we think of some painter, and indeed of a painter who is an Athenian, and that when we utter the word 'battle,' or 'Helen,' we think of a battle, indeed of a battle of hoplites, or of a beautiful woman, similar to those familiar to us in Hellenic sculpture. But we can think indifferently of any one of the numerous facts that those names recall. For this reason their content is indeterminate, and this indetermination of content is their emptiness.

All histories separated from their living documents resemble these examples and are empty narratives, and since they are empty they are without truth. Is it true or not that there existed a painter named Polygnotus and that he painted a portrait of Miltiades in the Pœcile? We shall be told that it is true, because one person or several people, who knew him and saw the work in question, bear witness to its existence. But we must reply that it was true for this or that witness, and that for us it is neither true nor false, or (which comes to the same thing) that it is true only on the evidence of those witnesses—that is to say, for an extrinsic reason, whereas truth always requires intrinsic reasons. And since that proposition is not true (neither true nor false), it is not useful either, because where there is nothing the king loses his rights, and where the elements of a problem are wanting the effective will and the effective need to solve it are also wanting, along with the possibility of its solution. Thus to quote those empty judgments is quite useless for our actual lives. Life is a present, and that history which has become an empty narration is a past: it is an irrevocable past, if not absolutely so, *καθ' αὑτό*, then certainly for the present moment.

The empty words remain, and the empty words are sounds, or the graphic signs which represent them, and they hold together and maintain themselves, not by an act of thought that thinks them (in which case they would soon be filled), but by an act of will, which thinks it useful for certain ends of its own to preserve those words, however empty or half empty they may be. Mere narrative, then, is nothing but a complex of empty words or formulas asserted by an act of the will.

Now with this definition we have succeeded in giving neither more nor less than the true distinction, hitherto sought in vain, between *history* and *chronicle*. It has been sought in vain, because it has generally been sought in a difference in the *quality* of the facts which each difference took as its object. Thus, for instance, the record of *individual* facts has been attributed to chronicle, to history that of *general* facts; to chronicle the record of *private*, to history that of *public* facts: as though the general were not always individual and the individual general, and the public were not always also private and the private public! Or else the record of *important* facts (memorable things) has been attributed to history, to chronicle that of the *unimportant*: as though the importance of facts were not relative to the situation in which we find ourselves, and as though for a man annoyed by a mosquito the evolutions of the minute insect were not of greater importance than the expedition of Xerxes! Certainly, we are sensible of a just sentiment in these fallacious distinctions—namely, that of placing the difference between history and chronicle in the conception of what *interests* and of what does not *interest* (the general interests and not the particular, the great interests and not the little, etc.). A just sentiment is also to be noted in other considerations that are wont to be adduced, such as the close bond between events that there is in history and the *disconnectedness* that appears on the other hand in chronicle, the *logical* order of the first, the purely *chronological* order of the second, the penetration of the first into the *core* of events and the limitation of the second to the superficial or *external*, and the like. But the differential character is here rather metaphorized than thought, and when metaphors are not employed as simple forms expressive of thought we lose a moment after what has just been gained. The truth is that chronicle and history are not distinguishable as two forms of history, mutually complementary, or as one subordinate to the other, but as two different spiritual *attitudes*. History is living chronicle, chronicle is dead history; history is contemporary history, chronicle is past history; history is principally an act of thought, chronicle an act of will. Every history becomes chronicle when it is no longer thought, but only recorded in abstract words, which were once upon a time concrete and expressive. The history of philosophy even is chronicle, when written or read by those who do not understand philosophy: history would even be what we are now disposed to read as chronicle, as when, for instance, the monk of Monte Cassino notes: 1001. *Beatus Dominicus migravit ad Christum.* 1002. *Hoc anno venerunt Saraceni super Capuam.* 1004. *Terremotus ingens hunc montem exagitavit*, etc.; for those facts were present to him when he wept over the death of the departed Dominic, or was terrified by the natural human scourges that convulsed his native land, seeing the hand of God in that succession of events. This does not prevent that history from assuming the form of chronicle when that same monk of Monte Cassino wrote down cold formulas, without representing to himself or thinking their content, with the sole intention of not allowing those memories to be lost and of handing them down to those who should inhabit Monte Cassino after him.

But the discovery of the real distinction between chronicle and history, which is a formal distinction (that is to say, a truly real distinction), not only frees us from the sterile and fatiguing search after material distinctions (that is to say, imaginary distinctions), but it also enables us to reject a very common presupposition—namely, that of the *priority* of chronicle in respect to history. *Primo annales* [chronicles] *fuere, post historiæ factæ sunt*, the saying of the old grammarian, Mario Vittorino, has been repeated, generalized, and universalized. But precisely the opposite of this is the outcome of the inquiry into the character and therefore into the genesis of the two operations or attitudes : *first comes history, then chronicle.* First comes the living being, then the corpse; and to make history the child of chronicle is the same thing as to make the living be born from the corpse, which is the residue of life, as chronicle is the residue of history.

III

History, separated from the living document and turned into chronicle, is no longer a spiritual act, but a thing, a complex of sounds and of other signs. But the document also, when separated from life, is nothing but a thing like another, a complex of sounds or of other signs—for example, the sounds and the letters in which a law was once communicated; the lines cut into a block of marble, which manifested a religious sentiment by means of the figure of a god; a heap of bones, which were at one time the expression of a man or of an animal.

Do such things as empty narratives and dead documents exist? In a certain sense, no, because external things do not exist outside the spirit; and we already know that chronicle, as empty narrative, exists in so far as the spirit produces it and holds it firmly with an act of will (and it may be opportune to observe once more that such an act carries always with it a new act of consciousness and of thought): with an act of will, which abstracts the sound from the thought, in which dwelt the certainty and concreteness of the sound. In the same way, these dead documents exist to the extent that they are the manifestations of a new life, as the lifeless corpse is really itself also a process of vital creation, although it appears to be one of decomposition and something dead in respect of a particular form of life. But in the same way as those empty sounds, which once contained the thought of a history, are eventually called *narratives*, in memory of the thought they contained, thus do those manifestations of a new life continue to be looked upon as remnants of the life that preceded them and is indeed extinguished.

Now observe how, by means of this string of deductions, we have put ourselves into the position of being able to account for the partition of historical *sources* into *narratives* and *documents*, as we find it among some of our modern methodologists, or, as it is also formulated, into *traditions* and *residues* or *remains* (*Überbleibsel*, *Überreste*). This partition is irrational from the empirical point of view, and may be of use as indicating the inopportunity of the introduction of a speculative thought into empiricism. It is so irrational that one immediately runs against the difficulty of not being able to distinguish what one wished to distinguish. An empty 'narrative' considered as a thing is tantamount to any other thing whatever which is called a 'document.' And, on the other hand, if we maintain the distinction we incur the further difficulty of having to base our historical construction upon two different orders of data (one foot on the bank and the other in the river)—that is to say, we shall have to recur to two parallel instances, one of which is perpetually referring us back to the other. And when we seek to determine the relation of the two kinds of sources with a view to avoiding the inconvenient parallelism, what happens is this: either the relation is stated to depend upon the superiority of the one over the other, and the distinction vanishes, because the superior form absorbs into itself and annuls the inferior form; or a third term is established, in which the two forms are supposed to become united with a distinction: but this is another way of declaring them to be inexistent in that abstractness. For this reason it does not seem to me to be without significance that the partition of accounts and documents should not have been adopted by the most empirical of the methodologists. They do not involve themselves in these subtleties, but content themselves with grouping the historical sources into those that are *written* and those that are *represented*, or in other similar ways. In Germany, however, Droysen availed himself of these distinctions between narratives and documents, traditions, etc., in his valuable *Elements of Historicism* (he had strong leanings toward philosophy), and they have been employed also by other methodologists, who are hybrid empiricists, 'systematists,' or 'pedants,' as they are looked upon in our Latin countries. This is due to the copious philosophical traditions of Germany. The pedantry certainly exists, and it is to be found just in that inopportune philosophy. But what an excellent thing is that pedantry and the contradictions which it entails, how it arouses the mind from its empirical slumbers and makes it see that in place of supposed things there are in reality spiritual acts, where the terms of an irreconcilable dualism were supposed to be in conflict, relation and unity, on the contrary, prevail! The partition of the sources into narratives and documents, and the superiority attributed to documents over narratives, and the alleged necessity of narrative as a subordinate but ineradicable element, almost form a mythology or allegory, which represents in an imaginative manner the relation between life and thought, between document and criticism in historical thought.

And document and criticism, life and thought, are the true *sources* of history—that is to say, the two elements of historical synthesis; and as such, they do not stand face to face with history, or face to face with the synthesis, in the same way as fountains are represented as being face to face with those who go to them with a pail, but they form part of history itself, they are within the synthesis, they form a constituent part of it and are constituted by it. Hence the idea of a history with its sources outside itself is another fancy to be dispelled, together with that of history being the opposite of chronicle. The two erroneous fancies converge to form one. Sources, in the extrinsic sense of the empiricists, like things, are equally with chronicle, which is a class of those things, not anterior but posterior to history. History would indeed be in a fix if it expected to be born of what comes after it, to be born of external things! Thing, not thought, is born of thing: a history derived from things would be a thing—that is to say, just the inexistent of which we were talking a moment ago.

But there must be a reason why chronicle as well as documents seems to precede history and to be its extrinsic source. The human spirit preserves the mortal remains of history, empty narratives and chronicles, and the same spirit collects the traces of past life, remains and documents, striving as far as possible to preserve them unchanged and to restore them as they deteriorate. What is the object of these acts of will which go to the preservation of what is empty and dead? Perhaps illusion or foolishness, which preserves a little while the worn-out elements of mortality on the confines of Dis by means of the erection of mausoleums and sepulchres? But sepulchres are not foolishness and illusion; they are, on the contrary, an act of morality, by which is affirmed the immortality of the work done by individuals. Although dead, they live in our memory and will live in the memory of times to come. And that collecting of dead documents and writing down of empty histories is an act of life which serves life. The moment will come when they will serve to reproduce past history, enriched and made present to our spirit.

For dead history revives, and past history again becomes present, as the development of life demands them. The Romans and the Greeks lay in their sepulchres, until awakened at the Renaissance by the new maturity of the European spirit. The primitive forms of civilization, so gross and so barbaric, lay forgotten, or but little regarded, or misunderstood, until that new phase of the European spirit, which was known as Romanticism or Restoration, 'sympathized' with them—that is to say, recognized them as its own proper present interest. Thus great tracts of history which are now chronicle for us, many documents now mute, will in their turn be traversed with new flashes of life and will speak again.

These revivals have altogether interior motives, and no wealth of documents or of narratives will bring them about; indeed, it is they themselves that copiously collect and place before themselves the documents and narratives, which without them would remain scattered and inert. And it will be impossible ever to understand anything of the effective process of historical thought unless we start from the principle that the spirit itself is history, maker of history at every moment of its existence, and also the result of all anterior history. Thus the spirit bears with it all its history, which coincides with itself. To forget one aspect of history and to remember another one is nothing but the rhythm of the life of the spirit, which operates by determining and individualizing itself, and by always rendering indeterminate and disindividualizing previous determinations and individualizations, in order to create others more copious. The spirit, so to speak, lives again its own history without those external things called narratives and documents; but those external things are instruments that it makes for itself, acts preparatory to that internal vital evocation in whose process they are resolved. The spirit asserts and jealously preserves 'records of the past' for that purpose.

What we all of us do at every moment when we note dates and other matters concerning our private affairs (chronicles) in our pocket-books, or when we place in their little caskets ribbons and dried flowers (I beg to be allowed to select these pleasant images, when giving instances of the collection of 'documents'), is done on a large scale by a certain class of workers called *philologists*, as though at the invitation of the whole of society. They are specially known as the *erudite* when they collect evidence and narrations, as *archæologists* and *archivists* when they collect documents and monuments, as the places where such objects are kept (the "silent white abodes of the dead") are called libraries, archives, and museums. Can there be any ill-feeling against these men of erudition, these archivists and archæologists, who fulfil a necessary and therefore a useful and important function? The fact remains that there is a tendency to mock at them and to regard them with compassion. It is true enough that they sometimes afford a hold for derision with their ingenuous belief that they have history under lock and key and are able to unlock the 'sources' at which thirsty humanity may quench its desire for knowledge; but we know that history is in all of us and that its sources are in our own breasts. For it is in our own breasts alone that is to be found that crucible in which the *certain* is converted into the *true*, and *philology*, joining with *philosophy*, produces *history*.

II

PSEUDO-HISTORIES

I

HISTORY, chronicle, and philology, of which we have seen the origin, are series of mental forms, which, although distinct from one another, must all of them be looked upon as physiological—that is to say, true and rational. But logical sequence now leads me from physiology to pathology—to those forms that are not forms but deformations, not true but erroneous, not rational but irrational.

The ingenuous belief cherished by the philologists that they have history locked up in their libraries, museums, and archives (something in the same manner as the genius of the *Arabian Nights*, who was shut up in a small vase in the form of compressed smoke) does not remain inactive, and gives rise to the idea of a history constructed with things, traditions, and documents (empty traditions and dead documents), and this affords an instance of what may be called *philological* history. I say the idea and not the reality, because it is simply impossible to compose a history with external things, whatever efforts may be made and whatever trouble be taken. Chronicles that have been weeded, chopped up into fragments, recombined, rearranged, always remain nevertheless chronicles—that is to say, empty narratives ; and documents that have been restored, reproduced, described, brought into line, remain documents—that is to say, silent things. Philological history consists of the pouring out of one or more books into a new book. This operation bears an appropriate name in current language and is known as 'compilation.' These compilations are frequently convenient, because they save the trouble of having recourse to several books at the same time; but they do not contain any historical thought. Modern chronological philologists regard medieval chroniclers and the old Italian historians (from Machiavelli and Guicciardini down to Giannone) with a feeling of superiority. These writers 'transcribed,' as they called it, their 'sources' in the parts of their books that are devoted to narrative —that is to say, chronicle. Yet they themselves do not and cannot behave otherwise, because when history is being composed from 'sources' as external things there is never anything else to do but to transcribe the sources. Transcription is varied by sometimes summarizing and sometimes altering the words, and this is sometimes a question of good taste and sometimes a literary pretence; it is also a verifying of quotations, which is sometimes a proof of loyalty and exactitude, sometimes a make-believe and a making oneself believe that the feet are planted firmly on the earth, on the soil of truth, believed to be narrative and quotation from the document. How very many of such philological historians there are in our time, especially since the so-called 'philological method' has been exaggerated—that is to say, a one-sided value has been attributed to it! These histories have indeed a dignified and scientific appearance, but unfortunately *fehlt leider! das geistige Band*, the spiritual tie is wanting. They really consist at bottom of nothing but learned or very learned 'chronicles,' sometimes of use for purposes of consultation, but lacking words that nourish and keep warm the minds and souls of men.

Nevertheless, since we have demonstrated that philological history really presents chronicles and documents and not histories, it might be asked upon what possible ground do we accuse it of irrationality and error, seeing that we have regarded the formation of chronicles, the collection of documents, and all the care that is expended upon them as most rational? But error never lies in the fact, but only in the 'claim' or 'idea' that accompanies the fact. And in this case the idea or claim is that which has been defined above as properly belonging to philological history—namely, that of composing histories with documents and narratives. This claim can be said to exercise a rational function also, to the extent that it lays down the claim, though without satisfying it, that history should go beyond the mere chronicle or document. But in so far as it makes the claim, without itself fulfilling it, this mode of history must be characterized as contradictory and absurd.

And since the claim is absurd, philological history remains without truth as being that which, like chronicle, has not got truth within it, but derives it from the authority to which it appeals. It will be claimed for philology that it tests authorities and selects those most worthy of faith. But without dwelling upon the fact that chronicle also, and chronicle of the crudest, most ignorant and credulous sort, proceeded in a like manner by testing and selecting those authorities which seemed to it to be the most worthy of faith, it is always a question of faith (that is to say, of the thought of others and of thought belonging to the past) and not of criticism (that is to say, of our own thought in the act), of verisimilitude and not of that certainty which is truth. Hence philological history can certainly be *correct*, but not *true* (*richtig* and not *wahr*). And as it is without truth, so is it without true historical interest—that is to say, it sheds no light upon an order of facts answering to a practical and ethical want ; it may embrace any matter indifferently, however remote it be from the practical and ethical soul of the compiler. Thus, as a pure philologist, I enjoy the free choice of indifference, and the history of Italy for the last half-century has the same value for me as that of the Chinese dynasty of the Tsin. I shall turn from one to the other, moved, no doubt, by a certain interest, but by an extra-historical interest, of the sort formed in the special circle of philology.

This procedure, which is without truth and without passion, and is proper to philological history, explains the marked contrast so constantly renewed between the philological historians and historians properly so called. These latter, intent as they are upon the solution of vital problems, grow impatient to find themselves offered in reply the frigid products of philology, or become angry at the persistent assertion that such is history, and that it must be treated in such a spirit and with such methods. Perhaps the finest explosion of such a feeling of anger and annoyance is to be found in the *Letters on the Study of History* (1751) of Bolingbroke, in which erudition is treated as neither more nor less than sumptuous ignorance, and learned disquisitions upon ancient or primitive history are admitted at the most as resembling those 'eccentric preludes' which precede concerts and aid in setting the instruments in tune and that can only be mistaken for harmony by some one without ear, just in the same way as only he who is without historic sense can confuse those exhibitions of erudition with true history. As an antithesis to them he suggests as an ideal a kind of 'political maps,' for the use of the intellect and not of the memory, indicating the *Storie fiorentine* of Machiavelli and the *Trattato dei benefici* of Fra Paolo as writings that approach that ideal. Finally he maintains that for true and living history we should not go beyond the beginning of the sixteenth century, beyond Charles V and Henry VIII, when the political and social history of Europe first appeared—a system which still persisted at the beginning of the eighteenth century. He then proceeds to paint a picture of those two centuries of history, for the use, not of the curious and the erudite, but of politicians. No one, I think, would wish to deny the just sentiment for history which animates these demands, set forth in so vivacious a manner. Bolingbroke, however, did not rise, nor was it possible for him to rise, to the conception of the death and rebirth of every history (which is the rigorously speculative concept of 'actual' and 'contemporary' history), owing to the conditions of culture of his time, nor did he suspect that primitive barbaric history, which he threw into a corner as useless dead leaves, would reappear quite fresh half a century later, as the result of the reaction against intellectualism and Jacobinism, and that this reaction would have as one of its principal promoters a publicist of his own country, Burke, nor indeed that it had already reappeared in his own time in a corner of Italy, in the mind and soul of Giambattista Vico. I shall not adduce further instances of the conflict between effective and philological historians, after this conspicuous one of Bolingbroke, because it is exceedingly well known, and the strife is resumed under our very eyes at every moment. I shall only add that it is certainly deplorable (though altogether natural, because blows are not measured in a struggle) that the polemic against the 'philologists' should have been transferred so as to include also the philologues pure and simple. For these latter, the poor learned ones, archivists and archæologists, are harmless, beneficent little souls. If they should be destroyed, as is sometimes prophesied in the heat of controversy, the fertility of the spiritual field would be not only diminished, but ruined altogether, and we should be obliged to promote to the utmost of our power the reintroduction of those coefficients of our culture, very much in the same way as is said to have been the case with French agriculture after the improvident harrying of the harmless and beneficent wasps which went on for several years.

Whatever of justified or justifiable is to be found in the statements as to the *uncertainty* and *uselessness* of history is also due to the revolt of the pure historic sense against philological history. This is to be assumed from observing that even the most radical of those opponents (Fontenelle, Volney, Delfico, etc.) end by admitting or demanding some form of history as not useless or uncertain, or not altogether useless and uncertain, and from the fact that all their shafts are directed against philological history and that founded upon authority, of which the only appropriate definition is that of Rousseau (in the *Émile*), as *l'art de choisir, entre plusieurs mensonges, celui qui ressemble mieux à la vérité.*

In all other respects—that is to say, as regards the part due to sensational and naturalistic assumptions—historical scepticism contradicts itself here, like every form of scepticism, for the natural sciences themselves, thus raised to the rank of model, are founded upon perceptions, observations, and experiments—that is to say, upon facts historically ascertained—and the 'sensations,' upon which the whole truth of knowledge is based, are not themselves knowledge, save to the extent that they assume the form of affirmations—that is to say, in so far as they are history.

But the truth is that philological history, like every other sort of error, does not fall before the enemy's attack, but rather solely from internal causes, and it is its own professors that destroy it, when they conceive of it as without connexion with life, as merely a learned *exercise* (note the many histories that are treatments of scholastic themes, undertaken with a view to training in the art of research, interpretation, and exposition, and the many others that are continuations of this direction outside the school and are due to tendency there imparted), and when they themselves evince uncertainty, surrounding every statement that they make with *doubts*. The distinction between *criticism* and *hypercriticism* has been drawn with a view to arresting this spontaneous dissolution of historical philology; thus we find the former praised and allowed, while the latter is blamed and forbidden. But the distinction is one of the customary sort, by means of which lack of intelligence disguised as love of moderation contrives to chip off the edges from the antitheses that it fails to solve. Hypercriticism is the prosecution of criticism; it is criticism itself, and to divide criticism into a more and a less, and to admit the less and deny the more, is extravagant, to say the least of it. No 'authorities' are certain while others are uncertain, but all are uncertain, varying in uncertainty in an extrinsic and conjectural manner. Who can guarantee himself against the false statement made by the usually diligent and trustworthy witness in a moment of distraction or of passion? A sixteenth-century inscription, still to be read in one of the old byways of Naples, wisely prays God (and historical philologists should pray to Him fervently every morning) to deliver us now and for ever from *the lies of honest men*. Thus historians who push criticism to the point of so-called hyper-criticism perform a most instructive philosophical duty when they render the whole of such work vain, and therefore fit to be called by the title of Sanchez's work *Quod nihil scitur*. I recollect the remark made to me when I was occupied with research work in my young days by a friend of but slight literary knowledge, to whom I had lent a very critical, indeed hypercritical, history of ancient Rome. When he had finished reading it he returned the book to me, remarking that he had acquired the proud conviction of being "the most learned of philologists," because the latter arrive at the conclusion that they know nothing as the result of exhausting toil, while he knew nothing without any effort at all, simply as a generous gift of nature.[1]

II

The consequence of this spontaneous dissolution of philological history should be the negation of history claimed to have been written with the aid of narratives and documents conceived as external things, and the consignment of these to their proper lower place as mere aids to historical knowledge, as it determines and redetermines itself in the development of the spirit. But if such consequences are distasteful and the project is persevered in of thus writing history in spite of repeated failures, the further problem then presents itself as to how the cold indifference of philological history and its

[1] See Appendix I

intrinsic uncertainty can be healed without changing those presumptions. The problem, itself fallacious, can receive but a fallacious solution, expressed by the substitution of the interest of *sentiment* for the lack of interest of thought and of *æsthetic* coherence of representation for the logical coherence here unobtainable. The new erroneous form of history thus obtained is *poetical history*.

Numerous examples of this kind of history are afforded by the affectionate biographies of persons much beloved and venerated and by the satirical biographies of the detested; patriotic histories which vaunt the glory and lament the misadventures of the people to which the author belongs and with which he sympathizes, and those that shed a sinister light upon the enemy people, adversary of his own ; universal history, illuminated with the ideals of liberalism or humanitarianism, that composed by a socialist, depicting the acts, as Marx said, of the "cavalier of the sorry countenance," in other words of the capitalist, that of the anti-Semite, who shows the Jew to be everywhere the source of human misfortune and of human turpitude and the persecution of the Jew to be the acme of human splendour and happiness. Nor is poetical history exhausted with this fundamental and general description of love and hate (love that is hate and hate that is love), for it passes through all the most intricate forms, the fine gradations of sentiment. Thus we have poetical histories which are amorous, melancholy, nostalgic, pessimistic, resigned, confident, cheerful, and as many other sorts as one can imagine. Herodotus celebrates the romance of the jealousies of the gods, Livy the epos of Roman virtue, Tacitus composes horrible tragedies, Elizabethan dramas in sculptural Latin prose. If we turn to the most modern among the moderns, we find Droysen giving expression to his lyrical aspiration toward the strong centralized state in his history of Macedonia, that Prussia of Hellas; Grote to his aspirations toward democratic institutions, as symbolized in Athens; Mommsen to those directed toward empire, as symbolized in Cæsar; Balbo pouring forth all his ardours for Latin independence, employing for that purpose all the records of Latin battles and beginning with nothing less than those between the Itali and Etrusci against the Pelasgi; Thierry celebrating the middle class in the history of the Third Estate represented by Jacques Bonhomme; the Goncourts writing voluptuous fiction round the figures of Mme de Pompadour, of Mme Du Barry, of Marie Antoinette, more careful of the material and cut of garments than of thoughts; and, finally, De Barante, in his history of the Dukes of Burgundy, having his eye upon knights and ladies, arms and love.

It may seem that the indifference of philological history is thus truly conquered and historical material dominated by a principle and criterion of *values*. This is the demand persistently addressed to history from all sides in our day by methodologists and philosophers. But I have avoided the word 'value' hitherto, owing to its equivocal meaning, apt to deceive many. For since history is history of the spirit, and since spirit is value, and indeed the only value that is possible to conceive, that history is clearly always history of values; and since the spirit becomes transparent to itself as thought in the consciousness of the historian, the value that rules the writing of history is the value of thought. But precisely for this reason its principle of determination cannot be the value known as the value of 'sentiment,' which is life and not thought, and when this life finds expression and representation, before it has been dominated by thought, we have poetry, not history. In order to turn poetical biography into truly historical biography we must repress our loves, our tears, our scorn, and seek what function the individual has fulfilled in social activity or civilization; and we must do the same for national history as for that of humanity, and for every group of facts, small or great, as for every order of events. We must supersede—that is to say, transform—values of *sentiment* with values of *thought*. If we do not find ourselves able to rise to this 'subjectivity' of thought, we shall produce poetry and not history: the historical problem will remain intact, or, rather, it will not yet have come into being, but will do so when the requisite conditions are present. The interest that stirs us in the former case is not that of life which becomes thought, but of life which becomes intuition and imagination.

And since we have entered the domain of poetry, while the historical problem remains beyond, erudition or philology, from which we seem to have started, remains something on this side—that is to say, is altogether surpassed. In philological history, notwithstanding the claims made by it, chronicles and documents persist in their crude natural and undigested state. But these are profoundly changed in poetical history; or, to speak with greater accuracy, they are simply dissolved. Let us ignore the case (common enough) of the historian who, with a view to obtaining artistic effects, intentionally mingles his inventions with the data provided by the chronicles and documents, endeavouring to make them pass for history—that is to say, he renders himself guilty of a lie and is the cause of confusion. But the alteration that is continuous and inherent to historiography consists of the choice and connexion of the details themselves, selected from the 'sources,' rather owing to motives of sentiment than of thought. This, closely considered, is really an invention or imagining of the facts ; the new connexion becomes concrete in a newly imagined fact. And since the data that are taken from the 'sources' do not always lend themselves with docility to the required connexion, it is considered permissible to *solliciter doucement les textes* (as, if I am not mistaken, Renan, one of the historian-poets, remarked) and to add imaginary particulars, though in a conjectural form, to the actual data. Vossius blamed those Grecian historians, and historians of other nations, who, when they invent fables, *ad effugiendam vanitatis notam satis fore putant si addant solemne suum 'aiunt,' 'fertur,' vel aliquid quod tantundem valeat.* But even in our own day it would be diverting and instructive to catalogue the forms of insinuation employed by historians who pass for being most weighty, with a view to introducing their own personal imaginings : 'perhaps,' 'it would seem,' 'one would say,' 'it is pleasant to think,' 'we may infer,' 'it is probable,' 'it is evident,' and the like ; and to note how they sometimes come to omit these warnings and recount things that they have themselves imagined as though they had seen them, in order to complete their picture, regarding which they would be much embarrassed if some one, indiscreet as an *enfant terrible*, should chance to ask them: "How do you know it ?" "Who told you this ?" Recourse has been had to the methodological theory of "imagination necessary for the historian who does not wish to become a mere chronicler," to an imagination, that is to say, which shall be reconstructive and integrating; or, as is also said, to "the necessity of integrating the historical datum with our personal psychology or psychological knowledge." This theory, similar to that of value in history, also contains an equivocation. For doubtless imagination is indispensable to the historian: empty criticism, empty narrative, the concept without intuition or imagination, are altogether sterile; and this has been said and said again in these pages, when we have demanded the vivid experience of the events whose history we have undertaken to relate, which also means their re-elaboration as intuition and imagination. Without this imaginative reconstruction or integration it is not possible to write history, or to read it, or to understand it. But this sort of imagination, which is really quite indispensable to the historian, is the imagination that is inseparable from the historical synthesis, the imagination in and for thought, the concreteness of thought, which is never an abstract concept, but always a relation and a judgment, not indetermination but determination. It is nevertheless to be radically distinguished from the free poetic imagination, dear to those historians who see and hear the face and the voice of Jesus on the Lake of Tiberias, or follow Heraclitus on his daily walks among the hills of Ephesus, or repeat again the secret colloquies between Francis of Assisi and the sweet Umbrian countryside.

Here too we shall be asked of what error, then, we can accuse poetical history, if it be poetry (a necessary form of the spirit and one of the dearest to the heart of man) and not history. But here also we must reply—in manner analogous to our reply in the case of philological history—that the error does not lie in what is done, but in what is claimed to be done: not in creating poetry, but in calling histories that are poetry *poetical histories*, which is a contradiction in terms. So far am I from entertaining the thought of objecting to poetry woven out of historical data that I wish to affirm that a great part of pure poetry, especially in modern times, is to be found in books that are called histories. The epic, for instance, did not, as is believed, die in the nineteenth century, but it is not to be found in the 'epic poems' of Botta, of Bagnoli, of Bellini, or of Bandettini, where it is sought by short-sighted classifiers of literature, but in narratives of the history of the Risorgimento, where are poured forth epic, drama, satire, idyll, elegy, and as many other 'kinds of poetry' as may be desired. The historiography of the Risorgimento is in great part a poetical historiography, rich in legends which still await the historian, or have met with him only occasionally and by chance, exactly like ancient or medieval epic, which, if it were really poetry, was yet believed by its hearers, and often perhaps by its composers themselves, to be history. And I claim for others and for myself the right to imagine history as dictated by my personal feeling; to imagine, for instance, an Italy as fair as a beloved woman, as dear as the tenderest of mothers, as austere as a venerated ancestress, to seek out her doings through the centuries and even to prophesy her future, and to create for myself in history idols of hatred and of love, to embellish yet more the charming, if I will, and to make the unpleasant yet more unpleasant. I claim to seek out every memory and every particular, the expressions of countenance, the gestures, the garments, the dwellings, every kind of insignificant particular (insignificant for others or in other respects, but not for me at that moment), almost physically to approach my friends and my mistresses, of both of which I possess a fine circle or harem in history. But it remains evident that when I or others have the intention of writing history, true history and not poetical history, we shall clear away myths and idols, friends and mistresses, devoting our attention solely to the problem of history, which is spirit or value (or if less philosophical and more colloquial terms be preferred, culture, civilization, progress), and we shall look upon them with the two eyes and the single sight of thought. And when some one, in that sphere or at that altitude, begins to talk to us of the sentiments that but a short while ago were tumultuous in our breasts, we shall listen to him as to one who talks of things that are henceforth distant and dead, in which we no longer participate, because the only sentiment that now fills our soul is the sentiment of truth, the search for historical truth.

III

With poetical history—that is to say, with the falling back of history into a form ideally anterior, that of poetry—the cycle of erroneous forms of history (or of erroneous theoretical forms) is complete. But my discourse would not perhaps be complete were I to remain silent as to a so-called form of history which had great importance in antiquity when it developed its own theory. It continues to have some importance in our own day, although now inclined to conceal its face, to change its garments, and to disguise itself. This is the history known in antiquity as *oratory* or *rhetoric*. Its object was to teach philosophy by example, to incite to virtuous conduct, to impart instruction as to the best political and military institutions, or simply to delight, according to the various intentions of the rhetoricians. And even in our own day this type of history is demanded and supplied not only in the elementary schools (where it seems to be understood that the bitter of wisdom should be imbibed by youth mingled with the sweet of fable), but among grown men. It is closely linked up with politics, where it is a question of politics, or with religion, philosophy, morality, and the like, where they are concerned, or with diversions, as in the case of anecdotes, of strange events, of scandalous and terrifying histories. But can this, I ask, be considered, I do not say history, but an erroneous (theoretical) form of history? The structure of rhetorical history presupposes a *history that already exists*, or at least a poetical history, narrated with a *practical end*. The end would be to induce an emotion leading to virtue, to remorse, to shame, or to enthusiasm; or perhaps to provide repose for the soul, such as is supplied by games; or to introduce into the mind a historical, philosophical, or scientific truth (*movere*, *delectare*, *docere*, or in whatever way it may be decided to classify these ends); but it will always be an end—that is to say, a practical act, which avails itself of the telling of the history as a means or as one of its means. Hence rhetorical history (which would be more correctly termed *practicistical* history) is composed of two elements, history and the practical end, converging into one, which is the practical act. For this reason one cannot attack it, but only its theory, which is the already mentioned theory, so celebrated in antiquity, of history as *opus oratorium*, as *φιλοσοφία ἐκ παραδειγμάτων*, as *ἀποδεικτική*, as *νίκης γύμνασμα* (if warlike), or *γνώμης παίδευμα* (if political), or as evocative of *ἡδονή*, and the like. This doctrine is altogether analogous to the hedonistic and pedagogic doctrine relating to poetry which at that time dominated. It was believed possible to assign an end to poetry, whereas an *extrinsic end* was assigned to it, and poetry was thus passed over without being touched. Practicistical history (which, however, is not history) is exempt from censure as a practical act: each one of us is not content with inquiring into history, but also acts, and in acting can quite well avail himself of the re-evocation of this or that image, with a view to stimulating his own work, or (which comes to the same thing) the work of others. He can, indeed, read and re-read all the books that have from time to time been of assistance to him, as Cato the younger had recourse to reading the *Phædo* in order to prepare himself for suicide, while others have prepared themselves for it by reading *Werther*, *Ortis*, or the poems of Leopardi. From the time of the Renaissance to the eighteenth century, many others prepared themselves for conspiracies and tyrannicides by reading Plutarch, and so much was this the case that one of them, the youthful Boscoli, when condemned to death for a conspiracy against the Medici, remarked in his last hour to Della Robbia (who recounts the incident), "Get Brutus out of my head!"—Brutus, not, that is to say, the history of Brutus that he had read and thought about, but that by which he had been fascinated and urged on to commit the crime. For the rest, true and proper history is not that Brutus which procreated the modern Bruti with their daggers, but Brutus as thought and situated in the world of thought.

One might be induced to assign a special place to the history now known as biased, because, on the one hand, it seems that it is not a simple history of sentiment and poetry, since it has an end to attain, and on the other because such end is not imposed upon it from without, but coincides with the conception of history itself. Hence it would seem fitting to look upon it as a form of history standing half-way between poetry and practicism, a mixture of the two. But mixed forms and hybrid products exist only in the fictitious classifications of empiricists, never in the reality of the spirit, and biased history, when closely examined, is really either poetical history or practicistical history. An exception must always be made of the books in which the two moments are sometimes to be found side by side, as indeed one usually finds true history and chronicle and the document and philological and poetical history side by side. What gives the illusion of a mingling or of a special form of history is the fact that many take their point of departure from poetical inspiration (love of country, faith in their country, enthusiasm for a great man, and so on) and end with practical calculations: they begin with poetry and end with the allegations of the special pleader, and sometimes, although more rarely, they follow an opposite course. This duplication is to be observed in the numerous histories of parties that have been composed since the world was a world, and it is not difficult to discover in what parts of them we have manifestations of poetry and in what parts of calculation. Good taste and criticism are continually effecting this separation for history, as for art and poetry in general.

It is true that good taste loves and accepts poetry and discriminates between the practical intentions of the poet and those of the historian-poet; but those intentions are received and admitted by the moral conscience, provided always that they are good intentions and consequently good actions; and although people are disposed to speak ill of advocates in general, it is certain that the honest advocate and the prudent orator cannot be dispensed with in social life. Nor has so-called practicistical history ever been dispensed with, either according to the Græco-Roman practice, which was that of proposing portraits of statesmen, of captains, and of heroic women as models for the soul, or according to that of the Middle Ages, which was to repeat the lives of saints and hermits of the desert, or of knights strong of arm and of unshakable faith, or in our own modern world, which recommends as edifying and stimulating reading the lives and 'legends' of inventors, of business men, of explorers, and of millionaires. Educative histories, composed with the view of promoting definite practical or moral dispositions, really exist, and every Italian knows how great were the effects of Colletta's and Balbo's histories and the like during the period of the Risorgimento, and everyone knows books that have 'inspired' him or inculcated in him the love of his own country, of his town and steeple.

This moral efficacy, which belongs to morality and not to history, has had so strong a hold upon the mind that the prejudice still survives of assigning a moral function to history (as also to poetry) in the field of teaching. This prejudice is still to be found inspiring even Labriola's pedagogic essay on *The Teaching of History*. But if we mean by the word 'history' both history that is thought as well as that which, on the contrary, is poetry, philology, or moral will, it is clear that 'history' will enter the educational process not under one form alone, but under all these forms. But as history proper it will only enter it under one of them, which is not that of moral education, exclusively or abstractly considered, but of the education or development of thought.

IV

Much is said, now even more than formerly, of the necessity of a 'reform of history,' but to me there does not seem to be anything to reform. Nothing to reform, in the sense attributed to such a demand—namely, that of moulding a *new form of history* or of creating for the first time *true history.* History is, has been, and always will be the same, what we have called living history, history that is (ideally) contemporary ; and chronicle, philological history, poetical history, and (let us call it history nevertheless) practicistical history are, have been, and always will be the same. Those who undertake the task of creating a new history always succeed in setting up philological history against poetical history, or poetical history against philological history, or contemporary history against both of them, and so on. Unless, indeed, as is the case with Buckle and the many tiresome sociologists and positivists of the last ten years, they lament with great pomposity and no less lack of intelligence as to what history is that it lacks the capacity of observation and of experiment (that is to say, the naturalistic abstraction of observation and experiment), boasting that they 'reduce history to natural science'—that is to say, by the employment of a circle, as vicious as it is grotesque, to a mental form which is its pale derivative.

In another sense, everything is certainly to be reformed in history, and history is at every moment labouring to render herself perfect—that is to say, is enriching herself and probing more deeply into herself. There is no history that completely satisfies us, because any construction of ours generates new facts and new problems and solicits new solutions. Thus the history of Rome, of Greece, and of Christianity, of the Reformation, of the French Revolution, of philosophy, of literature, and of any other subject is always being told afresh and always differently. But history reforms herself, remaining herself always, and the strength of her development lies precisely in thus enduring.

The demand for radical or abstract reform also cannot be given that other meaning of a reform of the 'idea of history,' of the discovery that is to be made or is finally made of the *true concept* of history. At all periods the distinction has to some extent been made between histories that are histories and those others that are works of imagination or chronicles. This could be demonstrated from the observations met with at all times among historians and methodologists, and from the confessions that even the most confused of them involuntarily let fall. It is also to be inferred with certainty from the nature itself of the human spirit, although the words in which those distinctions are expressed have not been written or are not preserved. And such a concept and distinction are renewed at every moment by history itself, which becomes ever more copious, more profound. This is to be looked upon as certain, and is for that matter made evident by the history of historiography, which has certainly accomplished some progress since the days of Diogenes of Halicarnassus and of Cicero to those of Hegel and of Humboldt. Other problems have been formed in our own day, some of which I attempt to solve in this book. I am well aware that it affords solutions only to some among the many, and especially that it does not solve (simply because it cannot) those that are not yet formed, but which will inevitably be formed in the future.

In any case it will be thought that the clearness

acquired by the historical consciousness as to the nature of its own work will at least avail to destroy the erroneous forms of history, that since we have shown that philological history or chronicle is not history, and that poetical history is poetry and not history, the 'facts' that correspond to those beliefs must disappear, or become ever more limited in extension, to the point of disappearing altogether in a near or distant future, as catapults have disappeared before guns and as we see carriages disappearing before automobiles.

And this would be truly possible were these erroneous forms to become concrete in 'facts,' were they not, as I have said above, mere 'claims.' If error and evil were a fact, humanity would have long ago abolished it—that is to say, superseded it, in the same way as it has superseded slavery and serfdom and the method of simple barter and so many other things that were facts, that is to say, its own transitory forms. But error (and evil, which is one with it) is not a fact; it does not possess empirical existence; it is nothing but the negative or dialectical moment of the spirit, necessary for the concreteness of the positive moment, for the reality of the spirit. For this reason it is eternal and indestructible, and to destroy it by abstraction (since it cannot be done by thought) is equivalent to imagining the death of the spirit, as confirmed in the saying that abstraction is death.

And without occupying further space with the exposition of a doctrine that would entail too wide a digression,[1] I shall observe that a glance at the history of history proves the salutary nature of error, which is not a Caliban, but rather an Ariel, who breathes everywhere, calling forth and exciting, but can never be grasped as a

[1] See *Logic as Science of Pure Concept*.—D. A.

solid thing. And with a view to seeking examples only in those general forms that have been hitherto examined, polemical and tendencious historiography is certainly to be termed error. This prevailed during the period of the énlightenment, and reduced history to a pleading against priests and tyrants. But who would have wished simply to return from this to the learned and apathetic history of the Benedictines and of the other authors of folios? The polemic and its direction expressed the need for living history, though not in an altogether satisfactory form, and this need was followed by the creation of a new historiography during the period of romanticism. The type of merely philological history, promulgated in Germany after 1820, and afterward disseminated throughout Europe, was also certainly error; but it was likewise an instrument of liberation from the more or less fantastic and arbitrary histories improvised by the philosophers. But who would wish to turn back from them to the 'philosophies of history'? The type of history, sometimes tendencious, but more often poetical, which followed in the wake of the national Italian movement, was also error —that is to say, it led to the loss of historical calm. But that poetical consciousness which surpassed itself when laying claim to historical truth was bound sooner or later to generate (as had been the case on a larger cale in the eighteenth century) a history linked with he interests of life without becoming servile and llowing itself to be led away by the phantoms of love nd hate suggested by them. Further examples could e adduced, but the example of examples is that which appens within each of us when we are dealing with istorical material. We see our sympathies and antiathies arise in turn as we proceed (our poetical history), our intentions as practical men (our rhetorical history), our chroniclistical memories (our philological history); we mentally supersede these forms in turn, and in doing so find ourselves in possession of a new and more profound historical truth. Thus does history affirm itself, distinguishing itself from non-histories and conquering the dialectical moments which arise from these. It was for this reason that I said that there is never *anything of anything* to reform in the *abstract*, but *everything of everything* in the *concrete*.

III

HISTORY AS HISTORY OF THE UNIVERSAL CRITICISM OF 'UNIVERSAL HISTORY'

I

RETURNING from this dialectical round to the concept of history as 'contemporary history,' a new doubt assails and torments us. For if the proof given has freed that concept from one of the most insistent forms of historical scepticism (the scepticism that arises from the lack of reliability of 'testimony'), it does not seem that it has been freed or ever can be freed from that other form of scepticism, more properly termed 'agnosticism,' which does not absolutely deny the truth of history, but denies to it *complete* truth. But in ultimate analysis this is to deny to it real knowledge, because unsound knowledge, half knowledge, also reduces the vigour of the part that it asserts to be known. It is, however, commonly asserted that only a part of history, a very small part, is known to us : a faint glimmer which renders yet more sensible the vast gloom that surrounds our knowledge on all sides.

In truth, what do we know of the origins of Rome or of the Greek states, and of the people who preceded the Greek and Roman civilizations in those countries, notwithstanding all the researches of the learned ? And if a fragment of the life of these people does remain to us, how uncertain is its interpretation! If some tradition has been handed down to us, how poor, confused, and contradictory it is! And we know still less of the people who preceded those people, of the immigrations from Asia and Africa into Europe or inversely, and of relations with other countries beyond the ocean, even with the Atlantis of the myths. And the monogenesis or polygenesis of the human race is a desperate head-splitter, open to all conjectures. The appearance upon the earth of the *genus homo* is open to vain conjectures, as is his affinity or relationship to the animals. The history of the earth, of the solar system, of the whole cosmos, is lost in the obscurity of its origin. But obscurity does not dwell alone among the 'origins': the whole of history, even that of modern Europe which is nearest to us, is obscure. Who can really say what motives determined a Danton or a Robespierre, a Napoleon or an Alexander of Russia? And how numerous are the obscurities and the lacunæ that relate to the acts themselves—that is to say, to their externalization! Mountains of books have been written upon the days of September, upon the eighteenth of Brumaire, upon the burning of Moscow; but who can tell how these things really happened? Even those who were direct witnesses are not able to say, for they have handed down to us diverse and conflicting narratives. But let us leave great history. Will it not at least be possible for us to know a little history completely, we will not say that of our country, of our town, or of our family, but the least little history of any one of ourselves, what he really wanted when (many years ago or yesterday) he abandoned himself to this or that motive of passion and uttered this or that word; how he reached this or that particular conclusion or decided upon some particular course of action; whether the motives that urged him in a particular direction were lofty or base, moral or egoistic, inspired by duty or by vanity, pure or impure

It is enough to make one lose one's head, as those scrupulous people are aware, who the more they attempt to perfect their examination of conscience the more they are confused. No other counsel can be offered to them than that of examining themselves certainly, but not overmuch, of looking rather ahead than behind, or only looking behind to the extent that it is necessary to look. We certainly know our own history and that of the world that surrounds us, but how little and how meagrely in comparison with our infinite desire for knowledge!

The best way of ending this vexation of spirit is that which I have followed, that of pushing it to its extreme limit, and then of imagining for a moment that all the interrogations mentioned, together with the infinite others that could be mentioned, have been satisfied; satisfied as interrogations that continued to the infinite can be satisfied—that is to say, by affording an immediate answer to them, one after the other, and by causing the spirit to enter the path of a vertiginous process of satisfactions, always obtained to the infinite. Now, were all those interrogations satisfactorily answered, were we in possession of all the answers to them, what should we do? The road of progress to the infinite is as wide as that to hell, and if it does not lead to hell it certainly leads to the madhouse. And that infinite, which grows bigger the moment we first touch it, does not avail us; indeed it fills us with fear. Only the poor finite assists us, the determined, the concrete, which is grasped by thought and which lends itself as base for our existence and as point of departure for our action. Thus even were all the particular infinities of infinite history offered for the gratification of our desire, there would be nothing else left for us to do but to clear our minds of them, to *forget* them, and to concentrate upon that particular point alone which corresponds to a problem and constitutes living, active history, *contemporary history.*

And this is what the spirit in its development accomplishes, because there is no fact that is not known at the moment of its being done, by means of the consciousness that germinates perpetually upon action; and there is no fact that is not forgotten sooner or later, but may be recalled, as we remarked when speaking of dead history revived at the touch of life, of the past that by means of the contemporaneous becomes again contemporaneous. Tolstoi got this thought fixed in his mind: not only is no one, not even a Napoleon, able to predetermine with exactitude the happenings of a battle, but no one can know how it really did happen, because on the very evening of its ending an artificial, legendary history appears, which only a credulous spirit could mistake for real history; yet it is upon this that professional historians work, integrating or tempering imagination with imagination. But the battle is known as it gradually develops, and then as the turmoil that it causes is dissipated, so too is dissipated the turmoil of that consciousness, and the only thing of importance is the actuality of the new situation and the new disposition of soul that has been produced, expressed in poetical legends or availing itself of artificial fictions. And each one of us at every moment knows and forgets the majority of his thoughts and acts (what a misfortune it would be if he did not do so, for his life would be a tiresome computation of his smallest movements !); but he does not forget, and preserves for a greater or less time, those thoughts and sentiments which represent memorable crises and problems relating to his future. Sometimes we assist with astonishment at the awakening in us of sentiments and thoughts that we had believed to be irrevocable. Thus it must be said that we know at every moment all the history that we need to know; and since what remains over does not matter to us, we do not possess the means of knowing it, or we shall possess it when the need arises. That 'remaining' history is the eternal phantom of the 'thing in itself,' which is neither 'thing' nor 'in itself,' but only the imaginative projection of the infinity of our action and of our knowledge.

The imaginative projection of the thing in itself, with the agnosticism that is its result, is caused in philosophy by the natural sciences, which posit a reality made extrinsic and material and therefore unintelligible. Chroniclism also occasions historical agnosticism in an analogous manner at the naturalistic moment of history, for it posits a dead and unintelligible history. Allowing itself to be seduced by this allurement it strays from the path of concrete truth, while the soul feels itself suddenly filled with infinite questions, most vain and desperate. In like manner, he who strays from or has not yet entered the fruitful path of a diligent life, feels his soul full to overflowing of infinite desires, of actions that cannot be realized, of pleasures out of reach, and consequently suffers the pains of a Tantalus. But the wisdom of life warns us not to lose ourselves in *absurd desires*, as the wisdom of thought warns us not to lose ourselves in *problems that are vain*.

II

But if we cannot know anything but the finite and the particular, always indeed only *this* particular and *this* finite, must we then renounce (a dolorous renunciation !)

knowledge of *universal history*? Without doubt, but with the double corollary that we are renouncing what we have never possessed, because we could not possess it, and that in consequence such renunciation is not at all painful.

'Universal history,' too, is not a concrete act or fact, but a 'claim,' and a claim due to chroniclism and to its 'thing in itself,' and to the strange proposal of closing the infinite progression, which had been improperly opened, by means of progress to the infinite. Universal history really tries to form a picture of all the things that have happened to the human race, from its origins upon the earth to the present moment. Indeed, it claims to do this from the origin of things, or the creation, to the end of the world, since it would not otherwise be truly universal. Hence its tendency to fill the abysses of prehistory and of the origins with theological or naturalistic fictions and to trace somehow the future, either with revelations and prophecies, as in Christian universal history (which went as far as Antichrist and the Last Judgment), or with previsions, as in the universal histories of positivism, democratism, and socialism.

Such was its claim, but the result turns out to be different from the intention, and it gets what it can —that is to say, a chronicle that is always more or less of a mixture, or a poetical history expressing some aspiration of the heart of man, or a true and proper history, which is not universal, but *particular*, although it embraces the lives of many peoples and of many times. Most frequently these different elements are to be discerned side by side in the same literary composition. Omitting chronicles more or less wide in scope (though always narrow), poetical histories, and the various contaminations of several different forms, we immediately perceive, not as a result of logical deduction alone, but with a simple glance at any one of the 'universal histories,' that 'universal histories,' in so far as they are histories, or in that part of them in which they are histories, resolve themselves into nothing else but 'particular histories'—that is to say, they are due to a particular interest centred in a particular problem, and comprehend only those facts that form part of that interest and afford an answer to that particular problem. For antiquity the example of the work of Polybius should suffice for all, since it was he who most vigorously insisted upon the need for a 'universal history' (*καθολικὴ ἱστορία, ἡ τῶν καθόλου πραγμάτων σύνταξις*). For the Christian period we may cite the *Civitas Dei* of Augustine, and for modern times the *Philosophy of History* of Hegel (he also called it universal history, or *philosophische Weltgeschichte*). But we observe here that the universal history which Polybius desired and created was that more vast, more complex, more political, and graver history which Roman hegemony and the formation of the Roman world required, and therefore that it embraced only those peoples which came into relation and conflict with Rome, and limited itself almost altogether to the history of political institutions and of military dispositions, according to the spiritual tendencies of the author. Augustine, in his turn, attempted to render intelligible the penetration of Paganism by Christianity, and with this object in view he made use of the idea of two enemy cities, the terrestrial and the celestial, of which the first was sometimes the adversary of and sometimes preparatory to the second. Finally, Hegel treated the same problem in his universal history as in his particular history of philosophy—that is to say, the manner in which the spirit of a philosophy of servitude to nature, or to the transcendental God, has elevated itself to the consciousness of liberty. He cut out prehistory from the philosophy of history, as he had cut it out from the history of philosophy, and considered Oriental history very summarily, since it did not offer much of interest to the prosecution of his design.

Naturalistic or cosmological romances will always be composed by those who feel inspired to write them, and they will always find eager and appreciative readers, especially among the lazy, who are pleased to possess the 'secret of the world' in a few pages. And more or less vast compilations will always be made of the histories of the East and the West, of the Americas and Africa and Oceania. The strength of a single individual does not suffice for these, even as regards their compilation, so we now find groups of learned men or compilers associated in that object (as though to give ocular evidence of the absence of all intimate connexion). We have even seen recently certain attempts at universal histories arranged on geographical principles, like so many histories set side by side—European, Asiatic, African, and so on—which insensibly assume the form of a historical dictionary. And this or that particular history can always usefully take the name of a 'universal history,' in the old sense of Polybius—that is to say, as opposed to books that are less actual, less serious, and less satisfactory, the books of those 'writers of particular things' (*οἱ τὰς ἐπὶ μέρους γράφοντες πράξεις*) who are led to make little things great (*τὰ μικρὰ μεγάλα ποιεῖν*) and to indulge in lengthy anecdotes unworthy of being recorded (*περὶ τῶν μηδὲ μνήμης ἀξίων*), and that owing to the lack of a criterion (*δι'* ἀκρισίαν). In this sense, those times and peoples whose politico-social development had produced, as it were, a narrowing of the historical circle would be well advised to break away from minute details and to envisage 'universal history'—that is to say, a vaster history, which lies beyond particular histories. This applies in particular to our Italy, which, since it had a universalistic function at the time of the Renaissance, had universal vision, and told the history of all the peoples in its own way, and then limited itself to local history, then again elevated itself to national history, and should now, even more than in the past, extend itself over the vast fields of the history of all times past and present. But the word 'universal,' which has value for the ends above mentioned, will never designate the possession of a 'universal history,' in the sense that we have refused to it. Such a history disappears in the world of illusions, together with similar Utopias, such, for instance, as the art that should serve as model for all times, or universal justice valid for all time.

III

But in the same way that by the dissipation of the illusion of universal art and of universal justice the intrinsically universal character of particular art and of particular justice is not cancelled (of the *Iliad* or of the constitution of the Roman family), to negate universal history does not mean to negate the universal in history. Here, too, must be repeated what was said of the vain search for God throughout the infinite series of the finite and found at every point of it : *Und du bist ganz vor mir!* That particular and that finite is determined, in its particularity and finitude, by thought, and therefore known together with the universal, the universal in that particular form. The merely finite and particular does not exist save as an abstraction. There is no abstract finite in poetry and in art itself, which is the reign of the individual; but there is the ingenuous finite, which is the undistinguished unity of finite and infinite, which will be distinguished in the sphere of thought and will in that way attain to a more lofty form of unity. And history is thought, and, as such, thought of the universal, of the universal in its concreteness, and therefore always determined in a particular manner. There is no fact, however small it be, that can be otherwise conceived (realized and qualified) than as universal. In its most simple form—that is to say, in its essential form—history expresses itself with judgments, inseparable syntheses of individual and universal. And the individual is called the *subject* of the judgment, the universal the *predicate*, by old terminological tradition, which it will perhaps be convenient to preserve. But for him who dominates words with thought, the *true subject* of history is just the *predicate*, and the *true predicate* the *subject*—that is to say, the universal is determined in the judgment by individualizing it. If this argument seems too abstruse and amounts to a philosophical subtlety, it may be rendered obvious and altogether different from a private possession of those known as philosophers by means of the simple observation that everyone who reflects, upon being asked what is the subject of the history of poetry, will certainly not reply Dante or Shakespeare, or Italian or English poetry, or the series of poems that are known to us, but *poetry*—that is to say, a universal; and again, when asked what is the subject of social and political history, the answer will not be Greece or Rome, France or Germany, or even all these and others such combined, but *culture*, *civilization*, *progress*, *liberty*, or any other similar word—that is to say, a universal.

And here we can remove a great stumbling-block to the recognition of the *identity of philosophy with history*. I have attempted to renovate, modify, and establish this doctrine with many analyses and with many arguments in another volume of my works.[1] It is, however, frequently very difficult, being rather an object of irresistible argument than of complete persuasion and adhesion. Seeking for the various causes of this difficulty, I have come upon one which seems to me to be the principal and fundamental. This is precisely the conception of history not as living contemporary history, but as history that is dead and belongs to the past, as *chronicle* (or philological history, which, as we know, can be reduced to chronicle). It is undeniable that when history is taken as chronicle its identity with philosophy cannot be made clear to the mind, because it does not exist. But when chronicle has been reduced to its proper practical and mnemonical function, and history has been raised to the knowledge of the *eternal present*, it reveals itself as all one with philosophy, which for its part is never anything but the thought of the eternal present. This, be it well understood, provided always that the dualism of ideas and facts has been superseded, of *vérités de raison* and *vérités de fait*, the concept of philosophy as contemplation of *vérités de raison*, and that of history as the amassing of brute facts, of coarse *vérités de fait*. We have recently found this tenacious dualism in the act of renewing itself, disguised beneath the axiom that *le propre de l'histoire est de savoir, le propre de la philosophie est de comprendre*. This amounts to the absurd distinction of

[1] In the *Logic*, especially in Part II, Chapter IV

knowing without understanding and of understanding without knowing, which would thus be the doubly disheartening theoretical fate of man. But such a dualism and the conception of the world which accompanies it, far from being true philosophy, are the perpetual source whence springs that imperfect attempt at philosophizing which is called *religion* when one is within its magic circle, *mythology* when one has left it. Will it be useful to attack transcendency, and to claim the character of immanence for reality and for philosophy? It will certainly be of use; but I do not feel the necessity of doing so, at any rate here and now.

And since history, properly understood, abolishes the idea of a *universal history*, so philosophy, immanent and identical with history, abolishes the idea of a *universa philosophy*—that is to say, of the *closed* system. The two negations correspond and are indeed fundamentally one (because closed systems, like universal histories, are cosmological romances), and both receive empirical confirmation from the tendency of the best spirits of our day to refrain from 'universal histories' and from 'definitive systems,' leaving both to compilers, to believers, and to the credulous of every sort. This tendency was implicit in the last great philosophy, that of Hegel, but it was opposed in its own self by old survivals and altogether betrayed in execution, so that this philosophy also converts itself into a cosmological romance. Thus it may be said that what at the beginning of the nineteenth century was merely a simple *presentiment* becomes changed into *firm consciousness* at the beginning of the twentieth. This defies the fears of the timid lest the knowledge of the universal should be thus compromised, and indeed maintains that only in this way can such knowledge be truly and perpetually acquired, because dynamically obtained. Thus history becoming *actual history* and philosophy becoming *historical philosophy* have freed themselves, the one from the anxiety of not being able to know that which is not known, only because it was or will be known, and the other from the despair of never being able to attain to definite truth—that is to say, both are freed from the phantom of the 'thing in itself.'

IV

IDEAL GENESIS AND DISSOLUTION OF THE 'PHILOSOPHY OF HISTORY'

I

THE conception of the so-called 'philosophy of history' is perpetually opposed to and resisted by the deterministic conception of history. Not only is this clearly to be seen from inspection, but it is also quite evident logically, because the 'philosophy of history' represents the transcendental conception of the real, determinism the immanent.

But on examining the facts it is not less certain that historical determinism perpetually generates the 'philosophy of history'; nor is this fact less evidently logical than the preceding, because determinism is naturalism, and therefore immanent, certainly, but insufficiently and falsely immanent. Hence it should rather be said that it wishes to be, but is not, immanent, and whatever its efforts may be in the contrary direction, it becomes converted into transcendency. All this does not present any difficulty to one who has clearly in mind the conceptions of the transcendent and of the immanent, of the philosophy of history as transcendency and of the deterministic or naturalistic conception of history as a false immanence. But it will be of use to see in more detail how this process of agreements and oppositions is developed and solved with reference to the problem of history.

"First collect the facts, then connect them causally"; this is the way that the work of the historian is represented in the deterministic conception. *Après la collection des faits, la recherche des causes*, to repeat the very common formula in the very words of one of the most eloquent and picturesque theorists of that school, Taine. Facts are brute, dense, real indeed, but not illumined with the light of science, not intellectualized. This intelligible character must be conferred upon them by means of the search for causes. But it is very well known what happens when one fact is linked to another as its cause, forming a chain of causes and effects: we thus inaugurate an infinite regression, and we never succeed in finding the cause or causes to which we can finally attach the chain that we have been so industriously putting together.

Some, maybe many, of the theorists of history get out of the difficulty in a truly simple manner: they break or let fall at a certain point their chain, which is already broken at another point at the other end (the effect which they have undertaken to consider). They operate with their fragment of chain as though it were something perfect and closed in itself, as though a straight line divided at two points should include space and be a figure. Hence, too, the doctrine that we find among the methodologists of history: that it is only necessary for history to seek out 'proximate' causes. This doctrine is intended to supply a logical foundation to the above process. But who can ever say what are the 'proximate causes'? Thought, since it is admitted that it is unfortunately obliged to think according to the chain of causes, will never wish to know anything but 'true' causes, be they near or distant in space and time (space, like time, *ne fait rien à l'affaire*). In reality, this theory is a fig-leaf, placed there to cover a proceeding of which the historian, who is a thinker and a critic, is ashamed, an act of will which is useful, but which for that very reason is wilful. The fig-leaf, however, is a sign of modesty, and as such has its value, because, if shame be lost, there is a risk that it will finally be declared that the 'causes' at which an arbitrary halt has been made are the 'ultimate' causes, the 'true' causes, thus raising the caprice of the individual to the rank of an act creative of the world, treating it as though it were God, the God of certain theologians, whose caprice is truth. I should not wish again to quote Taine just after having said this, for he is a most estimable author, not on account of his mental constitution, but of his enthusiastic faith in science; yet it suits me to quote him nevertheless. Taine, in his search for causes, having reached a cause which he sometimes calls the 'race' and sometimes the 'age,' as for instance in his history of English literature, when he reaches the concept of the 'man of the North' or 'German,' with the character and intellect that would be suitable to such a person—coldness of the senses, love of abstract ideas, grossness of taste, and contempt for order and regularity—gravely affirms: *Là s'arrête la recherche : on est tombé sur quelque disposition primitive, sur quelque trait propre à toutes les sensations, à toutes les conceptions d'un siècle ou d'une race, sur quelque particularité inséparable de toutes les démarches de son esprit et de son cœur. Ce sont là les grandes causes, les causes universelles et permanentes.* What that primitive and insurmountable thing contained was known to Taine's imagination, but criticism is ignorant of it; for criticism demands that the genesis of the facts or groups of facts designated as 'age' and 'race' should be given, and in demanding their genesis declares that they are neither 'universal' nor 'permanent,' because no universal and permanent 'facts' are known, as far as I am aware, certainly not *le Germain* and *l'homme du Nord*; nor are mummies facts, though they last some thousands of years, but not for ever—they change gradually, but they do change.

Thus whoever adopts the deterministic conception of history, provided that he decides to abstain from cutting short the inquiry that he has undertaken in an arbitrary and fanciful manner, is of necessity obliged to recognize that the method adopted does not attain the desired end. And since he has begun to think history, although by means of an insufficient method, no course remains to him save that of beginning all over again and following a different path, or that of going forward but changing his direction. The naturalistic presupposition, which still holds its ground ("first collect the facts, then seek the causes": what is more evident and more unavoidable than that?), necessarily leads to the second alternative. But to adopt the second alternative is to supersede determinism, it is to transcend nature and its causes, it is to propose a method opposite to that hitherto followed—that is to say, to renounce the category of cause for another, which cannot be anything but that of end, an extrinsic and transcendental end, which is the analogous opposite, corresponding to the cause. Now the search for the transcendental end is the 'philosophy of history.'

The consequent naturalist (I mean by this he who 'continues to think,' or, as is generally said, to draw the consequences) cannot avoid this inquiry, nor does he ever avoid it, in whatever manner he conceive his new inquiry. This he cannot even do, when he tries, by declaring that the end or 'ultimate cause' is unknowable, because (as elsewhere remarked) an unknowable affirmed is an unknowable in some way known. Naturalism is always crowned with a philosophy of history, whatever its mode of formulation: whether it explain the universe as composed of atoms that strike one another and produce history by means of their various shocks and gyrations, to which they can also put an end by returning to their primitive state of dispersion, whether the hidden God be termed Matter or the Unconscious or something else, or whether, finally, He be conceived as an Intelligence which avails itself of the chain of causes in order to actualize His counsels. And every philosopher of history is on the other hand a naturalist, because he is a dualist and conceives a God and a world, an idea and a fact in addition to or beneath the Idea, a kingdom of ends and a kingdom or sub-kingdom of causes, a celestial city and one that is more or less diabolical or terrene. Take any deterministic historical work and you will find or discover in it, explicit or understood, transcendency (in Taine, for example, it goes by the name of ' race ' or of ' *siècle*,' which are true and proper deities) ; take any work of ' philosophy of history ' and dualism and naturalism will be found there (in Hegel, for example, when he admits rebellious and impotent facts which resist or are unworthy the dominion of the idea). And we shall see more and more clearly how from the entrails of naturalism comes inevitably forth the ' philosophy of history.'

II

But the ' philosophy of history ' is just as contradictory as the deterministic conception from which it arises and to which it is opposed. Having both accepted and superseded the method of linking brute facts together, it no longer finds facts to link (for these have already been linked together, as well as might be, by means of the category of cause), but brute facts, on which it must confer rather a 'meaning' than a linking, representing them as aspects of a transcendental process, a theophany. Now those facts, in so far as they are brute facts, are mute, and the transcendency of the process requires an organ, not that of thought that thinks or produces facts, but an extra-logical organ, in order to be conceived and represented (such, for example, as thought which proceeds abstractly *a priori*, in the manner of Fichte), and this is not to be found in the spirit, save as a negative moment, as the void of effective logical thought. The void of logical thought is immediately filled with *praxis*, or what is called sentiment, which then appears as poetry, by theoretical refraction. There is an evident poetical character running through all 'philosophies of history.' Those of antiquity represented historical events as strife between the gods of certain peoples or of certain races or protectors of certain individuals, or between the god of light and truth and the powers of darkness and lies. They thus expressed the aspirations of peoples, groups, or individuals toward hegemony, or of man toward goodness and truth. The most modern of modern forms is that inspired by various national and ethical feelings (the Italian, the Germanic, the Slav, etc.), or which represents the course of history as leading to the kingdom of liberty, or as the passage from the Eden of primitive communism, through the Middle Ages of slavery, servitude, and wages, toward the restoration of communism, which shall no longer be unconscious but conscious, no longer Edenic but human. In poetry, facts are no longer facts but words, not reality but images, and so there would be no occasion to censure them, if it remained pure poetry.

But it does not so remain, because those images and words are placed there as ideas and facts—that is to say, as myths : progress, liberty, economy, technique, science are myths, in so far as they are looked upon as agents external to the facts. They are myths no less than God and the Devil, Mars and Venus, Jove and Baal, or any other cruder forms of divinity. And this is the reason why the deterministic conception, after it has produced the 'philosophy of history,' which opposes it, is obliged to oppose its own daughter in its turn, and to appeal from the realm of ends to that of causal connexions, from imagination to observation, from myths to facts.

The reciprocal confutation of historical determinism and the philosophy of history, which makes of each a void or a nothing—that is to say, a single void or nothing—seems to the eclectics as usual to be the reciprocal fulfilment of two entities, which effect or should effect an alliance for mutual support. And since eclecticism flourishes in contemporary philosophy, *mutato nomine*, it is not surprising that besides the duty of investigating the causes to history also is assigned that of ascertaining the 'meaning' or the 'general plan' of the course of history (see the works on the philosophy of history of Labriola, Simmel, and Rickert). Since, too, writers on method are wont to be empirical and therefore eclectic, we find that with them also history is divided into the history which unites and criticizes documents and reconstructs events, and 'philosophy of history' (see Bernheim's manual, typical of all of them). Finally, since ordinary thought is eclectic, nothing is more easy than to find agreement as to the thesis that simple history, which presents the series of facts, does not suffice, but that it is necessary that thought should return to the already constituted chain of events, in order to discover there the hidden design and to answer the questions as to whence we come and whither we go. This amounts to saying that a 'philosophy of history' must be posited side by side with history. This eclecticism, which gives substance to two opposite voids and makes them join hands, sometimes attempts to surpass itself and to mingle those two fallacious sciences or parts of science. Then we hear 'philosophy of history' defended, but with the caution that it must be conducted with 'scientific' and 'positive' method, by means of the search for the cause, thus revealing the action of divine reason or providence.[1] Ordinary thought quickly consents to this programme, but afterward fails to carry it out.[2]

There is nothing new here either for those who know: 'philosophy of history' to be constructed by means of 'positive methods,' transcendency to be demonstrated by means of the methods of false immanence, is the exact equivalent in the field of historical studies to that "metaphysic to be constructed by means of the experimental method" which was recommended by the neocritics (Zeller and others), for it claimed, not indeed to supersede two voids that reciprocally confute one another,

[1] See, for example, the work of Flint, but since, less radical than Flint, Hegel and the Hegelians themselves also ended in admitting the concourse of the two opposed methods, traces of this perversion are also to be found in their 'philosophies of history' Here, too, is to be noted the false analogy by which Hegel was led to discover the same relation between *a priori* and historical facts as between mathematics and natural facts. *Man muss mit dem Kreise dessen, worin die Prinzipien fallen, wenn man es so nennen will,* a priori *vertraut sein, so gut als Kepler mit den Ellipsen, mit Kuben und Quadraten und mit den Gedanken von Verhältnissen derselben* a priori *schon vorher bekannt sein musste, ehe er aus den empirischen Daten seine unsterblichen Gesetze, welche aus Bestimmungen jener Kreise von Vorstellungen bestehen, erfinden konnte* (Cf *Vorles ub d Philos d Gesch*, ed Brunstäd, pp 107–108)

[2] Not even the above-mentioned Flint carried it out, for he lost himself in preliminaries of historical documentation and never proceeded to the promised construction

but to make them agree together, and, after having given substance to them, to combine them in a single substance. I should not like to describe the impossibilities contained in the above as the prodigies of an alchemist (the metaphor seems to be too lofty), but rather as the medleys of bad cooks.

III

The true remedy for the contradictions of historical determinism and of the 'philosophy of history' is quite other than this. To obtain it, we must accept the result of the preceding confutation, which shows that both are futile, and reject, as lacking thought, both the 'designs' of the philosophy of history and the causal chains of determinism. When these two shadows have been dispersed we shall find ourselves at the starting-place: we are again face to face with disconnected brute facts, with facts that are connected, but not understood, for which determinism had tried to employ the cement of causality, the 'philosophy of history,' the magic wand of finality. What shall we do with these facts? How shall we make them clear rather than dense as they were, organic rather than inorganic, intelligible rather than unintelligible? Truly, it seems difficult to do anything with them, especially to effect their desired transformation. The spirit is helpless before that which is, or is supposed to be, external to it. And when facts are understood in that way we are apt to assume again that attitude of contempt of the philosophers for history which has been well-nigh constant since antiquity almost to the end of the eighteenth century (for Aristotle history was "less philosophical" and less serious than poetry, for Sextus Empiricus it was "unmethodical material"; Kant did not feel or understand history). The attitude amounts to this: leave ideas to the philosophers and brute facts to the historians—let us be satisfied with serious things and leave their toys to the children.

But before having recourse to such a temptation, it will be prudent to ask counsel of methodical doubt (which is always most useful), and to direct the attention precisely upon those brute and disconnected facts from which the causal method claims to start and before which we, who are now abandoned by it and by its complement, the philosophy of history, appear to find ourselves again. Methodical doubt will suggest above all things the thought that those facts are a *presupposition* that has *not been proved*, and it will lead to the inquiry as to *whether the proof can be obtained.* Having attempted the proof, we shall finally arrive at the conclusion that *those facts really do not exist.*

For who, as a matter of fact, affirms their existence? Precisely the spirit, at the moment when it is about to undertake the search for causes. But when accomplishing that act the spirit does not already possess the brute facts (*d'abord la collection des faits*) and then seek the causes (*après, la recherche des causes*); but it makes the *facts brute* by that very act—that is to say, it posits them itself in that way, because it is of use to it so to posit them. The search for causes, undertaken by history, is not in any way different from the procedure of naturalism, already several times illustrated, which abstractly analyses and classifies reality. And to illustrate abstractly and to classify implies at the same time to judge in classifying—that is to say, to treat facts, not as acts of the spirit, conscious in the spirit that thinks them, but as external brute facts. The *Divine Comedy* is that poem which we create again in our imagination in all its particulars as we read it and which we understand critically as a particular determination of the spirit, and to which we therefore assign its place in history, with all its surroundings and all its relations. But when this actuality of our thought and imagination has come to an end—that is to say, when that mental process is completed—we are able, by means of a new act of the spirit, separately to analyse its elements. Thus, for instance, we shall classify the concepts relating to 'Florentine civilization,' or to 'political poetry,' and say that the *Divine Comedy* was an effect of Florentine civilization, and this in its turn an effect of the strife of the communes, and the like. We shall also thus have prepared the way for those absurd problems which used to annoy de Sanctis so much in relation to the work of Dante, and which he admirably described when he said that they arise only when lively æsthetic expression has grown cold and poetical work has fallen into the hands of dullards addicted to trifles. But if we stop in time and do not enter the path of those absurdities, if we restrict ourselves purely and simply to the naturalistic moment, to classification, and to the classificatory judgment (which is also causal connexion), in an altogether practical manner, without drawing any deductions from it, we shall have done nothing that is not perfectly legitimate; indeed, we shall be exercising our right and bowing to a rational necessity, which is that of naturalizing, when naturalization is of use, but not beyond those limits. Thus the materialization of the facts and the external or causal binding of them together are altogether justified as pure naturalism. And even the maxim which bids us to stop at 'proximate' causes—that is to say, not to force classification so far that it loses all practical utility—will find its justification. To place the concept of the *Divine Comedy* in relation to that of 'Florentine civilization' may be of use, but it will be of no use whatever, or infinitely less use, to place it in relation to the class of 'Indo-European civilization' or to the 'civilization of the white man.'

IV

Let us then return with greater confidence to the point of departure, the true point of departure—that is to say, not to that of facts already disorganized and naturalized, but to that of the mind that thinks and constructs the fact. Let us raise up the debased countenances of the calumniated 'brute facts,' and we shall see the light of thought resplendent upon their foreheads. And that true point of departure will reveal itself not merely as a point of departure, but both as a point of arrival and of departure, not as the first step in historical construction, but the whole of history in its construction, which is also its self-construction. Historical determinism, and all the more 'philosophy of history,' leave the *reality of history* behind them, though they directed their journey thither, a journey which became so erratic and so full of useless repetitions.

We shall make the ingenuous Taine confess that what we are saying is the truth when we ask him what he means by the *collection des faits* and learn from him in reply that the collection in question consists of two stages or moments, in the first of which documents are revived in order to attain, *à travers la distance des temps, l'homme vivant, agissant, doué de passions, muni d'habitudes, avec sa voix et sa physionomie, avec ses gestes et ses habits, distinct et complet comme celui que tout à l'heure nous avons quitté dans la rue*; and in the second is sought and found *sous l'homme extérieur l'homme intérieur*, "*l'homme invisible*," "*le centre*," "*le groupe des facultés et des sentiments qui produit le reste*," "*le drame intérieur*," "*la psychologie*." Something very different, then, from *collections de faits*! If the things mentioned by our author really do come to pass, if we really do make live again in imagination individuals and events, and if we think what is within them—that is to say, if we think the synthesis of intuition and concept, which is thought in its concreteness—history is already achieved: what more is wanted? There is nothing more to seek. Taine replies: "We must seek causes." That is to say, we must slay the living 'fact' thought by thought, separate its abstract elements—a useful thing, no doubt, but useful for memory and practice. Or, as is the custom of Taine, we must misunderstand and exaggerate the value of the function of this abstract analysis, to lose ourselves in the mythology of races and ages, or in other different but none the less similar things. Let us beware how we slay poor facts, if we wish to think as historians, and in so far as we are such and really think in that way we shall not feel the necessity for having recourse either to the extrinsic bond of causes, historical determinism, or to that which is equally extrinsic of transcendental ends, philosophy of history. The fact historically thought has no cause and no end outside itself, but only in itself, coincident with its real qualities and with its qualitative reality. Because (it is well to note in passing) the determination of facts as *real* facts indeed, but of *unknown nature*, asserted but not understood, is itself also an illusion of naturalism (which thus heralds its other illusion, that of the 'philosophy of history'). In thought, reality and quality, existence and essence, are all one, and it is not possible to affirm a fact as real without at the same time knowing what fact it is—that is, without qualifying it.

Returning to and remaining in or moving in the concrete fact, or, rather, making of oneself thought that thinks the fact concretely, we experience the continual formation and the continual progress of our historical thought and also make clear to ourselves the history of historiography, which proceeds in the same manner. And we see how (I limit myself to this, in order not to allow the eye to wander too far) from the days of the Greeks to our own historical understanding has always been enriching and deepening itself, not because abstract causes and transcendental ends of human things have ever been recovered, but only because an ever increasing consciousness of them has been acquired. Politics and morality, religion and philosophy and art, science and culture and economy, have become more complex concepts and at the same time better determined and unified both in themselves and with respect to the whole. Correlatively with this, the histories of these forms of activity have become ever more complex and more firmly united. We know 'the causes' of civilization as little as did the Greeks; and we know as little as they of the god or gods who control the fortunes of humanity. But we know the theory of civilization better than did the Greeks, and, for instance, we know (as they did not know, or did not know with equal clearness and security) that poetry is an eternal form of the theoretic spirit, that regression or decadence is a relative concept, that the world is not divided into ideas and shadows of ideas, or into potencies and acts, that slavery is not a category of the real, but a historical form of economic, and so forth. Thus it no longer occurs to anyone (save to the survivals or fossils, still to be found among us) to write the history of poetry on the principle of the pedagogic ends that the poets are supposed to have had in view: on the contrary, we strive to determine the forms expressive of their sentiments. We are not at all bewildered when we find ourselves before what are called 'decadences,' but we seek out what new and greater thing was being developed by means of their dialectic. We do not consider the work of man to be miserable and illusory, and aspiration and admiration for the skies and for the ascesis joined thereunto and averse to earth as alone worthy of admiration and imitation. We recognize the reality of power in the act, and in the shadows the solidity of the ideas, and on earth heaven. Finally, we do not find that the possibility of social life is lost owing to the disappearance of the system of slavery. Such a disappearance would have been the catastrophe of reality, if slaves were natural to reality—and so forth.

This conception of history and the consideration of historiographical work in itself make it possible for us to be just toward historical determinism and to the 'philosophy of history,' which, by their continual reappearance, have continually pointed to the gaps in our knowledge, both historical and philosophical, and with their false provisional solutions have heralded the correct solutions of the new problems which we have been propounding. Nor has it been said that they will henceforth cease to exercise such a function (which is the beneficial function of Utopias of every sort). And although historical determinism and the 'philosophy of history' have no history, because they do not develop, they yet receive a content from the relation in which they stand to history, which does develop—that is to say, history develops in them, notwithstanding their covering, extrinsic to their content, which compels to think even him who proposes to schematize and to imagine without thinking. For there is a great difference between the determinism that can now appear, after Descartes and Vico and Kant and Hegel, and that which appeared after Aristotle; between the philosophy of history of Hegel and Marx and that of gnosticism and Christianity. Transcendency and false immanency are at work in both these conceptions respectively; but the abstract forms and mythologies that have appeared in more mature epochs of thought contain this new maturity in themselves. In proof of this, let us pause but a moment (passing by the various forms of naturalism) at the case of the 'philosophy of history.' We observe already a great difference between the philosophy of history, as it appears in the Homeric world, and that of Herodotus, with whom the conception of the anger of the gods is a simulacrum of the moral law, which spares the humble and treads the proud underfoot; from Herodotus to the Fate of the Stoics, a law to which the gods themselves are subjected, and from this to the conception of Providence, which appears in late antiquity as wisdom that rules the world; from this pagan providence again to Christianity, which is divine justice, evangelical preparation, and educative care of the human race, and so on, to the refined providence of the theologians, which as a rule excludes divine intervention and operates by means of secondary causes, to that of Vico, which operates as dialectic of the spirit, to the Idea of Hegel, which is the gradual conquest of the consciousness of self, which liberty achieves during the course of history, till we finally reach the mythology of progress and of civilization, which still persists and is supposed to tend toward the final abolition of prejudices and superstitions, to be carried out by means of the increasing power and divulgation of positive science.

In this way the 'philosophy of history' and historical determinism sometimes attain to the thinness and transparency of a veil, which covers and at the same time reveals the concreteness of the real in thought. Mechanical causes thus appear idealized, transcendent deities humanized, and facts are in great part divested of their brutal aspect. But however thin the veil may be, it remains a veil, and however clear the truth may be, it is not altogether clear, for at bottom the false persuasion still persists that history is constructed with the 'material' of brute facts, with the 'cement' of causes, and with the 'magic' of ends, as with three successive or concurrent methods. The same thing occurs with religion, which in lofty minds liberates itself almost altogether from vulgar beliefs, as do its ethics from the heteronomy of the divine command and from the utilitarianism of rewards and punishments. Almost altogether, but not altogether, and for this reason religion will never be philosophy, save by negating itself, and thus the 'philosophy of history' and historical determinism will become history only by negating themselves. The reason is that as long as they proceed in a positive manner dualism will also persist, and with it the torment of scepticism and agnosticism as a consequence.

The negation of the philosophy of history, in history understood concretely, is its ideal dissolution, and since that so-called philosophy is nothing but an abstract and negative moment, our reason for affirming that *the philosophy of history is dead* is clear. It is dead in its positivity, dead as a body of doctrine, dead in this way, with all the other conceptions and forms of the transcendental. I do not wish to attach to my brief (but in my opinion sufficient) treatment of the argument the addition of an explanation which to some will appear to be (as it appears to me) but little philosophical and even somewhat trivial. Notwithstanding, since I prefer the accusation of semi-triviality to that of equivocation, I shall add that since the criticism of the 'concepts' of cause and transcendental finality does not forbid the use of these 'words,' when they are simple words (to talk, for example, in an imaginative way of liberty as of a goddess, or to say, when about to undertake a study of Dante, that our intention is to 'seek the cause' or 'causes' of this or that work or act of his), so nothing forbids our continuing to talk of 'philosophy of history' and of philosophizing history, meaning the necessity of treating or of a better treatment of this or that historical problem. Neither does anything forbid our calling the researches of historical gnoseology 'philosophy of history,' although in this case we are treating the history, not properly of *history*, but of *historiography*, two things which are wont to be designated with the same word in Italian as in other languages. Neither do we wish to prevent the statement (as did a German professor years ago) that the 'philosophy of history' must be treated as 'sociology'—that is to say, the adornment with that ancient title of so-called sociology, the empirical science of the state, of society and of culture.

These denominations are all permissible in virtue of the same right as that invoked by the adventurer Casanova when he went before the magistrates in order to justify himself for having changed his name—"the right of every man to the letters of the alphabet." But the question treated above is not one of the letters of the alphabet. The 'philosophy of history,' of which we have briefly shown the genesis and the dissolution, is not one that is used in various senses, but a most definite mode of conceiving history—the transcendental mode.

V

THE POSITIVITY OF HISTORY

WE therefore meet the well-known saying of Fustel de Coulanges that there are certainly "history and philosophy, but not the philosophy of history," with the following: there is neither philosophy nor history, nor philosophy of history, but history which is philosophy and philosophy which is history and is intrinsic to history. For this reason, all the controversies—and foremost of all those concerned with *progress*—which philosophers, methodologists of history, and sociologists believe to belong to their especial province, and flaunt at the beginning and the end of their treatises, are reduced for us to simple problems of philosophy, with historical motivation, all of them connected with the problems of which philosophy treats.

In controversies relating to progress it is asked whether the work of man be fertile or sterile, whether it be lost or preserved, whether history have an end, and if so of what sort, whether this end be attainable in time or only in the infinite, whether history be progress or regress, or an interchange between progress and regress, greatness and decadence, whether good or evil prevail in it, and the like. When these questions have been considered with a little attention we shall see that they resolve themselves substantially into three points: the conception of *development*, that of *end*, and that of *value*. That is to say, they are concerned with the whole of reality, and with history only when it is precisely the whole of reality. For this reason they do not belong to supposed particular sciences, to the philosophy of history, or to sociology, but to philosophy and to history in so far as it is philosophy.

When the ordinary current terminology has been translated into philosophical terms it calls forth immediately the thesis, antithesis, and synthesis by means of which those problems have been thought and solved during the course of philosophy, to which the reader desirous of instruction must be referred. We can only mention here that the conception of reality as development is nothing but the synthesis of the two one-sided opposites, consisting of permanency without change and of change without permanency, of an identity without diversity and of a diversity without identity, for development is a perpetual surpassing, which is at the same time a perpetual conservation. From this point of view one of the conceptions that has had the greatest vogue in historical books, that of *historical circles*, is revealed as an equivocal attempt to issue forth from a double one-sidedness and a falling back into it, owing to an equivocation. Because either the series of circles is conceived as composed of identicals and we have only permanency, or it is conceived as of things diverse and we have only change. But if, on the contrary, we conceive it as circularity that is perpetually identical and at the same time perpetually diverse, in this sense it coincides with the conception of development itself.

In like manner, the opposite theses, as to the attainment or the impossibility of attainment of the end of history, reveal their common defect of positing the end as *extrinsic* to history, conceiving of it either as that which can be reached in time (*progressus ad finitum*), or as that which can never be attained, but only infinitely approximated (*progressus ad infinitum*). But where the end has been correctly conceived as *internal*—that is to say, all one with development itself—we must conclude that it is attained at every instant, and at the same time not attained, because every attainment is the formation of a new prospect, whence we have at every moment the satisfaction of possession, and arising from this the dissatisfaction which drives us to seek a new possession.[1]

Finally, the conceptions of history as a passage from evil to good (progress), or from good to evil (decadence, regression), take their origin from the same error of entifying and making extrinsic good and evil, joy and sorrow (which are the dialectical construction of reality itself). To unite them in the eclectic conception of an alternation of good and evil, of progress and regress, is incorrect. The true solution is that of progress understood not as a passage from evil to good, as though from one state to another, but as the passage from the good to the better, in which the evil is the good itself seen in the light of the better.

These are all philosophical solutions which are at variance with the superficial theses of controversialists (dictated to them by sentimental motives or imaginative combinations, really mythological or resulting in mythologies), to the same extent that they are in accordance with profound human convictions and with the tireless toil, the trust, the courage, which constitute their ethical manifestations.

By drawing the consequences of the dialectical con-

[1] For the complete development of these conceptions, see my study of *The Conception of Becoming*, in the *Saggio sullo Hegel seguito da altri scritti di storia della filosofia*, pp 149–175 (Bari, 1913). (English translation of the work on Hegel by Douglas Ainslie. Macmillan, London)

ception of progress something more immediately effective can be achieved in respect to the practice and history of historiography. For we find in that conception the origin of a historical maxim, in the mouth of every one, yet frequently misunderstood and frequently violated—that is to say, that to history pertains not to *judge*, but to *explain*, and that it should be not *subjective* but *objective*.

Misunderstood, because the judging in question is often taken in the sense of logical judgment, of that judgment which is thinking itself, and the subjectivity, which would thus be excluded, would be neither more nor less than the subjectivity of thought. In consequence of this misunderstanding we hear historians being advised to purge themselves of theories, to refrain from the disputes arising from them, to restrict themselves to facts, collecting, arranging, and squeezing out the sap (even by the statistical method). It is impossible to follow such advice as this, as may easily be seen, for such 'abstention from thought' reveals itself as really abstention from 'seriousness of thought,' as a surreptitious attaching of value to the most vulgar and contradictory thoughts, transmitted by tradition, wandering about idly in the mind, or flashing out as the result of momentary caprice. The maxim is altogether false, understood or misunderstood in this way, and it must be taken by its opposite—namely, that history must always judge strictly, and that it must always be energetically subjective without allowing itself to be confused by the conflicts in which thought engages or by the risks that it runs. For it is thought itself, and thought alone, which gets over its own difficulties and dangers, without falling even here into that frivolous eclecticism which tries to find a middle term between our judgment and that of others, and suggests various *neutral* and insipid forms of judgment.

But the true and legitimate meaning, the original motive for that 'judging,' that 'subjectivity,' which it condemns, is that history should not apply to the deeds and the personages that are its material the qualifications of good and evil, as though there really were good and evil facts in the world, people who are good and people who are evil. And it is certainly not to be denied that innumerable historiographers, or those who claim to be historiographers, have really striven and still strive along those lines, in the vain and presumptuous attempt to reward the good and punish the evil, to qualify historical epochs as representing progress or decadence—in a word, to settle what is good and what is evil, as though it were a question of separating one element from another in a compound, hydrogen from oxygen.

Whoever desires to observe intrinsically the above maxim, and by doing so to set himself in accordance with the dialectic conception of progress, must in truth look upon every trace or vestige of propositions affirming evil, regression, or decadence as real facts, as a sign of imperfection—in a word, he must condemn every trace or vestige of *negative* judgments. If the course of history is not the passage from evil to good, or alternative good and evil, but the passage from the good to the better, if history should explain and not condemn, it will pronounce only *positive* judgments, and will forge chains of good, so solid and so closely linked that it will not be possible to introduce into them even a little link of evil or to interpose empty spaces, which in so far as they are empty would not represent good but evil. A fact that seems to be only evil, an epoch that appears to be one of complete decadence, can be nothing but a *non-historical* fact—that is to say, one which has not been historically treated, not penetrated by thought, and which has remained the prey of sentiment and imagination.

Whence comes the phenomenology of good and evil, of sin and repentance, of decadence and resurrection, save from the consciousness of the agent, from the act which is in labour to produce a new form of life?[1] And in that act the adversary who opposed us is in the wrong; the state from which we wish to escape, and from which we are escaping, is unhappy; the new one toward which we are tending becomes symbolized as a dreamed-of felicity to be attained, or as a past condition to restore, which is therefore most beautiful in recollection (which here is not recollection, but imagination). Every one knows how these things present themselves to us in the course of history, manifesting themselves in poetry, in Utopias, in stories with a moral, in detractions, in apologies, in myths of love, of hate, and the like. To the heretics of the Middle Ages and to the Protestant reformers the condition of the primitive Christians seemed to be most lovely and most holy, that of papal Christians most evil and debased. The Sparta of Lycurgus and the Rome of Cincinnatus seemed to the Jacobins to be as admirable as France under the Carlovingians and the Capetians was detestable. The humanists looked upon the lives of the ancient poets and sages as luminous and the life of the Middle Ages as dense darkness. Even in times near our own has been witnessed the glorification of the Lombard communes and the depreciation of the Holy Roman Empire, and the very opposite of this, according as the facts relating to these

[1] For what relates to this section, see my treatment of *Judgments of Value*, in the work before cited.

historical events were reflected in the consciousness of an Italian longing for the independence of Italy or of a German upholding the holy German empire of Prussian hegemony. And this will always happen, because such is the phenomenology of the practical consciousness, and these practical valuations will always be present to some extent in the works of historians. As works, these are not and cannot ever be pure history, quintessential history; if in no other way, then in their phrasing and use of metaphors they will reflect the repercussion of practical needs and efforts directed toward the future. But the historical consciousness, as such, is logical and not practical consciousness, and indeed makes the other its object; history once lived has become in it thought, and the antitheses of will and feeling that formerly offered resistance have no longer a place in thought.

For if there are no good and evil facts, but facts that are always good when understood in their intimate being and concreteness, there are not opposite sides, but that wider side that embraces both the adversaries and which happens just to be historical consideration. Historical consideration, therefore, recognizes as of equal right the Church of the catacombs and that of Gregory VII, the tribunes of the Roman people and the feudal barons, the Lombard League and the Emperor Barbarossa. History never metes out justice, but always *justifies*; she could not carry out the former act without making herself unjust—that is to say, confounding thought with life, taking the attractions and repulsions of sentiment for the judgments of thought.

Poetry is satisfied with the expression of sentiment, and it is worthy of note that a considerable historian, Schlosser, wishing to reserve for himself the right and duty of judging historical facts with Kantian austerity and abstraction, kept his eyes fixed on the *Divine Comedy*—that is to say, a poetical work—as his model of treatment. And since there are poetical elements in all myths, we understand why the conception of history known as *dualistic*—that is to say, of history as composed of two currents, which mix but never resolve in one another their waters of good and evil, truth and error, rationality and irrationality—should have formed a conspicuous part, not only of the Christian religion, but also of the mythologies (for they really are such) of humanism and of illuminism. But the detection of this problem of the duality of values and its solution in the superior unity of the conception of development is the work of the nineteenth century, which on this account and on account of other solutions of the same kind (certainly not on account of its philological and archæological richness, which was relatively common to the four preceding centuries) has been well called 'the century of history.'

Not only, therefore, is history unable to discriminate between facts that are good and facts that are evil, and between epochs that are progressive and those that are regressive, but it does not begin until the psychological conditions which rendered possible such antitheses have been superseded and substituted by an act of the spirit, which seeks to ascertain what function the fact or the epoch previously condemned has fulfilled—that is to say, what it has produced of its own in the course of development, and therefore what it has produced. And since all facts and epochs are productive in their own way, not only is not one of them to be condemned in the light of history, but all are to be praised and venerated. A condemned fact, a fact that is repugnant, is not yet a historical proposition, it is hardly even the premiss of a historical problem to be formulated. A negative history is a non-history so long as its negative process substitutes itself for thought, which is affirmative, and does not maintain itself within its practical and moral bounds and limit itself to poetical expressions and empirical modes of representation, in respect of all of which we can certainly speak (speak and not think), as we do speak at every moment, of bad men and periods of decadence and regression.

If the vice of negative history arises from the separation, the solidification, and the opposition of the dialectical antitheses of good and evil and the transformation of the ideal moments of development into entities, that other deviation of history which may be known as *elegiac* history arises from the misunderstanding of another necessity of that conception—that is to say, the perpetual constancy, the perpetual conservation of what has been acquired. But this is also false by definition. What is preserved and enriched in the course of history is history itself, spirituality. The past does not live otherwise than in the present, as the force of the present, resolved and transformed in the present. Every particular form, individual, action, institution, work, thought, is destined to perish: even art, which is called eternal (and is so in a certain sense), perishes, for it does not live, save to the extent that it is reproduced, and therefore transfigured and surrounded with new light, in the spirit of posterity. Finally, truth itself perishes, particular and determined truth, because it is not rethinkable, save when included in the system of a vaster truth, and therefore at the same time transformed. But those who do not rise to the conception of pure historical consideration, those who attach themselves with their whole soul to an individual, a work, a belief, an institution, and attach themselves so strongly that they cannot separate themselves from it in order to objectify it before themselves and think it, are prone to attribute the immortality which belongs to the spirit in universal to the spirit in one of its particular and determined forms ; and since that form, notwithstanding their efforts, dies, and dies in their arms, the universe darkens before their gaze, and the only history that they can relate is the sad one of the agony and death of beautiful things. This too is poetry, and very lofty poetry. Who can do otherwise than weep at the loss of a beloved one, at separation from something dear to him, cannot see the sun extinguished and the earth tremble and the birds cease their flight and fall to earth, like Dante, on the loss of his beloved "who was so beautiful"? But history is never *history of death*, but *history of life*, and all know that the proper commemoration of the dead is the knowledge of what they did in life, of what they produced that is working in us, the history of their life and not of their death, which it behoves a gentle soul to veil, a soul barbarous and perverse to exhibit in its miserable nakedness and to contemplate with unhealthy persistence. For this reason all histories which narrate the death and not the life of peoples, of states, of institutions, of customs, of literary and artistic ideals, of religious conceptions, are to be considered false, or, we repeat, simply poetry, where they attain to the level of poetry. People grow sad and suffer and lament because that which was is no longer. This would resolve itself into a mere tautology (because if it was, it is evident that it is no longer), were it not conjoined to the neglect of recognizing what of that past has not perished—that is to say, that past in so far as it is not past but present, the eternal life of the past. It is in this neglect, in the incorrect view arising out of it, that the falsity of such histories resides.

It sometimes happens that historians, intent upon narrating those scenes of anguish in a lugubrious manner and upon celebrating the funerals which it pleases them to call histories, remain partly astounded and partly scandalized when they hear a peal of laughter, a cry of joy, a sigh of satisfaction, or find an enthusiastic impulse springing up from the documents that they are searching. How, they ask, could men live, make love, reproduce their species, sing, paint, discuss, when the trumps were sounding east and west to announce the end of the world? But they do not see that such an end of the world exists only in their own imaginations, rich in elegiac motives, but poor in understanding. They do not perceive that such importunate trumpet-calls have never in reality existed. These are very useful, on the other hand, for reminding those who may have forgotten it that history always pursues her indefatigable work, and that her apparent agonies are the travail of a new birth, and that what are believed to be her expiring sighs are moans that announce the birth of a new world. History differs from the individual who dies because, in the words of Alcmæon of Crete, he is not able *τὴν ἀρχὴν τῷ τέλει προσάψαι*, to join his beginning to his end: history never dies, because she always joins her beginning to her end.

VI

THE HUMANITY OF HISTORY

ENFRANCHISING itself from servitude to extra-mundane caprice and to blind natural necessity, freeing itself from transcendency and from false immanence (which is in its turn transcendency), thought conceives history as the work of man, as the product of human will and intellect, and in this manner enters that form of history which we shall call *humanistic.*

This humanism first appears as in simple contrast to nature or to extra-mundane powers, and posits dualism. On the one side is man, with his strength, his intelligence, his reason, his prudence, his will for the good ; on the other there is something that resists him, strives against him, upsets his wisest plans, breaks the web that he has been weaving and obliges him to weave it all over again. History, envisaged from the view-point of this conception, is developed entirely from the first of these two sides, because the other does not afford a dialectical element which can be continually met and superseded by the first, giving rise to a sort of interior collaboration, but represents the absolutely extraneous, the capricious, the accidental, the meddler, the ghost at the feast. Only in the former do we find rationality combined with human endeavour, and thus the possibility of a rational explication of history. What comes from the other side is announced, but not explained: it is not material for history, but at the most for chronicle.

This first form of humanistic history is known under the various names of *rationalistic*, *intellectualistic*, *abstract-*

istic, *individualistic*, *psychological* history, and especially under that of *pragmatic* history. It is a form generally condemned by the consciousness of our times, which has employed these designations, especially *rationalism* and *pragmatism*, to represent a particular sort of historiographical insufficiency and inferiority, and has made proverbial the most characteristic pragmatic explanations of institutions and events, as types of misrepresentation into which one must beware of falling if one wish to think history seriously. But as happens in the progress of culture and science, even if the condemnation be cordially accepted and no hesitation entertained as to drawing practical consequences from it in the field of actuality, there is not an equally clear consciousness of the reasons for this, or of the thought process by means of which it has been attained. This process we may briefly describe as follows.

Pragmatic finds the reasons for historical facts in man, but in man *in so far as he is an individual made abstract*, and thus opposed as such not only to the universe, but to other men, who have also been made abstract. History thus appears to consist of the mechanical action and reaction of beings, each one of whom is shut up in himself. Now no historical process is intelligible under such an arrangement, for the sum of the addition is always superior to the numbers added. To such an extent is this true that, not knowing which way to turn in order to make the sum come out right, it became necessary to excogitate the doctrine of 'little causes,' which were supposed to produce 'great effects.' This doctrine is absurd, for it is clear that great effects can only have real causes (if the illegitimate conceptions of great and small, of cause and effect, be applicable here). Such a formula, then, far from expressing the law of historical facts, unconsciously expresses the defects of the doctrine, which is inadequate for its purpose. And since the rational explanation fails, there arise crowds of fancies to take its place, which are all conceived upon the fundamental motive of the abstract individual. The pragmatic explanation of religions is characteristic of this; these are supposed to have been produced and maintained in the world by the economic cunning of the priests, taking advantage of the ignorance and credulity of the masses. But historical pragmatic does not always present itself in the guise of this egoistic and pessimistic inspiration. It is not fair to accuse it of egoism and utilitarianism, when the true accusation should, as we have already said, be levelled at its abstract individualism. This abstract individualism could be and sometimes was conceived even as highly moral, for we certainly find among the pragmatics sage legislators, good kings, and great men, who benefit humanity by means of science, inventions, and well-organized institutions. And if the greedy priest arranged the deceit of religions, if the cruel despot oppressed weak and innocent people, and if error was prolific and engendered the strangest and most foolish customs, yet the goodness of the enlightened monarch and legislator created the happy epochs, caused the arts to flourish, encouraged poets, aided discoveries, encouraged industries. From these pragmatic conceptions is derived the verbal usage whereby we speak of the age of Pericles, of that of Augustus, of that of Leo X, or of that of Louis XIV. And since fanciful explanations do not limit themselves merely to individuals physically existing, but also employ facts and small details, which are also made abstract and shut up in themselves, being thus also turned into what Vico describes as 'imaginative universals,' in like manner all those modes of explanation known as 'catastrophic' and making hinge the salvation or the ruin of a whole society upon the virtue of some single fact are also derived from pragmatic. Examples of this, which have also become proverbial, because they refer to concepts that have been persistently criticized by the historians of our time, are the fall of the Roman Empire, explained as the result of barbarian invasions, European civilization of the twelfth and thirteenth centuries, as the result of the Crusades, the renascence of classical literatures, as the result of the Turkish conquest of Constantinople and of the immigration of the learned Byzantines into Italy—and the like. And in just the same way as when the conception of the single individual did not furnish a sufficient explanation recourse was for that reason had to a multiplicity of individuals, to their co-operation and conflicting action, so here, when the sole cause adduced soon proved itself too narrow, an attempt was made to make up for the insufficiency of the method by the search for and enumeration of multiple historical causes. This enumeration threatened to proceed to the infinite, but, finite or infinite as it might be, it never explained the process to be explained, for the obvious reason that the continuous is never made out of the discontinuous, however much the latter may be multiplied and solidified. The so-called theory of the causes or factors of history, which survives in modern consciousness, together with several other mental habits of pragmatic, although generally inclined to follow other paths, is rather a confession of powerlessness to dominate history by means of individual causes, or causes individually conceived, than a theory; far from being a solution, it is but a reopening of the problem.

Pragmatic therefore fails to remain human—that is to say, to develop itself as rationality ; even in the human side to which it clings and in which it wishes to maintain and oppose itself to the natural or extra-natural ; and having already made individuals irrational and unhuman by making them abstract, it gradually has recourse to other historical factors, and arrives finally at natural causes, which do not differ at all in their abstractness from other individual causes. This means that pragmatic, which had previously asserted itself as humanism, falls back into naturalism, from which it had distinctly separated itself. And it falls into it all the more, seeing that, as has been noted, human individuals have been made abstract, not only among themselves, but toward the rest of the universe, which remains facing them, as though it were an enemy. What is it that really rules history according to this conception ? Is it man, or extra-human powers, natural or divine ? The claim that history exists only as an individual experience is not maintainable ; and in the pragmatic conception another agent in history is always presumed, an extra-human being which, at different times and to different thinkers, is known as fate, chance, fortune, nature, God, or by some other name. During the period at which pragmatic history flourished, and there was much talk of reason and wisdom, an expression of a monarchical or courtly tinge is to be found upon the lips of a monarch and of a philosopher who was his friend : homage was paid to *sa Majesté le Hasard !* Here too there is an attempt to patch up the difficulty and to seek eclectic solutions; in order to get out of it, we find pragmatic affirming that human affairs are conducted half by prudence and half by fortune, that intelligence contributes one part, fortune another, and so on. But who will assign the just share to the two competitors? Will not he who does assign it be the true and only maker of history? And since he who does assign it cannot be man, we see once again how pragmatic leads directly to transcendency and irrationality through its naturalism. It leads to irrationality, accompanied by all its following of inconveniences and by all the other dualisms that it brings with it and which are particular aspects of itself, such as the impossibility of development, regressions, the triumph of evil. The individual, engaged with external forces however conceived, sometimes wins, at other times loses; his victory itself is precarious, and the enemy is always victorious, inflicting losses upon him and making his victories precarious. Individuals are ants crushed by a piece of rock, and if some ant escapes from the mass that falls upon it and reproduces the species, which begins again the labour from the beginning, the rock will fall, or always may fall, upon the new generation and may crush all of its members, so that it is the arbiter of the lives of the industrious ants, to which it does much injury and no good. This is as pessimistic a view as can be conceived.

These difficulties and vain tentatives of pragmatic historiography have caused it to be looked upon with disfavour and to be rejected in favour of a superior conception, which preserves the initial humanistic motive and, removing from it the abstractness of the atomicized individual, assures it against any falling back into agnosticism, transcendency, or the despair caused by pessimism. The conception that has completed the criticism of pragmatic and the redemption of humanism has been variously and more or less well formulated in the course of the history of thought as mind or reason that constructs history, as the 'providence' of mind or the 'astuteness' of reason.

The great value of this conception is that it changes humanism from abstract to concrete, from monadistic or atomistic to idealistic, from something barely human into something cosmic, from unhuman humanism, such as that of man shut up in himself and opposed to man, into humanism that is really human, the humanity common to men, indeed to the whole universe, which is all humanity, even in its most hidden recesses—that is to say, spirituality. And history, according to this conception, as it is no longer the work of nature or of an extra-mundane God, so it is not the impotent work of the empirical and unreal individual, interrupted at every moment, but the work of that individual which is truly real and is the eternal spirit individualizing itself. For this reason it has no adversary at all opposed to it, but every adversary is at the same time its subject—that is to say, is one of the aspects of that dialecticism which constitutes its inner being. Again, it does not seek its principle of explanation in a particular act of thought or will, or in a single individual or in a multitude of individuals, or in an event given as the cause of other events, or in a collection of events that form the cause of a single event, but seeks and places it in the process itself, which is born of thought and returns to thought, and is intelligible through the auto-intelligibility of thought, which never has need of appealing to anything external to itself in order to understand itself. The explanation of history becomes so truly, because it coincides with its explication; whereas explanation by means of abstract causes is a breaking up of the process; the living having been slain, there is a forced attempt made to obtain life by setting the severed head again upon the shoulders.

When the historians of our day, and the many sensible folk who do not make a profession of philosophy, repeat that the history of the world does not depend upon the will of individuals, upon such accidents as the length of Cleopatra's nose, or upon anecdotes; that no historical event has ever been the result of deception or misunderstanding, but that all have been due to persuasion and necessity; that there is some one who has more intelligence than any individual whatever—the world; that the explanation of a fact is always to be sought in the entire organism and not in a single part torn from the other parts; that history could not have been developed otherwise than it has developed, and that it obeys its own iron logic; that every fact has its reason and that no individual is completely wrong; and numberless propositions of the same sort, which I have assembled promiscuously—they are perhaps not aware that with such henceforth obvious statements they are repeating the criticism of pragmatic history (and implicitly that of theological and naturalistic history) and affirming the truth of idealistic history. Were they aware of this, they would not mingle with these propositions others which are their direct contradiction, relating to causes, accidents, decadences, climates, races, and so on, which represent the detritus of the conception that has been superseded. For the rest, it is characteristic of the consciousness called common or vulgar to drag along with it an abundant detritus of old, dead concepts mingled with the new ones; but this does not detract from the importance of its enforced recognition of the new concept, which it substantially follows in its judgments.

Owing to the already mentioned resolution of all historiographical questions into general philosophy, it would not be possible to give copious illustrations of the new concept of history which the nineteenth century has accepted in place of the pragmatic conception without giving a lengthy exposition of general philosophy, which, in addition to the particular inconvenience its presence would have here, would lead to the repetition of things elsewhere explained. Taking the position that history is the work, not of the abstract individual, but of reason or providence, as admitted, I intend rather to correct an erroneous mode of expressing that doctrine which I believe that I have detected. I mean the form given to it by Vico and by Hegel, according to which Providence or Reason makes use of the particular ends and passions of men, in order to conduct them unconsciously to more lofty spiritual conditions, making use for this purpose of benevolent cunning.

Were this form exact, or were it necessary to take it literally (and not simply as an imaginative and provisional expression of the truth), I greatly fear that a shadow of dualism and transcendency would appear in the heart of the idealistic conception. For in this position of theirs toward the Idea or Providence, individuals would have to be considered, if not as *deluded* (satisfied indeed beyond their desires and hopes), then certainly as *illuded*, even though benevolently illuded. Individuals and Providence, or individuals and Reason, would not make one, but two ; and the individual would be inferior and the Idea superior—that is to say, dualism and the reciprocal transcendency of God and the world would persist. This, on the other hand, would not be at variance from the historical point of view with what has been several times observed as to the theological residue at the bottom of Hegel's, and yet more of Vico's, thought. Now the claim of the idealistic conception is that individual and Idea make one and not two—that is to say, perfectly coincide and are identified. For this reason, there must be no talking (save metaphorically) of the wisdom of the Idea and of the folly or illusion of individuals.

Nevertheless it seems indubitably certain that the individual acts through the medium of infinite illusions, proposing to himself ends that he fails to attain and attaining ends that he has not seen. Schopenhauer (imitating Hegel) has made popular the illusions of love, by means of which the will leads the individual to propagate the species; and we all know that illusions are not limited to those that men and women exercise toward one another (*les tromperies réciproques*), but that they enter into our every act, which is always accompanied by hopes and mirages that are not followed by realization. And the illusion of illusions seems to be this: that the individual believes himself to be toiling to live and to intensify his life more and more, whereas he is really toiling to die. He wishes to see his work completed as the affirmation of his life, and its completion is the passing away of the work; he toils to obtain peace in life, but peace is on the contrary death, which alone is peace. How then are we to deny this dualism between the illusion of the individual and the reality of the work, between the individual and the Idea? How are we to refute the only explanation which seems to compose in some measure the discord—namely, that the Idea turns the illusions of the individual to its own ends, even though this doctrine lead inevitably to a sort of transcendency of the Idea?

But the real truth is that what results from the observations and objections above exposed is not the illusion of the individual who loves, who tries to complete his work, who sighs for peace, but rather the illusion of him who believes that the individual is illuded: the illusory is the illusion itself. And this illusion appears in the phenomenology of the spirit as the result of the well-known abstractive process, which breaks up unity in an arbitrary manner and in this case separates the result from the process or actual acting, in which alone the former is real ; the accompaniment from the accompanied, which is all one with the accompaniment, because there is not spirit and its escort, but only the one spirit in its development, the single moments of the process, of the continuity, which is their soul; and so on. That illusion arises in the individual when he begins to reflect upon himself, and at the beginning of that reflection, which is at the same time a dialectical process. But in concrete reflection, or rather in concrete consciousness, he discovers that there is no end that has not been realized, as well as it could, in the process, in which it was never an absolute end—that is to say, an abstract end, but both a means and an end.

To return to the popular theory of Schopenhauer, only he who looks upon men as animals, or worse than animals, can believe that love is a process that leads only to the biological propagation of the species, when every man knows that he fecundates his own soul above all prior to the marriage couch, and that images and thoughts and projects and actions are created before children and in addition to them. Certainly, we are conscious of the moments of an action as it develops—that is to say, of its passage and not of its totality seen in the light of a new spiritual situation, such as we strive to obtain when, as we say, we leave the tumult behind us and set ourselves to write our own history. But there is no illusion, either now or then ; neither now nor then is there the abstract individual face to face with a Providence who succeeds in deceiving him for beneficial ends, acting rather as a doctor than as a serious educator, and treating the race of men as though they were animals to train and make use of, instead of men to educate—that is to say, develop.

After having concentrated the mind upon a thought of Vico and of Hegel, can it be possible to set ourselves down to examine those of others which afford material to the controversies of historians and methodologists of history of our time ? These represent the usual form in which appear the problems concerning the relation between the individual and the Idea, between pragmatic and idealistic history. Perhaps the patience necessary for the descent into low haunts is meritorious and our duty ; perhaps there may be some useful conclusion to be drawn from these common disputes ; but I must beg to be excused for not taking part in them and for limiting myself to the sole remark that the question which has been for some time discussed, whether history be the history of 'masses' or of 'individuals,' would be laughable in its very enunciation, if we were to understand by 'mass' what the word implies, a complex of individuals. And since it is not a good method to attribute laughable ideas to adversaries, it may be supposed that on this occasion what is meant by 'mass' is something else, which moves the mass of individuals. In this case, anyone can see that the problem is the same as that which has just been examined. The conflict between 'collectivistic' and 'individualistic' historiography will never be composed so long as the former assigns to collectivity the power that is creative of ideas and institutions, and the latter assigns it to the individual of genius, for both affirmations are true in what they include and false in what they exclude—that is to say, not only in their exclusion of the opposed thesis, but also in the tacit exclusion, which they both make, of totality as idea.

A warning as to a historiographical method, so similar in appearance to that which I have been defending as to be confounded with it, may perhaps be more opportune. This method, which is variously called *sociological*, *institutional*, and *of values*, preserves among the variety of its content and the inequality of mental level noticeable in its supporters the general and constant characteristic of believing that true history consists of the history of societies, institutions, and human values, not of individual values. The history of individuals, according to this view, is excluded, as being a parallel or inferior history, and its inferiority is held to be due either to the slight degree of interest that it is capable of arousing or to its lack of intelligibility. In the latter case (by an inversion on this occasion of the attitude of contempt which was noted in pragmatic history) it is handed over to chronicle or romance. But in such dualism as this, and in the disagreement which persists owing to that dualism, lies the profound difference between the empirical and naturalistic conceptions of value, of institutions, and of societies, and the idealistic conception. This conception does not contemplate the establishment of an abstract history of the spirit, of the abstract universal, side by side with or beyond abstract individualistic or pragmatic history; but the understanding that individual and idea, taken separately, are two equivalent abstractions, each equally unfitted for supplying its subject to history, and that true history is the history of the individual in so far as he is universal and of the universal in so far as individual. It is not a question of abolishing Pericles to the advantage of politics, or Plato to the advantage of philosophy, or Sophocles to the advantage of tragedy; but to think and to represent politics, philosophy, and tragedy as Pericles, Plato, and Sophocles, and these as each one of the others in one of their particular moments. Because if each one of these is the shadow of a dream outside its relation with the spirit, so likewise is the spirit outside its individualizations, and to attain to universality in the conception of history is to render both equally secure with that security which they mutually confer upon one another. Were the existence of Pericles, of Sophocles, and of Plato indifferent, would not the existence of the idea have for that very reason been pronounced indifferent? Let him who cuts individuals out of history but pay close attention and he will perceive that either he has not cut them out at all, as he imagined, or he has cut out with them history itself.

VII

CHOICE AND PERIODIZATION

SINCE a fact is historical in so far as it is thought, and since nothing exists outside thought, there can be no sense whatever in the question, What are *historical facts* and what are *non-historical facts*? A non-historical fact would be a fact that has not been thought and would therefore be non-existent, and so far no one has yet met with a non-existent fact. A historical thought links itself to and follows another historical thought, and then another, and yet another; and however far we navigate the great sea of being, we never leave the well-defined sea of thought.

But it remains to be explained how the illusion is formed that there are two orders of facts, historical and non-historical. The explanation is easy when we recollect what has been said as to the chroniclizing of history which dies as history, leaving behind it the mute traces of its life, and also as to the function of erudition or philology, which preserves these traces for the ends of culture, arranging scattered items of news, documents, and monuments in an orderly manner. News, documents, and monuments are innumerable, and to collect them all would not only be impossible, but contrary to the ends themselves of culture, which, though aided in its work by the moderate and even copious supply of such things, would be hindered and suffocated by their exuberance, not to say infinity. We consequently observe that the annotator of news transcribes some items and omits the rest; the collector of papers arranges and ties up in a bundle a certain number of them, tearing up or burning or sending to the dealer in such things a very large quantity, which forms the majority ; the collector of antiques places some objects in glass cases, others in temporary safe custody, others he resolutely destroys or allows to be destroyed ; if he does otherwise, he is not an intelligent collector, but a maniacal amasser, well fitted to provide (as he has provided) the comic type of the antiquarian for fiction and comedy. For this reason, not only are papers jealously collected and preserved in public archives, and lists made of them, but efforts are also made to discard those that are useless. It is for this reason that in the recensions of philologists we always hear the same song in praise of the learned man who has made a 'sober' use of documents, of blame for him who has followed a different method and included what is vain and superfluous in his volumes of annals, of selections from archives, or of collections of documents. All learned men and philologists, in fact, *select*, and all are advised to *select*. And what is the logical criterion of this selection ? There is none : no logical criterion can be named that shall determine what news or what documents are or are not useful and important, just because we are here occupied with a practical and not with a scientific problem. Indeed, this lack of a logical criterion is the foundation of the sophism that tyrannizes over maniacal collectors, who reasonably affirm that everything can be of use, and would therefore unreasonably preserve everything—they wear themselves out in accumulating old clothes and odds and ends of all sorts, over which they mount guard with jealous affection. The criterion is the choice itself, conditioned, like every economic act, by knowledge of the actual situation, and in this case by the practical and scientific needs of a definite moment or epoch. This selection is certainly conducted with intelligence, but not with the application of a philosophic criterion, and is justified only in and by itself. For this reason we speak of the fine tact, or scent, or instinct of the collector or learned man. Such a process of selection may quite well make use of apparent logical distinctions, as those between public and private facts, capital and secondary documents, beautiful or ugly, significant or insignificant monuments; but in final analysis the decision is always given from practical motives, and is summed up in the act of preserving or neglecting. Now from this preserving or neglecting, in which our action is realized, is afterward invented an *objective* quality, attributed to facts, which leads to their being spoken of as 'facts that are worthy' and 'facts that are not worthy of history,' of 'historical' and 'non-historical' facts. But all this is an affair of imagination, of vocabulary, and of rhetoric, which in no way changes the substance of things.

When history is confounded with erudition and the methods of the one are unduly transferred to the other, and when the metaphorical distinction that has just been noted is taken in a literal sense, we are asked how it is possible to avoid going astray in the infinity of facts, and with what criterion it is possible to effect the separation of 'historical' facts from 'those that are not worthy of history.' But there is no fear of going astray in history, because, as we have seen, the problem is in every case prepared by life, and in every case the problem is solved by thought, which passes from the confusion of life to the distinctness of consciousness; a given problem with a given solution: a problem that generates other problems, but is never a problem of choice between two or more facts, but on each occasion a creation of the unique fact, the fact thought. Choice does not appear in it, any more than in art, which passes from the obscurity of sentiment to the clearness of the representation, and is never embarrassed between the images to be chosen, because itself creates the image, the unity of the image.

By thus confounding two things, not only is an insoluble problem created, but the very distinction between facts that can and facts that cannot be neglected is also denaturalized and rendered void. This distinction is quite valid as regards erudition, for facts that can be neglected are always facts—that is to say, they are traces of facts, in the form of news, documents, and monuments, and for this reason one can understand how they can be looked upon as a class to be placed side by side with the other class of facts that cannot be neglected. But non-historical facts—that is to say, facts that have not been thought—would be nothing, and when placed beside historical facts—that is to say, thought as a species of the same genus—they would communicate their nullity to those also, and would dissolve their own distinctness, together with the concept of history.

After this, it does not seem necessary to examine the characteristics that have been proposed as the basis for this division of facts into historical and non-historical. The assumption being false, the manner in which it is treated in its particulars remains indifferent and without importance in respect to the fundamental criticism of the division itself. It may happen (and this is usually the case) that the characteristics and the differences enunciated have some truth in themselves, or at least offer some problem for solution : for example, when by historical facts are meant general facts and by non-historical facts those that are individual. Here we find the problem of the relation of the individual and the universal. Or, again, by historical facts are sometimes meant those that treat of history proper, and by non-historical the stray references of chronicles, and here we find the problem as to the relation between history and chronicle. But regarded as an attempt to decide logically of what facts history should treat and what neglect, and to assign to each its quality, such divisions are all equally erroneous.

The *periodization* of history is subject to the same criticism. To *think* history is certainly *to divide it into periods*, because thought is organism, dialectic, drama, and as such has its periods, its beginning, its middle, and its end, and all the other ideal pauses that a drama implies and demands. But those pauses are ideal and therefore inseparable from thought, with which they are one, as the shadow is one with the body, silence with sound: they are identical and changeable with it. Christian thinkers divided history into that which preceded and that which followed the redemption, and this periodization was not an addition to Christian thought, but Christian thought itself. We modern Europeans divide it into antiquity, the Middle Ages, and modern times. This periodization has been subject to a great deal of refined criticism on the part of those who hold that it came to be introduced anyhow, almost dishonestly, without the authority of great names, and without the advice of the philosophers and the methodologists being asked on the matter. But it has maintained itself and will maintain itself so long as our consciousness shall persist in its present phase. The fact of its having been insensibly formed would appear to be rather a merit than a demerit, because this means that it was not due to the caprice of an individual, but has followed the development of modern consciousness itself. When antiquity has nothing more to tell us who still feel the need of studying Greek and Latin, Greek philosophy and Roman law; when the Middle Ages have been superseded (and they have not been superseded yet); when a new social form, different from that which emerged from the ruins of the Middle Ages, has supplanted our own; then the problem itself and the historical outlook which derives from it will also be changed, and perhaps antiquity and the Middle Ages and modern times will all be contained within a single epoch, and the pauses be otherwise distributed. And what has been said of these great periods is to be understood of all the others, which vary according to the variety of historical material and the various modes of viewing it. It has sometimes been said that every periodization has a 'relative' value. But we must say 'both relative and absolute,' like all thought, it being understood that the periodization is intrinsic to thought and determined by the determination of thought.

However, the practical needs of chroniclism and of learning make themselves felt here also. Just as in metrical treatises the internal rhythm of a poem is resolved into external rhythm and divided into syllables and feet, into long and short vowels, tonic and rhythmic accents, into strophes and series of strophes, and so on, so the internal time of historical thought (that time which is thought itself) is derived from chroniclism converted into external time, or temporal series, of which the elements are spatially separated from one another. Scheme and facts are no longer one, but two, and the facts are disposed according to the scheme, and divided according to the scheme into major and minor cycles (for example, according to hours, days, months, years, centuries, and millenniums, where the calculation is based upon the rotations and revolutions of the earth upon itself and round the sun). Such is *chronology*, by means of which we know that the histories of Sparta, Athens, and Rome filled the thousand years preceding Christ, that of the Lombards, the Visigoths, and the Franks the first millennium after Christ, and that we are still in the second millennium. This mode of chronology can be pursued by means of particularizing incidents thus: that the Empire of the West ended in A.D. 476 (although it did not really end then or had already ended previously); that Charlemagne the Frank was crowned Emperor at Rome by Pope Leo III in the year 800; that America was discovered in 1492, and that the Thirty Years War ended in 1648. It is of the greatest use to us to know these things, or (since we really *know* nothing in this way) to acquire the capacity of so checking references to facts that we are able to find them easily and promptly when occasion arises. Certainly no one thinks of speaking ill of chronologies and chronographies and tables and synoptic views of history, although in using them we run the risk (and in what thing done by man does he not run a risk?) of seeing worthy folk impressed with the belief that the number produces the event, as the hand of the clock, when it touches the sign of the hour, makes the clock strike; or (as an old professor of mine used to say) that the curtain fell upon the acting of ancient history in 476, to rise again immediately afterward on the beginning of the Middle Ages.

But such fancies are not limited to the minds of the

ingenuous and inattentive; they constitute the base of that error owing to which a distinction of periods, which shall be what is called *objective and natural*, is desired and sought after. Christian chronographers had already introduced this ontological meaning into chronology, making the millenniums of the world's history correspond with the days of the creation or the ages of man's life. Finally, Ferrari in Italy and Lorenz in Germany (the latter ignorant of his Italian predecessor) conceived a theory of historical periods according to generations, calculated in periods of thirty-one years and a fraction, or of thirty-three years and a fraction, and grouped as tetrads or triads, in periods of a hundred and twenty-five years or a century. But, without dwelling upon numerical and chronographic schemes, all doctrines that represent the history of nations as proceeding according to the stages of development of the individual, of his psychological development, of the categories of the spirit, or of anything else, are due to the same error, which is that of rendering periodization external and natural. All are mythological, if taken in the naturalistic sense, save when these designations are employed empirically—that is to say, when chronology is used in chroniclism and erudition in a legitimate manner. We must also repeat a warning as to the care to be employed in recognizing important problems, which sometimes have first appeared through the medium of those erroneous inquiries, and as to the truths that have been seen or caught a glimpse of by these means. This exempts us (as we remarked above in relation to the criteria of choice) from examining those doctrines in the particularity of their various determinations, because in this respect, if their assumption be obviously fantastic, their value is consequently *nil*.

Nil, as the value of all those æsthetic constructions is *nil* which claim to pass from the abstractions, by means of which they reduce the organism of the work of art to fragments for practical ends, to the explanation of the nature of art and to the judgment and history of the creations of human imagination.

VIII

DISTINCTION (SPECIAL HISTORIES) AND DIVISION

THE conception of history that we have reached—namely, that which has not its documents outside itself, but in itself, which has not its final and causal explanation outside itself, but within itself, which has not philosophy outside itself, but coincides with philosophy, which has not the reason for its definite form and rhythm outside itself, but within itself—identifies history with the act of thought itself, which is always philosophy and history together. And with this it debarrasses it of the props and plasters applied to it as though to an invalid in need of external assistance. For they really did produce an infirmity through their very insistence in first imagining and then treating a non-existent infirmity.

Doubtless the autonomy thus attained is a great advantage; but at first sight it is not free from a grave objection. When all the fallacious distinctions formerly believed in have been cancelled, it seems that nothing remains for history as an act of thought but the immediate consciousness of the individual-universal, in which all distinctions are submerged and lost. And this is mysticism, which is admirably adapted for feeling oneself at unity with God, but is not adapted for thinking the world nor for acting in the world.

Nor does it seem useful to add that unity with God does not exclude consciousness of diversity, of change, of becoming. For it can be objected that consciousness of diversity either derives from the individual and intuitive element, and in this case it is incomprehensible how such an element can subsist in its proper form of intuition, in thought, which always universalizes; or if it is said to be the result of the act of thought itself, then the distinction, believed to have been abolished, reappears in a strengthened form, and the asserted indistinct simplicity of thought remains shaken. A mysticism which should insist upon particularity and diversity, a *historical mysticism*, in fact, would be a contradiction in terms, for mysticism is unhistorical and anti-historical by its very nature.

But these objections retain their validity precisely when the act of thought is conceived in the mystical manner—that is to say, not as an act of thought, but as something negative, the simple result of the negation by reason of empirical distinctions, which certainly leaves thought free of illusions, but not yet truly full of itself. To sum up, mysticism, which is a violent reaction from naturalism and transcendency, yet retains traces of what it has denied, because it is incapable of substituting anything for it, and thus maintains its presence, in however negative a manner. But the really efficacious negation of empiricism and transcendency, their positive negation, is brought about not by means of mysticism, but of *idealism*; not in the immediate, but in the *mediated* consciousness; not in indistinct unity, but in the unity that is *distinction*, and as such truly *thought*.

The act of thought is the consciousness of the spirit that is consciousness; and therefore that act is auto-consciousness. And auto-consciousness implies distinction in unity, distinction between subject and object, theory and practice, thought and will, universal and particular, imagination and intellect, utility and morality, or however these distinctions of and in unity are formulated, and whatever may be the historical forms and denominations which the eternal system of distinctions, *perennis philosophia*, may assume. To think is to judge, and to judge is to distinguish while unifying, in which the distinguishing is not less real than the unifying, and the unifying than the distinguishing—that is to say, they are real, not as two diverse realities, but as one reality, which is dialectical unity (whether it be called unity or distinction).

The first consequence to be drawn from this conception of the spirit and of thought is that when empirical distinctions have been overthrown history does not fall into the indistinct; when the will-o'-the-wisps have been extinguished, darkness does not supervene, because the light of the distinction is to be found in history itself. History is thought by judging it, with that judgment which is not, as we have shown, the evaluation of sentiments, but the intrinsic knowledge of facts. And here its unity with philosophy is all the more evident, because the better philosophy penetrates and refines its distinctions, the better it penetrates the particular; and the closer its embrace of the particular, the closer its possession of its own proper conceptions. Philosophy and historiography progress together, indissolubly united.

Another consequence to be deduced from the above, and one which will perhaps seem to be more clearly connected with the practice of historiography, is the refutation of the false idea of a *general history*, superior to *special histories*. This has been called a history of histories, and is supposed to be true and proper history, having beneath it political, economic, and institutional histories, moral history or the history of the sentiments and ethical ideals, the history of poetry and art, the history of thought and of philosophy. But were this so, a dualism would arise, with the usual result of every dualism, that each one of the two terms, having been ill distinguished, reveals itself as empty. In this case, either general history shows itself to be empty, having nothing to do when the special histories have accomplished their work, or particular histories do so, when they fail even to pick up the crumbs of the banquet, all of which has been voraciously devoured by the other. Sometimes recourse is had to a feeble expedient, and to general history is accorded the treatment of one of the subjects of the special histories, the latter being then grouped apart from that. Of this arrangement the best that can be said is that it is purely verbal and does not designate a logical distinction and opposition, and the worst that can happen is that a real value should be attributed to it, because in this case a fantastic hierarchy is established, which makes it impossible to understand the genuine development of the facts. And there is practically no special history that has not been promoted to be a general history, now as *political* or *social* history, to which those of literature, art, philosophy, religion, and the lesser sides of life should supply an appendix ; now as *history of the ideas or progress of the mind*, where social history and all the others are placed in the second line; now as *economic history*, where all the others are looked upon as histories or chronicles of 'superstructures' derived from economic development in an illusory manner, while the former is held to have developed in some mysterious way by means of unknown powers, without thought and will, or producing thought and will, in fancies and velleities, like so many bubbles on the surface of its course. We must be firm in maintaining against the theory of *general* history that there *does not exist anything real but special histories*, because thought thinks facts to the extent that it discerns a special aspect of them, and only and always constructs histories of ideas, of imaginations, of political actions, of apostolates, and the like.

But it is equally just and advantageous to maintain the opposite thesis: that *nothing exists but general history*. In this way is refuted the false notion of the speciality of histories, understood as a juxtaposition of specialities. This fallacy is correctly noted by the critics in all histories which expose the various orders of facts one after the other as so many strata and (to employ the critics' word) compartments or little boxes, containing political history, industrial and commercial history, history of customs, religious history, history of literature and of art, and so on, under so many separate headings. These divisions are merely literary; they may possess some utility as such, but in the case under consideration they do not fulfil merely a literary function, but attempt that of historical understanding, and thereby give evidence of their defect, in thus presenting these histories as without relation between one another, not dialecticized, but aggregated. It is quite clear that *history* remains to be written after the writing of those *histories* in this disjointed manner. Abstract distinction and abstract unity are both equally misunderstandings of concrete distinction and concrete unity, which is relation.

And when the relation is not broken and history is thought in the concrete, it is seen that to think one aspect is to think all the others at the same time. Thus it is impossible to understand completely the doctrine, say, of a philosopher, without having to some extent recourse to the personality of the man himself, and, by distinguishing the philosopher from the man, at the same time qualifying not only the philosopher but the man, and uniting these two distinct characteristics as a relation of life and philosophy. The same is to be said of the distinction between the philosopher as philosopher and as orator or artist, as subject to his private passions or as rising to the execution of his duty, and so on. This means that we cannot think the history of philosophy save as at the same time social, political, literary, religious, and ethical history, and so on. This is the source of the illusion that one in particular of these histories is the whole of them, or that that one from which a start is made, and which answers to the predilections and to the competence of the writer, is the foundation of all the others. It also explains why it is sometimes said that the 'history of philosophy' is also the 'philosophy of history,' or that 'social history' is the true 'history of philosophy,' and so on. A history of philosophy thoroughly thought out is truly the whole of history (and in like manner a history of literature or of any other form of the spirit), not because it annuls the other in itself, but because all the others are present in it. Hence the demand that historians shall acquire universal minds and a doctrine that shall also be in a way universal, and the hatred of specialist historians, pure philosophers, pure men of letters, pure politicians, or pure economists, who, owing precisely to their one-sidedness, fail even to understand the speciality that they claim to know in its purity, but possess only in skeleton form—that is to say, in its abstractness.

And here a distinction becomes clear to us, with which it is impossible to dispense in thinking history: the distinction between *form* and *matter*, owing to which, for example, we understand art by referring it to matter (emotions, sentiments, passions, etc.) to which the artist has given form; or philosophy by referring it to the facts which gave rise to the problems that the thinker formulated and solved; or the action of the politician by referring it to the aspirations and ideas with which he was faced, and which supplied the material he has shaped with genius, as an artist of practical life—that is to say, we understand these things by always distinguishing an *external* from an *internal* history, or an external history that is made into an internal history. This distinction of matter and form, of external and internal, would give rise again to the worst sort of dualism, would lead us to think of the pragmatical imagination of man who strives against his enemy nature, if it did not assume an altogether internal and dialectical meaning in its true conception. Because from what has been said it is easy to see that external and internal are not two realities or two forms of reality, but that external and internal, matter and form, both appear in turn as form in respect to one another; and this materialization of each to idealize itself in the other is the perpetual movement of the spirit as relation and circle: a circle that is progress just because neither of these forms has the privilege of functioning solely as form, and neither has the misfortune of functioning solely as matter. What is the matter of artistic and philosophical history? What is called social and moral history? And what is the matter of this history? Artistic and philosophical history. From this clearing up of the relation between matter and form, that false mode of history is refuted which sets facts on one side and ideas on the other, as two rival elements, and is therefore never able to pay its debt and show how ideas are generated from facts and facts from ideas, because that generation must be conceived in its truth as a perpetually rendering vain of one of the elements in the unity of the other.

If history is based upon distinction (unity) and coincides with philosophy, the high importance that research into the autonomy of one or the other special history attains in historiographical development is perfectly comprehensible, but this is merely the reflection of philosophical research, and is often troubled and lacking in precision. All know what a powerful stimulus the new conception of imagination and art gave to the conception of history, and therefore also to mythology and religion, which were being developed with slowness and difficulty during the eighteenth to triumph at the beginning of the nineteenth century. This is set down to the creation of the history of poetry and myth in the works of Vico in the first place and then of Herder and others, and of the history of the figurative arts in the works of Winckelmann and others. And to the clearer conception of philosophy, law, customs, and language is due their renewal in the respective historiographical fields, at the hands of Hegel, Savigny, and Humboldt, and other creators and improvers of history, celebrated on this account. This also explains why there has been so much dispute as to whether history should be described as history of the state or as history of culture, and as to whether the history of culture represents an original aspect beyond that of the state or greater than it, as to whether the progress narrated in history is only intellectual or also practical and moral, and so on. These discussions must be referred to the fundamental philosophical inquiry into the forms of the spirit, their distinction and relation, and to the precise mode of relation of each one to the other.[1]

But although history distinguishes and unifies, it never *divides*—that is to say, *separates*; and the *divisions of history* which have been and are made do not originate otherwise than as the result of the same practical and abstractive process that we have seen break up the actuality of living history to collect and arrange the inert materials in the temporal scheme, rendered extrinsic. Histories already produced, and as such past, receive in this way titles (every thought is 'without title' in its actuality—that is to say, it has only itself for title), and each one is separated from the other, and all of them, thus separated, are classified under more or less general empirical conceptions, by means of classifications that more or less cross one another. We may admire copious lists of this sort in the books of methodologists, all of them proceeding, as is inevitable, according to one or the other of these general criteria: the criterion of the *quality* of the objects (histories of religions, customs, ideas, institutions, etc., etc.), and that of *temporal-spatial* arrangement (European, Asiatic, American, ancient, medieval, of modern times, of ancient Greece, of ancient Rome, of modern Greece, of the Rome of the Middle Ages, etc.); in conformity with the abstract procedure which, when dividing the concept, is led to posit on the one hand *abstract forms of the spirit* (objects) and on the other *abstract intuitions* (space and time). I shall not say that those titles and divisions are useless, nor even those tables, but shall limit myself to the remark that the history of philosophy, of art, or of any other ideally distinct history, when understood as a definite book or discourse, becomes empirical for

[1] See Appendix II

the reason already given, that true distinction is ideal, and a discourse or a book in its concreteness contains not only distinction but unity and totality, and to look upon either as incorporating only one side of the real is arbitrary. And I shall also observe that as there are histories of philosophy and of art in the empirical sense, so also nothing forbids our talking in the same sense of a general history, separate from special histories, indeed even of a history of progress and one of decadence, of good and evil, of truth and error.

The confusion between division and distinction—that is to say, between the empirical consideration that breaks up history into special histories and the philosophical consideration which always unifies and distinguishes as it unifies—is the cause of errors analogous to those that we have seen to result from such a process. To this are due above all the many disquisitions on the 'problem' and on the 'limits' of this or that history or group of special histories empirically constituted. The problem does not exist, and the limits are impossible to assign because they are conventional, as is finally recognized with much trouble, and as could be recognized with much less trouble if a start were made, not from the periphery, but from the centre—that is to say, from gnoseological analysis. A graver error is the creation of an infinity of *entia imaginationis*, taken for metaphysical entities and forms of the spirit, and the pretension that arises from this of developing the history of abstractions as though they were so many forms of the spirit with independent lives of their own, whereas the spirit is one. Hence the innumerable otiose problems with fantastic solutions met with in historical books, which it is here unnecessary to record. Every one is now able to draw these obvious consequences for himself and to make appropriate reflections concerning them. It is further obvious that the *entia imaginationis*, in the same way as the 'choice' of facts, and the chronological schematization or dating of them, enter as a subsidiary element into any concrete exposition of historical thought, because the distinction of thinking and abstraction is an ideal distinction, which operates only in the unity of the spirit.

IX

THE 'HISTORY OF NATURE' AND HISTORY

WE must cease the process of classifying referred to just now, and also that of the illusion of naturalism connected with it, by means of which imaginary entities created by abstraction are changed into historical facts and classificatory schemes into history, if we wish to understand the difference between history that is history and that due to what are called the natural sciences. This is also called history—'*history of nature*'—but is so only in name.

Some few years ago a lively protest was made [1] against the confusion of these two forms of mental labour, one of which offers us genuine history, such as might, for instance, be that of the Peloponnesian War or of Hannibal's wars or of ancient Egyptian civilization, and the other a spurious history, such as that known as the history of animal organisms, of the earth's structure or geology, of the formation of the solar system or cosmogony. It was observed with reason that in many treatises the one has been wrongly connected with the other—that is to say, history of civilization with history of nature, as though the former follows the latter historically. The bottomless abyss between the two was pointed out. This has been observed, however, in a confused way by all, and better by historians of purely historical temperament, who have an instinctive

[1] By the economist Professor Gottl, at the seventh congress of German historians, held at Heidelberg. The lecture can be read in print under the anything but clear or exact title of *Die Grenzen der Geschichte* (Leipzig, Duncker u. Humblot, 1904).

repugnance for natural history and hold themselves carefully aloof from it. It was remembered with reason that the history of historians has always the individually determinate as its object, and proceeds by internal reconstruction, whereas that of the naturalists depends upon types and abstractions and proceeds by analogies. Finally, this so-called history or *quasi-history* was very accurately defined as an apparently chronological arrangement of things spatially distinct, and it was proposed to describe it with a new and proper name, that of *Metastoria.*

Indeed, constructions of this sort are really nothing but classificatory schemes, from the more simple to the more complex. Their terms are obtained by abstract analyses and generalization, and their series appears to the imagination as a history of the successive development of the more complex from the more simple. Their right to exist as classificatory schemes is incontestable, and their utility is also incontestable, for they avail themselves of imagination to assist learning and to aid the memory.

This only becomes contestable when they are estranged from themselves, lose their real nature, lay claim to illegitimate functions, and take their imaginary historicity too seriously. We find this in the metaphysic of naturalism, especially in *evolutionism*, which has been its most recent form. This is due, not so much to the men of science (who are as a rule cautious and possess a more or less clear consciousness of the limits of those schemes and series) as to the dilettante scientists and dilettante philosophers to whom we owe the many books that undertake to narrate the origin of the world, and which, aided by the acrisia of their authors, run on without meeting any obstacle, from the cell, indeed from the nebula, to the French Revolution, and even to the socialist movements of the nineteenth century. 'Universal histories,' and therefore cosmological romances (as we have already remarked in relation to universal histories), are composed, not of pure thought, which is criticism, but of thought mingled with imagination, which finds its outlet in myths. It is useless to prove in detail that the evolutionists of to-day are creators of myths, and that they weary themselves with attempts to write the first chapters of Genesis in modern style (their description is more elaborate, but they confuse such description with history in a manner by no means inferior to that of Babylonian or Israelitish priests), because this becomes evident as soon as such works are placed in their proper position. Their logical origin will at once make clear their true character.

But setting aside these scientific monstrosities, already condemned by the constant attitude of restraint and scepsis toward them on the part of all scientifically trained minds—condemned, too, by the very fact that they have had to seek and have found their fortune at the hands of the crowd or 'great public,' and have fallen to the rank of popular propaganda—we must here determine more precisely how these classificatory schemes of historiographical appearance are formed and how they operate. With this object, it is well to observe that classificatory schemes and apparent histories do not appear to be confined to the field of what are called the natural sciences or sub-human world, but appear also in that of the moral sciences or sciences of the human world. And to adduce simple and perspicuous examples, it often happens that in the abstract analysis of language and the positing of the types of the parts of speech, noun, verb, adjective, pronoun, and so on, or in the analysis of the word into syllables and sounds, or of style into proper or metaphorical words and into various classes of metaphors, we construct classes that go from the more simple to the more complex. This gives rise to the illusion of history of language, exposed as the successive acquisition of the various parts of speech or as the passage from the single sound to the syllable (monosyllabic languages), from the syllable to the aggregate of syllables (plurisyllabic languages), from words to propositions, metres, rhymes, and so on. These are imaginary histories that have never been developed elsewhere than in the studies of scientists. In like manner, literary styles that have been abstractly distinguished and arranged in series of increasing complexity (for example, lyric, epic, drama) have given rise and continue to give rise to the thought of a schematic arrangement of poetry, which, for example, should appear during a first period as lyric, a second as epic, a third as drama.

The same has happened with regard to the classifications of abstract political, economic, philosophical forms, and so on, all of which have been followed by their shadows in the shape of imaginative history. The repugnance that historians experience in attaching their narratives to naturalistic-mythological prologues—that is to say, in linking together in matrimony a living being and a corpse—is also proved by their reluctance to admit scraps of abstract history into concrete history, for they at once reveal their heterogeneity in regard to one another by their mere appearance. De Sanctis has often been reproached for not having begun his *History of Italian Literature* with an account of the origins of the Italian language and of its relations with Latin, and even with the linguistic family of Indo-European languages, and of the races that inhabit the various parts of Italy. An attempt has even been made to correct the design of that classic work by supplying, with a complete lack of historical sense, the introductions and additions that are not needed. But de Sanctis, who took great pains to select the best point of departure for the narrative of the history of Italian literature, and finally decided to begin with a brief sketch of the state of culture at the Suabian court and of the Sicilian poetical school, did not hesitate a moment in rejecting all abstractions of languages and races which to his true historical sense did not appear to be reconcilable with the *tenzone* of Ciullo, with the rhythms of Friar Jacob, or with the ballades of Guido Cavalcanti, which are quite concrete things.

We must also remember that plans for classification and pseudo-historical arrangements of their analogies are created not only upon the bodies of histories that are living and really reproducible and rethinkable, but also upon those that are dead—that is to say, upon news items, documents, and monuments. This observation makes more complete the identification of imaginary histories arising from the natural sciences with those which have their source in the moral sciences. The foundation of both is therefore very often not historical intelligence, but, on the contrary, the lack of it, and their end not only that of aiding living history and keeping it alive, but also the mediate end of assisting in the prompt handling of the remains and the cinders of the vanished world, the inert residues of history.

The efficacy of this enlargement of the concept of abstract history, which is analogical or naturalizing in respect to the field known as 'spiritual' (and thus separated from that empirically known as 'natural'), cannot be doubted by one who knows and remembers the great consequences that philosophy draws from the resolution of the realistic concept of 'nature' in the idealistic conception of 'construction,' which the human spirit makes of reality, looking upon it as nature. Kant worked upon the solution of this problem indefatigably and with subtlety; he gave to it the direction that it has followed down to our own days. And the consequence that we draw from it, in respect to the problem that now occupies us, is that an error was committed when, moved by the legitimate desire of distinguishing abstract from concrete history, naturalizing history from thinking history, genuine from fictitious history, a sort of agnosticism was reached, as a final result, by means of limiting history to the field of humanity, which was said to be cognoscible, and declaring all the rest to be the object of metastoria and the limit of human knowledge. This conclusion would lead again to a sort of dualism, though in a lofty sphere. But if metastoria also appears, as we have seen, in the human field, it is clear that the distinction as formulated stands in need of correction; and the agnosticism founded upon it vacillates and falls. There is not a double object before thought, man and nature, the one capable of treatment in one way, the other in another way, the first cognizable, and the second uncognizable and capable only of being constructed abstractly; but thought always thinks history, the history of reality that is one, and beyond thought there is nothing, for the natural object becomes a myth when it is affirmed as object, and shows itself in its true reality as nothing else but the human spirit itself, which schematized history that has been lived and thought, or the materials of the history that has already been lived and thought. The saying that nature has no history is to be understood in the sense that nature as a rational being capable of thought has not history, because it is not—or, let us say, it is nothing that is real. The opposite saying, that nature is also formative and possesses historical life, is to be taken in the other sense that reality, the sole reality (comprehending man and nature in itself, which are only empirically and abstractly separate), is all development and life.

What substantial difference can ever be discovered on the one hand between geological stratifications and the remains of vegetables and animals, of which it is possible to construct a prospective and indeed a serial arrangement, but which it is never possible to rethink in the living dialectic of their genesis, and on the other hand the relics of what is called human history, and not only that called prehistorical, but even the historical documents of our history of yesterday, which we have forgotten and no longer understand, and which we can certainly classify and arrange in a series, and build castles in the air about or allow our fancies to wander among, but which it is no longer possible really to think again? Both cases, which have been arbitrarily distinguished, are reducible to one single case. Even in what is called 'human history' there exists a 'natural history,' and what is called 'natural history' also was once 'human' history—that is to say, spiritual, although to us who have left it so far behind it seems to be almost foreign, so mummified and mechanicized has it become, if we glance at it but summarily and from the outside. Do you wish to understand the true history of a Ligurian or Sicilian neolithic man? First of all, try if it be possible to make yourself mentally into a Ligurian or Sicilian neolithic man; and if it be not possible, or you do not care to do this, content yourself with describing and classifying and arranging in a series the skulls, the utensils, and the inscriptions belonging to those neolithic peoples. Do you wish to understand the history of a blade of grass? First and foremost, try to make yourself into a blade of grass, and if you do not succeed, content yourself with analysing the parts and even with disposing them in a kind of imaginative history. This leads to the idea from which I started in making these observations about historiography, as to history being *contemporary* history and chronicle being *past* history. We take advantage of the idea and at the same time confirm that truth by solving with its aid the antithesis between a history that is 'history' and a 'history of nature,' which, although it is history, was supposed to obey laws strangely at variance with those of the only history. It solves this antithesis by placing the second in the lower rank of *pseudo-history*.

APPENDIX I

ATTESTED EVIDENCE

IF true history is that of which an interior verification is possible, and is therefore history ideally contemporary and present, and if history by witnesses is lacking in truth and is not even false, but just neither false nor true (not a *hoc est* but a *fertur*), a legitimate question arises as to the origin and function of those innumerable propositions resumed from evidence critically thrashed out and 'held to be true,' although not verified, and perhaps never to be verified, but nevertheless employed even in most serious historical treatment.

When we are writing the history of the doctrine known as the *coincidentia oppositorum*, or of the poem called *I sepolcri*, the Latin of the Cardinal di Cusa and the verse of Foscolo obviously belong to us, both as to the thoughts and the actual words, pronounced by ourselves to ourselves, and the certainty of those historical facts is at the same time logical truth. But that the *De docta ignorantia* was written between the end of 1439 and the early part of 1440, and Foscolo's poem on the return of the poet to Italy after his long military service in France, is evidence founded upon proofs, as to which we can only say that they are to be considered valid, because they have been to some extent *attested*, but we cannot claim them to be *true*. No amount of acute mental labour upon them can prevent another document or the better reading of an old document destroying them. Nevertheless, no one will treat of the works of the Cusan or of Foscolo without availing himself of the biographical details as to their authors which have been preserved.

An esteemed methodologist of our day has been tempted to found the faith placed in this order of evidence upon a sort of telepathy of the past, an almost spiritualistic revival. But there is nothing so mysterious in the genesis of that belief as to need a risky and fantastic explanation, to which even Horace's Jew would not give credence. On the contrary, it is a question of something that we can observe in process of formation in our private life of every day. We are noting down in our diary, for instance, certain of our acts, or striking the balance of our account. After a certain interval has elapsed those facts fade from memory and the only way of affirming to ourselves that they have happened and must be considered true is the evidence of our notes: the document bears witness; trust the book. We behave in a similar way in respect to the statements of others on the authority of their diaries or account-books. We presume that if the thing has been written down it answers to the truth. Doubtless this assumption, like every assumption, may turn out to be false in fact, owing to the note having been made in a moment of distraction or of hallucination, or too late, when the memory of the fact was already imprecise and lacking in certainty, or because it was capriciously made or made with the object of deceiving others. But just for this reason, written evidence is not usually accepted with closed eyes; its verisimilitude is examined and we confront it with other written evidence, we investigate the probity and accuracy of the writer or witness. It is just for this reason that the penal code threatens with pains and penalties those who alter or falsify documents. And although these and other subtle and severe precautions do not in certain cases prevent fraud, deception, and error (in the same way that the tribunals established for the purpose of condemning the guilty often send away the guilty unpunished and sometimes condemn the innocent), yet the use of documents and evidence works out on the whole in accordance with the truth; it is held to be useful and worthy of support and encouragement, because the injuries that it is liable to cause are greatly inferior to those that it prevents.

Now what men do with regard to their private affairs in daily life may be said to be done on a large scale by the human race when it delivers itself of the load of innumerable facts and fixes them externally where they are recoverable in a weakened form as unverifiable documentary evidence, yet are nevertheless such that as a whole we are justified in looking upon them and treating them as true. Historical faith then is not the result of telepathy or spiritualism, but of a wise *economic* provision, which the spirit continues to realize. In this way we understand historical work directed toward the prevention of alterations and deformations, and its acceptation of certain testimony, as 'what must be held to be true in the present state of science,' and its graduation of the rest as uncertain, probable, and most probable to be sometimes accepted in the expectation of ulterior inquiries. Finally, it explains the dislike of 'hypercriticism' when, not content with a constant refinement of criticism, hypercriticism contests the value of the most ingenuous and authoritative testimony. The reason is that it thus breaks the rules of the game that is being played *sub regula*, and only serves at the most to remind those apt to forget it that history by evidence is at bottom an altogether external history, never fundamental, true history, which is contemporary and present.

This genesis or nature of 'attested' evidence already contains the answer to the other question as to its function. It is clear that this cannot be to posit true history or to take its place, but to supply it with those secondary particulars which it would not be worth while to make the effort of keeping alive and complete in the mind, for this effort would result in damaging what is most important to us. Finally, whether the *De docta ignorantia* were written some time earlier or later is something that may quite well be determined by a different interpretation of this or that thought of Cusanus, but it does not affect the function that the doctrine of the coincidence of opposites exercises in the formation of logical science. Again, whether the *Sepolcri* was composed or planned prior to Foscolo's visit to France would without doubt change to some extent our representation of the gradual development of the soul and genius of the poet, but it would hardly at all change our mode of interpreting his great ode. Those who despair of historical truth, owing to the lack of a verifiable certainty of some particulars, or to the uncertainty and dubiety that surrounds it, resemble him who, having forgotten the chronicle of his life in this or that year, should think that he did not know himself in his present condition, which is both the recapitulation of his past and carries with it his past in all that it really concerns him to know. But, on the other hand, attested evidence that has been held to be true is a stimulus to us to search ourselves more closely, an enrichment of what we have found by means of analysis and meditation and a confirmation or proof of our thoughts, which are not to be neglected, especially when true evidence and attested evidence agree with one another. To refuse the assistance and the facilities afforded by attested evidence, owing to the fear that some of it may prove false, or because all of it possesses an external and somewhat general and vague character, would be to refuse *the authority of the human race*, and so to commit the sin of Descartes and of Malebranche. This great refusal does not concern or assist the understanding of history. All that does matter and does assist is that authority—including the authority of the human race—should never be allowed to take the place of *the thought of humanity*, to which, in any case, belongs the first place.

APPENDIX II

ANALOGY AND ANOMALY OF SPECIAL HISTORIES

IN the course of the preceding theoretical explanations we have denied both the idea of a *universal history* (in time and space) [1] and that of a *general history* (of the spirit in its indiscriminate generality or unity),[2] and have insisted instead upon the opposite view with its two clauses : that history is always *particular* and always *special*, and that these two determinations constitute precisely concrete and effective *universality* and concrete and effective *unity*. What has been declared impossible, then, does not represent in any way a loss, for it is on the one hand fictitious universality or the universality of *fancy*, and on the other abstract *universality*, or, if it be preferred, *confused* universality. So-called universal histories have therefore shown themselves to be particular histories, which have assumed that title for purposes of literary notoriety, or as collections, views, and chroniclistical compilations of particular histories, or, finally, as romances. In like manner, general inclusive histories are either so only in name, or set different histories side by side, or they are metaphysical and metaphorical playthings.

As a result of this double but converging negation, it is also advisable to refute a common and deeply rooted belief (which we ourselves at one time shared to some extent)[3] that we should arrive at the re-establishment of the universality of the fancy: or that there are some

[1] *Supra*, pp 55-59 [2] *Supra*, pp 119-122. [3] In the *Æsthetic*, I, ch xvii.

among the special histories, constituted according to the various forms of the spirit (general and individual only in so far as every form of the spirit is the whole spirit in that form), which require universal treatment and others only treatment as monographs. The typical instance generally adduced is that of the difference between the history of philosophy and the history of poetry or of art. The subject of the former is supposed to be the one great philosophical problem that interests all men, of the latter the sentimental or imaginative problems of particular moments, or at the most of particular artists. Thus the former is supposed to be continuous, the latter discontinuous, the former capable of complete universal vision, the second only of a sequence of particular visions. But a more 'realistic' conception of philosophy deprives it of this privilege as compared with the history of art and poetry or of any other special history; for, appearances notwithstanding, it is not true that men have concentrated upon one philosophical problem only, whose successive solutions, less and less inadequate, compose a single line of progress, the universal history of the human spirit, affording support and unification to all other histories. The opposite is the truth: the philosophical problems that men have treated of and will treat of are infinite, and each one of them is always particularly and individually determined. The illusion as to the uniqueness of the problem is due to logical misapprehension, increased by historical contingencies, whence a problem which owing to religious motives seemed supreme has been looked upon as unique or fundamental, and groupings and generalizations made for practical ends have been held to be real identity and unity.[1] 'Universal'

[1] See Appendix III.

histories of philosophy, too, like the others, when we examine them with a good magnifying glass, are revealed as either particular histories of the problem that engages the philosopher-historian, or arbitrary artificial constructions, or tables and collections of many different historical sequences, in the manner of a manual or encyclopædia of philosophical history. Certainly nothing forbids the composition of abridgments of philosophical histories, containing classifications of particular problems and representing the principal thinkers of all peoples and of all times as occupied with one or another class of problem. This, however, is always a chroniclistical and naturalistic method of treating the history of philosophy, which only really lives when a new thinker connects the problems already set in the past and its intrinsic antecedents with the definite problem that occupies his attention. He provisionally sets aside others with a different connexion, though without for that reason suppressing them, intending rather to recall them when another problem makes their presence necessary. It is for this reason that even in those abridgments that seem to be the most complete and 'objective' (that is to say, 'material') a certain selection does appear, due to the theoretical interest of the writer, who never altogether ceases to be a historiographer-philosopher. The procedure is in fact just that of the history of art and poetry, where what is really historical treatment, living and complete, is the thought or criticism of individual poetical personalities, and the rest a table of criticisms, an abridgment due to contiguity of time or place, affinity of matter or similarity of temperament, or to degrees of artistic excellence. Nor must we say that every philosophic problem is linked to all the others and is always a problem of the whole of philosophy, thus differing from the cases of poetry and art, for there is no diversity here either, and the whole of history and the entire universe are immanent in every single work of art.

Now that we have likewise reduced philosophies of history to the rank of particular histories, it is scarcely necessary to demonstrate that the demand being made in several quarters for a 'universal' or 'general' history of science is without foundation. For such a history would be impossible to write, even if we were able to identify or compare the history of science with that of philosophy. But it is doubly impossible both because there are comprised under the name of 'science' such diverse forms as sciences of observation and mathematical sciences, and also because in each of these classes themselves the several disciplines remain separate, owing to the irreducible variety of data and postulates from which they spring. If, as we have pointed out, every particular philosophical problem links and places itself in harmony with all other philosophical problems, every scientific problem tends, on the contrary, to shut itself up in itself, and there is no more destructive tendency in science than that of 'explaining' all the facts by means of a 'single principle,' substituting, that is to say, an unfruitful metaphysic for fruitful science, allowing an empty word to act as a magic wand, and by 'explaining everything' to 'explain' nothing at all. The unity admitted by the history of the sciences is not that which connects one theory with another and one science with another in an imaginary general history of science, but that which connects each science and each theory with the intellectual and social complex of the moment in which it appeared. But even here too we must utter the warning that in thus explaining their true nature we do not wish to contest the right to existence of tables and encyclopædias of the history of science, far less to throw discredit upon the present direction of studies, by means of which, at the call of the history of the sciences, useful research is stimulated in directions that have been long neglected. Nor do we intend to move any objection to histories of science in the form of tables and encyclopædias on the ground that it is impossible for the same student to be equally competent as to problems of quite different nature, such as are those of the various sciences; for it is inconceivable that a philosopher exists with a capacity equal to the understanding of each and every philosophical problem (indeed, the mind of the best solver of certain problems is usually the more closed to others); or that a critic and historian of poetry and art exists who tastes and enjoys equally all forms of poetry and art, however versatile he be. Each one has his sphere marked out more or less narrowly, and each is universal only by means of his particularity.

Finally, we shall not repeat the same demonstration for political history and ethics, where the claim to represent the whole of history in a single line of development has had less occasion to manifest itself. It is usually more readily admitted there that every history is particular—that is to say, determined by the political and ethical problem or problems with which history is concerned in time and place, and which every history therefore occasionally rethinks from the beginning.

The *analogy*, then, between different kinds of special history is to be considered perfect, and the *anomaly* between them excluded, for they all obey the principle of particularity, that is, particular universality (whatever be the appearance to the contrary). But if, as histories, they all proceed according to the nature of what we have explained as historiography, in so far as they are *special* each one conforms to the concept of its speciality. It is in this sense alone that each one is anomalous in respect to the others, preserving, that is to say, its own peculiar nature. We have explained that the claim to treat the history of poetry and of art in the same way as philosophy is erroneous, not only because it misconceives the true concept of history, but also because it misrepresents the nature of art, conceiving it as philosophy and dissipating it in a dialectic of concepts, or because it leaves out, in the history of art, just that by reason of which art is art, looking upon it as something secondary, or at best giving it a place beside the social or conceptual activities. This error is precisely analogous to that of those who from time to time suggest what they term the 'psychological' reform of philosophy—that is to say, they would like to treat it as dependent upon the psychology of philosophers and of the social environment, thus placing it on a level, sometimes with the history of the sentiments, at others with that of fancies and Utopias, or with what is not the history of philosophizing. Such persons lack the knowledge of what *philosophy* is, as the others lack the knowledge of *poetry* and *art*. Anyone desirous of arriving at a rapid knowledge of the difference between the history of philosophy and the history of poetry should observe how the one, owing to the nature of its object, is led to examine theories in so far as they are the *work of pure mind*, and therefore to develop a history in which thoughts represent the *dramatis personæ*, while the other is led by the nature of its object to examine works of art in so far as they are *works of imagination*, which gives expression to movements of feeling, and therefore to develop a history of imaginative and sensitive points of view. The former, therefore, though it does not neglect actions, events, and imagination, regards them as the *humus* of pure thought and takes the form of a history of concepts *without persons*, either real or imaginary, while the latter, which also does not neglect actions, events, and thoughts in its turn regards them as the *humus* of imaginary creations and takes the form of a history of ideal or imaginary *personalities*, which have divested themselves of the ballast of practical interests and of the curb of concepts. The plans, too, which they draw up and with which they cannot dispense, any more than can any human dialectic, answer to these different tendencies—that is to say, with the one they are schemes or general types of modes of thinking, with the other schemes containing ideal personalities.

If the history of philosophy has several times tried to devour the history of poetry and art, it may also be said to have several times tried to devour the *history of practice*, that of politics and ethics, or 'social history,' as people prefer to call it in our day. It has also been asserted that such history should be set free from the chroniclism in which it had become involved and assume a scientific and rigorous form. To do this, it was needful to reduce it to a history of 'ideas,' which are the true and essential practical acts, because they generate them—that is to say, the error which we noted above in respect to poetry and art has here been repeated. What is peculiar to practical acts has been neglected, and only the 'ideas,' which are their antecedents and consequents, have been retained. But on other occasions the 'ideas' to which it was claimed to reduce practical acts were not really ideas or intellectual formations, but truly practical acts, sentiments, dispositions, customs, institutions. The originality of political and ethical history was thus unconsciously confirmed. Its object is just what can be designated with the single word *institutions*, taking the word in its widest signification—that is to say, understanding by it all practical arrangements of human individuals and societies, from the most recondite sentiments to the most obvious modes of life (which, too, are always will in action). All are equally historical productions, the sole effective historical productions perceivable according to the practical form of the spirit. If the patrimony of judgments, as the capital with and upon which our modern thought works, is the result of a long history, of which we become conscious from time to time, illustrating now one and now another of its particular aspects at the solicitation of new needs, so also what we can now practically *do*, all our sentiments as so-called civilized men—courage, honour, dignity, love, modesty, and the like—all our institutions in the strict sense of the term (which are themselves due to attitudes of the spirit, utilitarian or moral)—the family, the state, commerce, industry, military affairs, and so on—have a long history; and according as one or other of those sentiments or institutions enters upon a crisis, as the result of new wants, we attempt to ascertain its true 'nature'—that is to say, its historical genesis. Any-one who has followed the developments of modern social historiography with care and attention has been able to see clearly that its aim is precisely to arrange the *chroniclistic chaos* of disaggregated notes of events in *ordered series of histories of social values*, and that its field of research is the history of the human soul in its practical aspect; either when it produces general histories of *civilization* (always due to particular motives and limited by them), or when it presents histories *of classes, peoples, social currents, sentiments, institutions,* and so forth.

Biography, too (only when not limited to a mere chroniclistic collection of the experiences of an individual or to a poetical portrait, improperly regarded as a historical work), is the history of an 'institution' in the philosophical acceptation of the word and forms part of the history of practice: because the individual, in the same way as a people or a social class, is the formation of a character, or complex of specific attitudes and actions consequent upon them; and it is of this that historical biography consists, not of the individual looked upon as external or private or physical, or whatever it be called.

We might be expected to indicate the place or function of the *history of science* and of *religion,* in order to render to a certain extent complete this rapid review of special histories, in which general history realizes itself in turn —it never exists outside of them. But if science differs from philosophy in being partly theoretical and partly practical, and religion is an attempt to explain reality by means of myth and to direct the work of man according to an ideal, it is evident that the history of science enters to some extent into the history of philosophical thought and to some extent forms part of that of needs and institutions; indeed, since the moment which sets science to work and endows it with its peculiar character is the practical or suitable moment, it really belongs to the history of institutions in the very wide sense described; and the history of religion forms to some extent part of the history of institutions and to some extent part of the history of philosophy; indeed, since the dominating moment is here mythical conception or philosophical effort, the history of religion is substantially that of philosophy. Other more particular disquisitions in connexion with this argument would be out of place in the present treatise, which is not especially concerned with the theory and methodology of particular special histories (coincident with the treatment of the various spheres of philosophy, æsthetics, logic, etc.), and aims only at indicating the directions in which they must necessarily develop.[1]

[1] It will be of further use to draw attention here, in a note, to the already mentioned distinction between the history of practice in *politics* and in *ethics*, because thus alone can be set at rest the variance which runs through historiography, between political history or history of states and history of humanity or of civilization, especially from the eighteenth century onward In Germany it is one of the elements in the intricate debate between *Geschichte* and *Kulturgeschichte*, and it has sometimes been described as a conflict between French historiography (Voltaire and his followers), or *histoire de la civilisation*, and the Germanic (Moser and his followers), or history of the state One side would absorb and subject the history of culture or social history to that of the state, the other would do the opposite; and the eclectics, as usual, without knowing much about it, place the one beside the other, inert, history of politics and history of civilization, thus destroying the unity of history The truth is that political history and history of civilization have the same relations between one another in the practical field as those between the history of poetry or of art and the history of philosophy or thought in the theoretical field. They correspond to two eternal moments of the spirit—that of the pure will, or economic moment, and that of the ethical will. Hence we also see why some will always be attracted rather by the one than the other form of history · according as to whether they are moved chiefly by political or chiefly by moral interests

APPENDIX III

PHILOSOPHY AND METHODOLOGY

HAVING established the unity of philosophy and historiography, and shown that the division between the two has but a literary and didactic value, because it is founded upon the possibility of placing in the foreground of verbal exposition now one and now the other of the two dialectical elements of that unity, it is well to make quite clear what is the true object of the treatises bearing the traditional title of philosophic 'theory' or 'system': to what (in a word) *philosophy can be reduced.*

Philosophy, in consequence of the new relation in which it has been placed, cannot of necessity be anything but the *methodological moment of historiography*: a dilucidation of the categories constitutive of historical judgments, or of the concepts that direct historical interpretation. And since historiography has for content the concrete life of the spirit, and this life is life of imagination and of thought, of action and of morality (or of something else, if anything else can be thought of), and in this variety of its forms remains always one, the dilucidation moves in distinguishing between æsthetic and logic, between economic and ethic, uniting and dissolving them all in the philosophy of the spirit. If a philosophical problem shows itself to be altogether sterile for the historical judgment, we have there the proof that such problem is otiose, badly stated, and in reality does not exist. If the solution of a problem—that is to say, of a philosophical proposition—instead of making history more intelligible, leaves it obscure or confounds it with others, or leaps over it and lightly condemns or negates it, we have there the proof that such proposition and the philosophy with which it is connected are arbitrary, though it may preserve interest in other respects, as a manifestation of sentiment or of imagination.

The definition of philosophy as 'methodology' is not at first exempt from doubts, even on the part of one ready to accept in general the tendency that it represents; because philosophy and methodology are terms often contrasted, and a philosophy that leads to a methodology is apt to be tainted with empiricism. But certainly the methodology of which we are here speaking is not at all empirical; indeed, it appears just for the purpose of correcting and taking the place of the empirical methodology of professional historians and of other such specialists in all that greater part of it where it is a true and proper, though defective, attempt toward the philosophical solution of the theoretical problems raised by the study of history, or toward philosophical methodology and philosophy as methodology.

If, however, the above-mentioned dispute is settled as soon as stated, this cannot be said of another, where our position finds itself opposed to a widely diffused and ancient conception of philosophy as the solver of the mystery of the universe, knowledge of ultimate reality, revelation of the world of noumena, which is held to be beyond the world of phenomena, in which we move in ordinary life and in which history also moves. This is not the place to give the history of that idea; but we must at least say this, that its origin is religious or mythological, and that it persisted even among those philosophers who were most successful in directing thought toward our earth as the sole reality, and initiated the new philosophy as methodology of the judgment or of historical knowledge. It persisted in Kant, who admitted it as the limit of his criticism; it persisted in Hegel, who framed his subtle researches in logic and philosophy of the spirit in a sort of mythology of the Idea.

Nevertheless, the diversity of the two conceptions manifested itself in an ever-increasing ratio, finding expression in various formulas of the nineteenth century, such as *psychology against metaphysic*, a philosophy of *experience and immanence*, *aprioristic* against *transcendental* philosophy, *positivism* against *idealism* ; and although the polemic was as a rule ill conducted, going beyond the mark and ending by unconsciously embracing that very metaphysic, transcendency, and apriority, that very abstract idealism, which it had set out to combat, the sentiment that inspired it was legitimate. And the philosophy of methodology has made it its own, has combated the same adversary with better arms, has certainly insisted upon a psychological view, but a speculative psychological view, immanent in history, but dialectically immanent, differing in this from positivism, that while the latter made necessary the contingent, it made the contingent necessary, thus affirming the right of thought to the hegemony. Such a philosophy is just philosophy as history (and so history as philosophy), and the determination of the philosophical moment in the purely categorical and methodological moment.

The greater vigour of this conception in respect to the opposite, the superiority of philosophy as *methodology* over philosophy as *metaphysic*, is shown by the capacity of the former to solve the problems of the latter by criticizing them and pointing out their origin. Metaphysic, on the other hand, is incapable of solving not only the problems of methodology, but even its own problems, without having recourse to the fantastic and arbitrary. Thus questions as to the reality of the external world, of soul-substance, of the unknowable, of dualisms and of antitheses, and so forth, have disappeared in gnoseological doctrines, which have substituted better conceptions for those which we formerly possessed concerning the logic of the sciences, explaining those questions as eternally renascent aspects of the dialectic or phenomenology of knowledge.

The view of philosophy as metaphysic is, however, so inveterate and so tenacious that it is not surprising that it should still give some sign of life in the minds of those who have set themselves free of it in general, but have not applied themselves to eradicating it in all its particulars, nor closed all the doors by which it may return in a more or less unexpected manner. And if we rarely find it openly and directly displayed now, we may yet discern or suspect it in one or other of its aspects or attitudes, persisting like kinks of the mind, or unconscious preconceptions, which threaten to drive philosophy as methodology back into the wrong path, and to prepare the return, though but for a brief period, of the metaphysic that has been superseded.

It seems to me opportune to provide here a clear statement of some of these preconceptions, tendencies, and habits, pointing out the errors which they contain and entail.

First of all the survivals of the past that are still common comes the view of philosophy as having a fundamental problem to solve. Now the conception of a fundamental problem is intrinsically at variance with that of philosophy as history, and with the treatment of philosophy as methodology of history, which posits, and cannot do otherwise than posit, the *infinity* of philosophical problems, all certainly connected with one another, but not one of which can be considered fundamental, for just the same reason that no single part of an organism is the foundation of all the others, but each one is in its turn foundation and founded. If, indeed, methodology take the substance of its problems from history, history in its most modest but concrete form of history of ourselves, of each one of us as an individual, this shows us that we pass on from one to another particular philosophical problem at the promptings of our life as it is lived, and that one or the other group or class of problems holds the field or has especial interest for us, according to the epochs of our life. And we find the same to be the case if we look at the wider but less definite spectacle afforded by the already mentioned general history of philosophy—that is to say, that according to times and peoples, philosophical problems relating sometimes to morality, sometimes to politics, to religion, or to the natural sciences and mathematics, have in turn the upper hand. Every particular philosophical problem has been a problem of the whole of philosophy, either openly or by inference, but we never meet with a *general problem of philosophy*, owing to the contradiction thereby implied. And if there does seem to be one (and it certainly does seem so), it is really a question of appearances, due to the fact that modern philosophy, which comes to us from the Middle Ages and was elaborated during the religious struggles of the Renaissance, has preserved a strong imprint of *theology* in its didactic form, not less than in the psychological disposition of the greater part of those addicted to it.

Hence arises the fundamental and almost unique importance usurped by the problem of thought and being, which after all was nothing more than the old problem of this world and the next, of earth and heaven, in a critical and gnoseological form. But those who destroyed or who initiated the destruction of heaven and of the other world and of transcendental philosophy by immanent philosophy began at the same moment to corrode the conception of a fundamental problem, although they were not fully aware of this (for we have said above that they remained trammelled in the philosophy of the Thing in Itself or in the Mythology of the Idea). That problem was rightly fundamental for religious spirits, who held that the whole intellectual and practical dominion of the world was nothing, unless they had saved their own souls or their own thought in another world, in the knowledge of a world of noumena and reality. But such it was not destined to remain for the philosophers, henceforth restricted to the world alone or to nature, which has no skin and no kernel and is all of a piece. What would happen were we to resume belief in a fundamental problem, dominating all others? The other problems would either have to be considered as all dependent upon it and therefore solved with it, or as problems no longer philosophical but empirical. That is to say, all the problems appearing every day anew in science and life would lose their value, either becoming a tautology of the fundamental solution or being committed to empirical treatment. Thus the distinction between philosophy and methodology, between metaphysic and philosophy of the spirit, would reappear, the first transcendental as regards the second, the second aphilosophical as regards the first.

Another view, arising from the old metaphysical conception of the function of philosophy, leads to the rejection of distinction in favour of *unity*, thus conforming to the theological conception that all distinctions are unified by absorption in God, and to the religious point of view, which forgets the world and its necessities in the vision of God. From this ensues a disposition which may be described as something between indifferent, accommodating, or weak, in respect of particular problems, and the pernicious doctrine of the double faculty is almost tacitly renewed, that is, of intellectual intuition or other superior cognoscitive faculty, peculiar to the philosopher and leading to the vision of true reality, and of criticism or thought prone to interest itself in the contingent and thus greatly inferior in degree and free to proceed with a lack of speculative rigour not permissible in the other. Such a disposition led to the worst possible consequences in the philosophical treatises of the Hegelian school, where the disciples (differing from the master) generally gave evidence of having meditated but little or not at all upon the problems of the various spiritual forms, freely accepting vulgar opinions concerning them, or engaging in them with the indifference of men sure of the essential, and therefore cutting and mutilating them without pity, in order to force them into their pre-established schemes with all haste, thus getting rid of difficulties by means of this illusory arrangement. Hence the emptiness and tiresomeness of their philosophies, from which the historian, or the man whose attention is directed to the understanding of the particular and the concrete, failed to learn anything that could be of use to him in the direction of his own studies and in the clearer formulation of his own judgments. And since the mythology of the idea reappeared in positivism as mythology of evolution, here too particular problems (which are indeed the only philosophical problems) received merely schematic and empty treatment and did not progress at all. Philosophy as history and methodology of history restores honour to the virtue of acuteness or discernment, which the theological unitarianism of metaphysic tended to depreciate: discernment, which is prosaic but severe, hard and laborious but prolific, which sometimes assumes the unsympathetic aspect of scholasticism and pedantry, but is also of use in this aspect, like every discipline, and holds that the neglect of distinction for unity is also intimately opposed to the conception of philosophy as history.

A third tendency (I beg to be allowed to proceed by enumeration of the various sides of the same mental attitude for reasons of convenience), a third tendency also seeks the *definitive* philosophy, untaught by the historical fact that no philosophy has ever been definitive or has set a limit to thought, or has ever been thoroughly convinced that the perpetual changing of philosophy with the world which perpetually changes is not by any means a defect, but is the nature itself of thought and reality. Or, rather, such teaching, and the proposition that follows it, do not fail altogether of acceptance, and they are led to believe that the spirit, ever growing upon itself, produces thoughts and systems that are ever new. But since they have retained the presupposition of a fundamental problem which (as we have said) substantially consists of the ancient problem of religion alone, and each problem well determined implies a single solution, the solution given of the 'fundamental problem' naturally claims to be the definitive solution of the problem of philosophy itself.

A new solution could not appear without a new problem (owing to the logical unity of problem and solution); but that problem, which is superior to all the others, is on the contrary the only one. Thus a definitive philosophy, assumed in the conception of the fundamental problem, is at variance with historical experience, and more irreconcilably, because in a more evidently logical manner, with philosophy as history, which, admitting infinite problems, denies the claim for and the expectation of a definitive philosophy. Every philosophy is definitive for the problem which it solves, but not for the one that appears immediately afterward, at the foot of the first, nor for the other problems which will arise from the solution of this. To close the series would be to turn from philosophy to religion and to rest in God.

Indeed, the fourth preconception, which we now proceed to state, and which links itself with the preceding, and, together with all the preceding, to the theological nature of the old metaphysic, concerns the *figure of the philosopher*, as Buddha or the Awakened One, who posits himself as superior to others (and to himself in the moments when he is not a philosopher), because he holds himself to be free from human passions, illusions, and agitations by means of philosophy. This is the case with the believer, who fixes his mind upon God and shakes off earthly cares, like the lover, who feels himself blessed in the possession of the beloved and defies the whole world. But the world soon takes its revenge both upon the believer and the lover, and does not fail to insist upon its rights. Such an illusion is impossible for the philosophical historian, who differs from the other in feeling himself irresistibly involved in the course of history, as at once both subject and object, and who is therefore led to negate felicity or beatitude, as he negates every other abstraction (because, as has been well said, *le bonheur est le contraire de la sensation de vivre*), and to accept life as it is, as joy that overcomes sorrow and perpetually produces new sorrows and new unstable joys. And history, which he thinks as the only truth, is the work of tireless thought, which conditions practical work, as practical work conditions the new work of thought. Thus the primacy formerly attributed to the contemplative life is now transferred not to active life, but to life in its integrity, which is at once thought and action. And every man is a philosopher (in his circle, however wide or narrow it may appear), and every philosopher is a man, indissolubly linked to the conditions of human life, which it is not given to anyone to transcend. The mystical or apocalyptic philosopher of the Græco-Roman decadence was well able to separate himself from the world : the great thinkers, like Hegel, who inaugurated the epoch of modern philosophy, although they denied the primacy of the abstract contemplative life, were liable to fall back into the error of belief in this supremacy and to conceive a sphere of absolute spirit, a process of liberation through art, religion, and philosophy, as a means of reaching it ; but the once sublime figure of the philosopher blessed in the absolute, when we try to revive it in this modern world of ours, becomes tinged with the comic. It is true that satire has now but little material upon which to exercise itself, and is reduced to aiming its shafts at the 'professors of philosophy' (according to the type of philosopher that has been created by modern universities, which is partly the heir of the 'master of theology' of the Middle Ages : against the professors, that is to say, to the extent that they continue to repeat mechanically abstract general propositions, and seem to be unmoved by the passions and the problems that press upon them from all sides and vainly ask for more concrete and actual treatment. But the function and the social figure of the philosopher have profoundly changed, and we have not said that the manner of being of the 'professors of philosophy' will not also change in its turn—that is to say, that the way of teaching philosophy in the universities and schools is not on the verge of experiencing a crisis, which will eliminate the last remains of the medieval fashion of formalistic philosophizing. A strong advance in philosophical culture should lead to this result: that all students of human affairs, jurists, economists, moralists, men of letters—in other words, all students of historical matters—should become conscious and disciplined philosophers, and that thus the philosopher in general, the *purus philosophus*, should find no place left for him among the professional specifications of knowledge. With the disappearance of the philosopher 'in general' would also disappear the last social vestige of the teleologist or metaphysician, and of the Buddha or Awakened One.

There is also a prejudice which to some extent inquinates the manner of *culture* of students of philosophy. They are accustomed to have recourse almost exclusively to the books of philosophers, indeed of philosophers 'in general,' of the metaphysical system-makers, in the same way as the student of theology formed himself upon the sacred texts. This method of culture, which is perfectly consequent when a start is made from the presupposition of a fundamental or single problem, of which it is necessary to know the different diverging and progressive solutions which have been attempted, is altogether inconsequent and inadequate in the case of a historical and immanent philosophy, which draws its material from all the most varied impressions of life and from all intuitions and reflections upon life. That form of culture is the reason for the aridity of the treatment of certain particular problems, for which is necessary a continued contact with daily experience (art and art criticism for æsthetic, politics, economy, judicial trials for the philosophy of rights, positive and mathematical sciences for the gnoseology of the sciences, and so on). To it is also due the aridity of treatment of those parts of philosophy themselves which are traditionally considered to constitute 'general philosophy,' for they too had their origin in life, and we must refer them back to life if we are to give a satisfactory interpretation of their propositions; we must plunge them into life again to develop them and to find in them new aspects. The *whole of history* is the foundation of philosophy as history, and to limit its foundation to the *history of philosophy* alone, and of 'general' or 'metaphysical' philosophy, is impossible, save by unconsciously adhering to the old idea of philosophy, not as methodology but as metaphysic, which is the fifth of the prejudices that we are enumerating.

This enumeration can be both lengthened and ended with the mention of a sixth preconception, relating to *philosophical exposition*. Owing to this, philosophy is expected to have either an architectural form, as though it were a temple consecrated to the Eternal, or a warm poetical form, as though it were a hymn to the Eternal. But these forms were part of the old content, and that form is now changed. Philosophy shows itself to be a dilucidation of the categories of historical interpretation rather than the grandiose architecture of a temple or a sacred hymn running on conventional lines.

Philosophy is discussion, polemic, rigorous didactic exposition, which is certainly coloured with the sentiments of the writer, like every other literary form, able also at times to raise its voice (or on the other hand to become slight and playful, according to circumstances), but not constrained to observe rules which appear to be proper to a theological or religious content. Philosophy treated as methodology has, so to speak, caused philosophical exposition to descend from poetry to prose.

All the preconceptions, habits, and tendencies which I have briefly described should in my opinion be carefully sought out and eliminated, for it is they that impede philosophy from taking the form and proceeding in the mode suitable and adequate to the consciousness of the unity with history which it has reached. If we look merely at the enormous amount of psychological observations and moral doubts accumulated in the course of the nineteenth century by poetry, fiction, and drama, those voices of our society, and consider that in great part it remains without critical treatment, some idea can be formed of the immense amount of work that falls to philosophy to accomplish. And if on the other hand we observe the multitude of anxious questions that the great European War has everywhere raised—as to the state, as to history, as to rights, as to the functions of the different peoples, as to civilization, culture, and barbarism, as to science, art, religion, as to the end and ideal of life, and so on—we realize the duty of philosophers to issue forth from the theologico-metaphysical circle in which they remain confined even when they refuse to hear of theology and metaphysic. For notwithstanding their protests, and notwithstanding the new conception accepted and professed by them, they really remain intellectually and spiritually attached to the old ideas.

Even the *history itself of philosophy* has hitherto been renewed only to a small extent, in conformity with the new conception of philosophy. This new conception invites us to direct our attention to thoughts and thinkers, long neglected or placed in the second rank and not considered to be truly philosophers because they did not treat directly the 'fundamental problem' of philosophy or the great *peut-être*, but were occupied with 'particular problems.' These particular problems, however, were destined to produce eventually a change of view as regards the 'general problem,' which emerged itself reduced to the rank of a 'particular' problem. It is simply the result of prejudice to look upon a Machiavelli, who posited the conception of the modern state, a Baltasar Gracian, who examined the question of acuteness in practical matters, a Pascal, who criticized the spirit of Jesuitry, a Vico, who renewed all the sciences of the spirit, or a Hamann, with his keen sense of the value of tradition, as minor philosophers, I do not say in comparison with some metaphysician of little originality, but even when compared with a Descartes or a Spinoza, who dealt with *other* but not *superior* problems. A schematic and bloodless history of philosophy corresponded, in fact, with the philosophy of the 'fundamental problem.' A far richer, more varied and pliant philosophy should correspond with philosophy as methodology, which holds to be philosophy not only what appertains to the problems of immanency, of transcendency, of this world and the next, but everything that has been of avail in increasing the patrimony of guiding conceptions, the understanding of actual history, and the formation of the reality of thought in which we live.

PART II

CONCERNING THE HISTORY OF HISTORIOGRAPHY

I

PRELIMINARY QUESTIONS

WE possess many works relating to the history of historiography, both special, dealing with individual authors, and more or less general, dealing with groups of authors (histories of historiography confined to one people and to a definite period, or altogether 'universal' histories). Not only have we bibliographical works and works of erudition, but criticism, some of it excellent, especially in the case of German scientific literature, ever the most vigilant of all in not leaving unexplored any nook or cranny of the dominion of knowledge. It cannot, therefore, form part of my design to treat the theme from its foundations: but I propose to make a sort of appendix or critical annotation to the collection of books and essays that I have read upon the argument. I will not say that these are all, or even that they are all those of any importance, but they are certainly a considerable number. By means of this annotation I shall try to establish, on the one hand, in an exact manner and in conformity with the principles explained, the method of such a history, regarding which I observe that there still exist confusion and perplexity, even among the best, which lead to errors of judgment or at least of plan, and on the other hand I shall try to outline the principal periods in a summary manner, both with the view of exemplifying the method established, and, as it were, of illustrating historically the concepts exposed in the preceding theoretical pages, which might otherwise retain here and there something of an abstract appearance.

Beginning with methodical delimitations, I shall note in the first place that in a history of historiography as such, historical writings cannot be looked upon from the point of view proper to a *history of literature*—that is to say, as expressions of individual sentiments, as forms of art. Doubtless they are this also, and have a perfect right to form part of histories of literature, as the treatises and systems of the philosophers, the writings of Plato and Aristotle, of Bruno, of Leibnitz, and of Hegel; but in this case both are regarded not as works of history and of philosophy, but of literature and poetry; and the empirical scale of values which constitute the different modes of history in the cases of the same authors is different, because in a history of literature the place of a Plato will always be more considerable than that of an Aristotle, that of a Bruno than that of a Leibnitz, owing to the greater amount of passion and the greater richness of artistic problems contained in the former of each pair. The fact that in many volumes of literary history such diversity of treatment is not observed, and historians are talked of historically and not in a literary manner and philosophers philosophically rather than in a literary manner, is due to the substitution in such works of incoherent compilation for work that is properly critical and scientific. But the distinction between the two aspects is important for this reason also, that erroneous judgments, praise, and censure, alike unjustified, are apt to appear, owing to the careless transference of the scale of values from one history to another.

The slight esteem in which Polybius was held in antiquity and for some time after, because 'he did not write well' in comparison with the splendour of Livy or with the emotional intensity of Tacitus, is an instance of this, as is likewise in Italy the excessive praise lavished upon certain historians who were little more than correct and elegant writers of prose in comparison with others who were negligent and crude in their form, but serious students. Ulrici,[1] in his youthful book on ancient historiography, which despite its heaviness and verbosity of exposition has great merits, after having discussed the 'scientific value' of that historiography, also speaks at great length of 'artistic value'; but setting aside what of arbitrary is to be found in some of the laws that he applies to historiography as art, in conformity with the æsthetic ideas of his time, it is evident that the second subject of which he treats does not coalesce with the first and is only placed side by side with it in the same way as those sections of works dealing with historical method are not connected but simply juxtaposed, and after having studied in their own way the formation of historical thought, the collection of materials or 'heuristic,' up to final 'comprehension,' begin to discuss the form of the 'exposition,' and in so doing continue without being aware of it the method of rhetorical treatises on the art of history composed during the Renaissance. These have their chief exponent in Vossius (1623). We cannot abstain from sometimes mentioning the literary form of the works of historians, nor from according their laurels to works of remarkable literary value, while noting their unsatisfactory historiographical methods; but to touch here and there upon, to discuss, to characterize, to eliminate, is of secondary importance and

[1] *Charakteristik der antiken Historiographie* (Berlin, 1833).

does not form part of the proper function of historiography, whose object is the *development of historiographical thought.*

The distinction between this history and that of *philology* or *erudition* is less apparent but not less indubitable, always, be it well understood, in the sense explained, of a distinction that is not a separation. This warning should be understood in respect of other exclusions that we are about to effect, without our being obliged to repeat it at every step ; for the connexion between history and philology is undeniable, not less than that between history and art, or history and practical life. But that does not prevent philology in itself being the collection, the rearrangement, the purification of material, and not history. Owing to this quality it forms a part rather of the history of culture than of that of thought. It would be impossible to disassociate it from the history of libraries, archives, museums, universities, seminaries, *écoles des chartes*, academical and editorial enterprises, and from other institutions and proceedings of an entirely practical nature. Fueter has therefore been right in excluding from his theme in his recent work on the history of modern historiography[1] "the history of merely philological research and criticism." This has not prevented him from taking store where apposite of the school of Biondo or of that of Maurini, or of the perfecting of the method of seeking for the sources attained by the German school in the nineteenth century. The confusion and lack of development observable in the old and solid work of Wachler[2] is perhaps due to his having failed to make

[1] *Geschichte der neueren Historiographie* (München u Berlin, Oldenburg, 1911).

[2] *Geschichte der historischen Forschung und Kunst seit der Wiederherstellung der literarischen Cultur in Europa* (Gottingen, 1812–20)

this distinction, to which recourse can also be had with advantage elsewhere. Wachler's work, entitled and conceived as "history of *research* and of the *historical art* from the Renaissance of letters in Europe onward," ended by assuming the appearance of a repertory or bibliographical catalogue.

The obstacles to be encountered by the distinction between the history of historiography and that of the *practical tendencies*, or tendencies of the *social and political spirit*, are more intricate. These indeed become incorporated with or at least leave their mark upon the works of historians; but it is just because we can only with difficulty perceive the line of demarcation that it is indispensable to make it quite clear. Such tendencies, such social and political spirit, belong rather to the matter than to the theoretical form of history; they are not so much historiography as history in the act and in its *fieri*. Machiavelli is a historian in so far as he tries to understand the course of events; he is a politician, or at least a publicist, when he posits and desires a prince, founder of a strong national state, as his ideal, reflecting this in his history. This history, in so far as it portrays that ideal and the inspiration and teaching that accompany it, here and there becomes fable (*fabula docet*). Thus Machiavelli belongs partly to the history of thought in the Renaissance and partly to the history of the practice of the Renaissance. Nor does this happen solely in political and social historiography, but also in literary and artistic, because there is not perhaps a critic in the world, however unprejudiced and broad in his ideas, who does not manifest tendencies in the direction of a literary renovation of his epoch together with his actual judgments and reconstructions. Now to the extent that he does this, even if it be in the same book and on the same page or in the same period, he is no longer a critic, but a practical reformer of art. In one domain of history alone is this pacific accompaniment of interpretations and aspirations impossible—in the history of philosophy, because when, as here, there is a difference between historical interpretation and the tendency of the philosopher, the difference reveals the insufficiency of the interpretation itself: in other words, if the theory of the historian of philosophy is at war with the theories of which he claims to expound the history, his theory must be false, just because it does not avail to justify the history of the theories. But this exception does not annul the distinction in other fields; indeed, it confirms it, and is not an exception in the empirical sense, as it appears to be: thought distinguishes and is distinguished from sentiment and will, but it is not distinguished from itself, precisely because it is the principle of distinction. A methodological corollary of this distinction between history of historiography and history of practical tendencies is that the introduction into the first of considerations belonging to the second is to be held erroneous. Here I think Fueter has sinned to some extent in the book to which I have already referred, where he divides his material into humanistic, political, party, imperial, particularist, Protestant, Catholic, Jesuitic, illuministic, romanticist, erudite, lirico-subjective, national, statolatral, historiographical, and the like. Only some of the above divisions belong to, or can properly be reduced to, historiographical concepts, while the majority refer to social and political life. Hence the lack of sound organization that we observe in this book, which is yet so lively and ingenious: its divisions follow one another without sufficient logicality, continuity, and necessity, and are not the result of a single thought which posits them and develops itself through them. If, on the other hand, the genuinely historiographical portions, which have become mingled with it, should be eliminated, what remained could certainly be organized, but as social and political history, no longer as historiography, because the works of historians would be consulted only as documents showing the tendencies of the times in which they were written. Machiavelli, for instance, (to use the same example) would there figure as an Italian patriot and defender of absolute power, while Vico (a much greater historian than Machiavelli) would not be able to appear at all, or hardly at all, because his relation with the political life of his time was remote and general.

What I have been expounding may be resumed by saying that the history of historiography is neither *literary* history nor the history of cultural, social, political, moral doings, which are of a *practical* nature, but that it is certainly all these things, by reason of the unbreakable unity of history, though with it the *accent* does not fall upon practical facts, but rather upon *historiographical thought*, which is its proper subject.

Having pointed out or recalled these distinctions, which, as we have seen, are sometimes neglected with evil results, we must now utter a warning against other distinctions, employed without rational basis, which rather overcloud and trouble the history of historiography than shed light upon it.

Fueter (I cite him again, although the error is not peculiar to him) declares that he has dealt in his book with *historiographical theories* and with *historical method* only in so far as they seem to have had influence upon actual historiography The history of historicity (here is the reason he gives for the method he has followed) is as little the history of historiography as is the history of dramatic theories the history of the drama. This he considers to be proved by the fact that theory and practice often follow different paths, as, for instance, in Lope de Vega, whose theory of the drama and actual dramatic work were two different things, to such an extent that it was said of the Spanish dramatist that although he reverenced the poetical art, when he sat down to compose "he locked up the correct rules under seven keys." This argument is without doubt specious, and I was myself formerly seduced by it; but it is fallacious, as I realized when I thought it over again, and I now affirm it to be an error with all the conviction and authority of one who criticizes an error at one time his own. The argument is founded upon a false analogy between the production of art and that of history. Art, which is the work of the imagination, can be well distinguished from the theory of art, which is the work of reflection; artistic genius produces the former, the speculative intellect the latter, and it often happens with artists that the speculative intellect is inferior to their genius, so that they do one thing and say another, or say one thing and do another, without its being possible to accuse them of logical incoherence, because the incoherence is between two discordant thoughts, never between a thought and an act of the imagination. But history and theory of history are both of them works of thought, bound to one another in the same way as thought is bound to itself, since it is one. Thus no historian but possesses in a more or less reflective way his theory of history, because, not to put too fine a point upon it, every historian implicitly or explicitly conducts a polemic against other historians (against other 'versions' and 'judgments' of a fact), and how could he ever conduct a polemic or criticize others if he did not himself possess a *conception* of what history is and ought to be, to which to refer, a *theory* of history? The artist, on the other hand, in so far as he is an artist, does not polemize or criticize, but forms. It may quite well happen that an erroneous theory of historiography is expounded, while on the contrary the history as narrated may turn out to be well constructed. This is, of course, to be incoherent, but is so neither more nor less than when progress is effected in one branch of historiography, while there is backwardness in another. There may obtain, on the contrary, an excellent theory of history, where history itself is bad; but in the same way that in one field of historiography there is the sense of and striving for a better method, while there is adherence to old methods in all the other fields. The history of historiography is the history of historical thought; and here it is impossible to distinguish theory of history from history.

Another exclusion which Fueter declares that he has made is that of the *philosophy of history*. He does not give the reason for this, but allows it to be understood, for he evidently holds that philosophies of history do not possess a purely scientific character and are lacking in truth. But not only are what are called 'philosophies of history' erroneous conceptions of history, but so also are the naturalistic or deterministic conceptions opposed to them, and all the various forms of pseudo-history which have been described above, philological history, poetical history, rhetorical history. I do not find that he has excluded these from his history, any more than he has really excluded the theological and transcendental conception of history (philosophy of history); indeed, he constantly refers to it. Justice and logic would insist upon all or none being excluded —all really excluded, and not merely in words. But to exclude all of them, it may be said, would be anything but intelligent, because how could the history of history ever be told in such a void? What is this history but the struggle of scientific historiography against inadequate scientific formulas? Certainly the former is the protagonist, but how could a drama be presented with a protagonist lacking antagonists? And even if historical philology be not considered directly, but referred back to philology, if poetical history be referred back to literature, rhetorical or practical to social and political history, it would nevertheless be necessary always to take account of the conversion that often occurs of those various mental constructions into assertions of reality, taken in exchange for and given the value of true and proper histories. In this sense they become in turn *deterministic* or *transcendental* conceptions of history, and both of them logical or illogical representations of all the others, and end by becoming equivalent to one another dialectically, and are always before the eyes of the historian, because the perpetual condition and the perpetual sign of the progress of historical thought reside in their movement, which passes from transcendency or false immanence to pure immanence, to return to them and enter into a more profound conception of immanency. To exclude philosophies of history from the history of historiography does not, therefore, seem to me to be justifiable, for the same reason as it seems to be unjustifiable to exclude from it historiographical theories, which are the consciousness that historiography acquires of itself: owing to their homogeneity, I say, owing indeed to their identity with history, of which they do not form accidental ingredients or material elements, but constitute the very essence. A proof of this is to be found in the *Historical Philosophy of France* of Flint. He proceeds from a presumption that is perhaps the opposite of that of Fueter—that is to say, he treats of the philosophy of history, and not of history, but finds it impossible to maintain the dykes between the two. His treatise, therefore, when artificial obstacles have been overcome, runs like a single river and reveals to our view the whole history of historical French thought, to which Bossuet and Rollin, Condorcet and Voltaire, Auguste Comte and Michelet or Tocqueville equally belong.

At this point it will probably be objected (although Fueter does not propound this objection, it is probable that it is at the back of his mind) that what is desired in a history of historiography is not so much a history of *historical thought* as a history of *history in the concrete*: of the *Storie fiorentine* of Machiavelli, of the *Siècle de Louis XIV* of Voltaire, or of the *Romische Geschichte* of Niebuhr: that would be a *general* history, while what is desired is a *specific* history. But it is well to pay close attention to the meaning of such a request and to the possibility of what is asked. If I set out to write the history of the *Storie fiorentine* of Machiavelli, in respect to the particular material with which it deals, I shall rewrite the history of Florence, criticizing and completing Machiavelli, and shall thus be, for instance, a Villari, a Davidsohn, or a Salvemini. If I set out to write the history of the material of Voltaire's work, I shall criticize Voltaire and outline a new *Siècle de Louis XIV*, as has been done, for example, by Philippson. And if I set to work to examine and rethink the work of Niebuhr in respect to its particular material, I shall be a new historian of Rome, a Mommsen or (to quote the most recent writers) a Hector Pais or a Gaetano de Sanctis. But is this what is desired? Certainly not. But if this be not desired, if the particular materials of those histories are not to be taken account of, what else remains save the 'way' in which they have been conceived, the 'mental form' by means of which they construct their narratives, and therefore their theory and their historical 'thought'?

Now, if this truth be admitted (and I do not see how it can be contested) it is not possible to reject an ulterior consequence which, although it is wont to arouse in some the sensation of a paradox, does not do so in us, for we find it altogether in accordance with the conception of the identity of history with philosophy that we have defended. Is a thought that is not thought conceivable? Is it permissible to distinguish between the *thought of the historian* and the *thought of the philosopher*? Are there perhaps two different thoughts in the world? To persist in maintaining that the thought of the historian thinks the fact and not the theory is prevented by the preceding admission, if by nothing else: that the historian always thinks at least both the theory of history and the historical fact. But this admission entails his thinking the theory of all the things that he narrates, together with the theory of history. And indeed he could not narrate without understanding them. Fueter extols the merit of Winckelmann, who was the first to conceive a history, not of artists, but of art, of a pure spiritual activity, and that of Giannone, who was the first to attempt a history of the life of jurisprudence. But these writers made the progress they did because they had a new and more accurate conception of art and of rights, and if they went wrong as to certain points, that is because they did not always think those conceptions with equal exactitude. Winckelmann, for instance, materialized the spiritual activity of the artist when he posited an abstract, fixed material ideal of beauty, and gave an abstract history of artistic styles without regard to the temperaments, historical circumstances, and individualities of the artists themselves. Giannone failed to supersede the dualism of Church and State. Without indulging in other too particular examples, it is evident at the first glance that ancient historiography concords with the ancient conception of religion of the state, of ethic, and of the whole of reality; the medieval with Christian theology and ethic; that of the first half of the nineteenth century with the idealistic and romantic philosophy, that of the second half with naturalistic and positivistic philosophy. Thus, *ex parte historicorum*, there is no way of distinguishing historical and philosophical thought, which are perfectly commingled in the narratives. But there is also no possibility of maintaining such a distinction *ex parte philosophorum* either, because, as all know, or at least say, each period has the philosophy proper to it, which is the consciousness of that period, and as such is its history, at least in germ; or, as we have put it, philosophy and history coincide. And if they coincide, the history of philosophy and the history of historiography also coincide: the one is not only not distinguishable from the other, but is not even subordinate to the other, for it is all one with it.

The historiography of philosophy has already begun to open its arms, inviting and receiving the works of the historians. Every day it understands better that a history of Greek thought is not complete without taking count of Herodotus, Thucydides, and Polybius, nor of Roman thought without Livy and Tacitus, nor of the thought of the Renaissance without Machiavelli and Guicciardini. It must open them yet wider and clasp to its bosom even the humble medieval historiographers who noted the *Gesta episcoporum* or *Historiolæ translationum* or *Vitæ sanctorum*, or who bear witness to the Christian faith, according to their powers and in their own way, it is true, but not less than the great Augustine according to his powers. It must receive not only the hagiographical writers, but even obtuse philologists or sociologists who have amused us during the last decades and bear witness to the creed of positivism not otherwise than as Spencer or Haeckel in their systems. By means of this amplification of concepts and enrichment of material, the historiography of philosophy will place itself in the position of being able to show that philosophy is a force diffused throughout life, and not the particular invention and cult of certain men who are philosophers, and will obtain the means that have hitherto been lacking to effect a close conjunction with the whole historical movement.

In its turn the history of historiography will gain by the fusion, because it will find its own directive principles in philosophy, and by its means will be rendered capable of understanding both the problems of history in general and those of its various aspects as history of art and of philosophy, of economic and moral life. To seek elsewhere the criterion of explanation is vain. Fueter, who takes a glance at the most recent historiography, that posterior to 1870, at the end of his book, discerns in it the new consciousness that gives the highest place to political and military power and marks the end of the old liberalism, the strengthening of such consciousness by means of the Darwinian theories concerning the struggle for life, the influence of a more intense economical and industrial life and a greater intensity of world politics, the repercussion of Egyptian and Orientalistic discoveries, which have aided in disproving the illusion of Europe as the centre of the world, the attraction exercised by the theory of races, and so on. These observations are just, but they do not reach the heart and brain of the most recent historiography; they merely revolve round its body. The heart or brain is, as I have observed, *naturalism*, the ideal of historical culture inspired and to be inspired by the natural sciences. So true is this that Fueter himself burns a few grains of incense before this idol, sighing for a form of history that shall be beautiful with the beauty of a well-made machine, rivalling a book on physics such as the *Theory of Tones* of Helmholtz. The truth is that the ideal of the natural sciences, instead of being the perfection, is one of the many crises that historical thought has passed through and will pass through. Historical thought is dialectic of development, and not by any means a deterministic explanation by means of causes which does not explain anything because it does not develop anything. But whatever we may think of this, it is certain that naturalism—that is, the criticism of naturalism—can alone supply the clue for unravelling the web of the historiography of the last ten years ; the same events and historical movements enumerated above have acted in the particular way in which they have acted owing to being constantly framed in naturalistic thought.

For the rest, nothing forbids, and it may even serve a useful purpose, that the history of philosophy and the history of historiography should receive literary treatment in different books, for altogether practical reasons, such, for instance, as the abundance of material and the different training and acquirements needed for the treatment of the different classes of material. But what is *apparently disunited* by practice thought *really unifies*; and this real unification is what I have wished to inculcate, without the pedantic idea ever passing through my mind of dictating rules for composing books, as to which it is desirable to leave all liberty of inclusion and exclusion to writers, in conformity with their various intentions.

II

GRÆCO-ROMAN HISTORIOGRAPHY

AFTER what we have said as to the nature of periodization,[1] the usual custom, to which I too bow here, of beginning the history of historiography with that of the Greeks, and with the Greeks of the fifth or sixth century before Christ, will be taken for what it is really worth, but it must not be thought that we thus intend to announce the beginning of historiography, its first appearance in the world, when, on the contrary, all we wish to say is that our interest in the investigation of its course becomes more vivid at that point. History, like philosophy, has no historical beginning, but only an ideal or metaphysical beginning, in so far as it is an activity of thought, which is outside time. Historically speaking, it is quite clear that prior to Herodotus, prior to the logographs, prior indeed to Hesiod and to Homer, history was already, because it is impossible to conceive of men who do not think and do not narrate their deeds in some way or other. This explanation might seem to be superfluous if the confusion between historical beginning and ideal beginning had not led to the fancy of a 'first philosophical step,' made by Thales or Zeno, or by somebody else, by means of which thinking the first stone is supposed to have been laid, as it was believed that by thinking another last step the pinnacle of the edifice of philosophy was or would be attained. But Thales and Herodotus should really be called rather the 'sons' of our interest in the development of those

[1] See pp 112-116.

disciplines than the 'fathers' of philosophy and history, and it is we whom those sons salute as their 'fathers.' We have not usually much interest in what occurred prior to them or among people more distant than they from our point of view, not only because there is a scarcity of surviving documents concerning them, but above all because they are forms of thought which have but little connexion with our own actual problems.

From its point of view, too, the distinction that we laid down between history and philology suggests refraining from the search hitherto made for the beginnings of Græco-Roman historiography by means of composing lists of magistrates and of adding to these brief mention of wars, treatises, embassies from colonies, religious festivities, earthquakes, inundations, and the like, in the *ὦροι* and in the *annales pontificum*, in archives and museums made in temples, or indeed in the chronological nails fixed to the walls, spoken of by Perizonius. Such things are extrinsic to historiography and form the precedent, not of it, but of chronicle and philology, which were not born for the first time in the nineteenth or seventeenth century, or at any rate during the Alexandrine period, but belong to all times, for in all times men take note of what they remember and attempt to preserve such memorials intact, to restore and to increase them. The precedent of history cannot be something different from history, but is history itself, as philosophy is the precedent of philosophy and the living of the living. Nevertheless the thought of Herodotus and of the logographs really does unite itself with religions, myths, theogonies, cosmogonies, genealogies, and with legendary and epical tales, which were not indeed poetry, or were not only poetry but also thoughts—that is to say, metaphysics and histories.

The whole of later historiography developed from them by a dialectical process, for which they supplied the presuppositions—that is to say, concepts, propositions of fact and fancy mingled, and with that the stimulus better to seek out the truth and to dissipate fancies. This dissipation took place more rapidly at the time which it is usual to fix by convention as the beginning of Greek historiography.

At that time thought deserts mythological history and its ruder form, prodigious or miraculous history, and enters earthly or human history—that is to say, the general conception that is still ours, so much so that it has been possible for an illustrious living historian to propose the works of Thucydides as an example and model to the historians of our times. Certainly that exit and that entrance did not represent for the Greeks a complete breaking with the past; and since earthly history could not have been altogether wanting in the past, so it is not to be believed that the Greeks from the sixth and seventh centuries onward should have abandoned all faith in mythology and prodigies. These things persisted not only with the people and among lesser or vulgar historiographers, but also left their traces among some of the greatest. Nevertheless, looking at the whole from above, as one should look at it, it is evident that the environment is altogether changed from what it was. Even the many fables that we read in Herodotus, and which were to be read in the logographs, are rarely (as has been justly observed) put forward ingenuously, but are usually given as by one who collects what others believe, and does not for that reason accept those beliefs, even if he does not openly evince his disbelief; or he collects them because he does not know what to substitute for them, and rather as matter for reflection and inquiry: *quæ nec confirmare argumentis neque refellere in animo est*, as Tacitus says, when he recounts the fables of the Germans: *plura transcribo quam credo*, declared Quintus Curtius. Herodotus is certainly not Voltaire, nor is he indeed Thucydides (Thucydides, 'the atheist'); but certainly he is no longer Homer or Hesiod.

The following are a few examples of leading problems which ancient historians had before them, dictated by the conditions and events of Greek and Roman life; they were treated from a mental point of view, which no longer found in those facts episodes of the rivalry of Aphrodite and Hera (as formerly in the Trojan War), but varying complex human struggles, due to human interests, expressing themselves in human actions. How did the wars between the Greeks and the Persians originate and develop? What were the origins of the Peloponnesian War? of the expedition of Cyrus against Artaxerxes? How was the Roman power formed in Latium, and how did it afterward extend in Italy and in the whole world? How did the Romans succeed in depriving the Carthaginians of the hegemony of the Mediterranean? What were the political institutions developed in Athens, Rome, and Sparta, and what form did the social struggle take in those cities? What did the Athenian *demos*, the Roman *plebs*, the *eupatrides*, and the *patres* desire? What were the virtues, the dispositions, the points of view, of the various peoples which entered into conflict among themselves, Athenians, Lacedemonians, Persians, Macedonians, Romans, Gauls, and Germans? What were the characters of the great men who guided the destinies of the peoples, Themistocles, Pericles, Alexander, Hannibal, and Scipio?

These problems were solved in a series of classical

works by Thucydides, Xenophon, Polybius, Livy, Tacitus, etc., and they will certainly not be blamed for failing to exhaust their themes—that is, for failing to sound the bottom of the universe, because there is no sounding the bottom of the universe—nor because they solve those problems only in the terms in which they had proposed them, neither more nor less than as we solve the problems of our day in our own terms. Nor must we forget that since modern historiography is still much as it was left by the Greeks, the greater part of those events are still thought as they were by the ancients, and although something has been added and a different light illumines the whole, the work of the ancient historians is preserved in our own: a true "eternal possession," as Thucydides intended that his history should be.

And just as historical thought had become invigorated in its passage from the mythological to the human stage, so did research and philology grow. Herodotus was already travelling, asking questions, and listening to answers, distinguishing between the things that he had seen with his own eyes and those which depended upon hearsay, opinion, and conjecture; Thucydides was submitting to criticism different traditions relating to the same fact, and even inserting documents in his narrative. Later appeared legions of learned men and critics, who compiled 'antiquities' and 'libraries,' and busied themselves also with the reading of texts, with chronology and geography, thus affording great assistance to historical studies. Such a fervour of philological studies was eventually attained that it was recognized as necessary to draw a clear distinction between the 'histories of antiquaries' (of which a considerable number survive either entire or in fragments) and 'histories of historians,' and Polybius several times said that it is easy to compose history from books, because it suffices to take up one's residence in a city where there exist rich libraries, but that true history requires acquaintance with political and military affairs and direct knowledge of places and of people; and Lucian repeated that it is indispensable for the historian to have political sense, *ἀδίδακτον φυσέως δῶρον*, a gift of nature not to be learned (the maxims and practices praised as quite novel by Moser and Niebuhr are therefore by no means new). The fact is that a more profound theoretical consciousness corresponded with a more vigorous historiography, so inseparable is the theory of history from history, advancing with it. It was also known that history should not be made a simple instrument of practice, of political intrigue, or of amusement, and that its function is above all to aim at truth: *ne quid falsi dicere audeat, ne quid veri non audeat.* In consequence of this, partisanship, even for one's own country, was condemned (although it was recognized that solicitude and sympathy were permissible); and *quidquid Græcia mendax audet in historia* was blamed. It was known that history is not chronicle (*annales*), which is limited to external things, recording (in the words of Asellio, the ancient Roman historian) *quod factum, quoque anno gestum sit*, whereas history tries to understand *quo consilio, quaque ratione gesta sint.* And it was also known that history cannot set herself the same task as poetry. We find Thucydides referring with disdain to histories written with the object of gaining the prize in oratorical competitions, and to those which indulge in fables to please the vulgar. Polybius too inveighed against those who seek to emphasize moving details, and depict women dishevelled and in tears, and dreadful scenes, as though composing tragedies and as though it were their business to create the marvellous and pleasing and not impart truth and instruction. If it be a fact that rhetorical historiography (a worsening of the imaginative and poetic) abounded in antiquity and introduced its false gold even into some masterpieces, the general tendency of the better historians was to set themselves free of ornate rhetoricians and of cheap eloquence. But the ancient historians will never fail of lofty poetical power and elevation for this reason (not even the 'prosaic' Polybius, who sometimes paints most effective pictures), but will ever retain what is proper to lofty historical narrative. Cicero and Quintilian, Diogenes and Lucian, all recognize that history must adopt *verba ferme poetarum*, that it is *proxima poetis et quodammodo carmen solutum*, that *scribitur ad narrandum, non ad demonstrandum*, that *ἔχει τι ποιητικόν*, and the like. What the best historians and theorists sought at that time was not the aridity and dryness of mathematical or physical treatment (such as we often hear desired in our day), but gravity, abstention from fabulous and pleasing tales, or if not from fabulous then from frivolous tales, in fact from competition with the rhetoricians and composers of histories that were romances or gross caricatures of such. Above all they desired that history should remain faithful to real life, since it is the instrument of life, and a form of knowledge useful to the statesman and to the lover of his country, and by no means docile to the capricious requirements of the unoccupied seeking amusement.

This theory of historiography, which may be found here and there in a good many special treatises and in general treatises on the art of speech, finds nowhere such complete and conscious expression as in the frequent polemical interludes of Polybius in his *Histories*, where the polemic itself endows it with precision, concreteness, and savour. Polybius is the Aristotle of ancient historiography : an Aristotle who is both historical and theoretical, completing the Stagirite, who in the vast expanse of his work had taken but little interest in history properly so called. And since so great a part of the ancient narratives lives in our own, so there is not one of the propositions recorded that has not been included and has not been worthy of being included in our treatises. And if, for example, the maxim that history should be narrated by men of the world and not by the simply erudite or by philologists, that it is born of practice and assists in practice, has been often neglected, the blame falls on those who neglect it. A further blunder committed by such writers has been to forget completely the τι ποιητικόν and to pay court to an ideal of history something like an anatomical map or a treatise of mechanics.

But the defect that ancient historiography exposes to our gaze is of another sort. The ancients did not observe it as a defect, or only sometimes, in a vague and fugitive manner, without attaching weight to it, for otherwise they would have remedied it when it occurred. The modern spirit inquires how the sentiments and conceptions which are now our ideal patrimony, and the institutions in which they are realized, have been gradually formed. It wishes to understand the revolutionary passages from primitive and Oriental to Græco-Roman culture, how modern ethic was attained through ancient ethic, the modern through the ancient state, the vast industry and international commerce of the modern world through the ancient mode of economic production, the passage from the myths of the Aryans to our philosophies, from Mycenean to French or Swedish or Italian art of the twentieth century. Hence there are special histories of culture, of philosophy, of poetry, of the sciences, of technique, of economy, of morality, of religions, and so on, which are preferred to histories of individuals or of states themselves, in so far as they are abstract individuals. They are illuminated and inspired throughout with the ideas of liberty, of civilization, of humanity, and of progress. All this is not to be found in ancient historiography, although it cannot be said to be altogether absent, for with what could the mind of man have ever been occupied, save by human ideals or 'values'? Nor should the error be made of considering 'epochs' as something compact and static, whereas they are various and in motion, or of rendering those divisions natural and external which, as has been demonstrated, are nothing but the movement of our thought as we think history, a fallacy linked with the other one concerning the absolute beginning of history and the rendering temporal of the forms of the spirit. Whoever is gifted with the patience of the collector will meet here and there with suggestions and buddings of those historiographical conceptions of which, generally speaking, we have denied the existence in the writings of the ancients. He who finds diversion in modernizing the old may travesty the thoughts of the ancients, as they have been travestied, so as to render them almost altogether similar to those of the moderns. In the first book of Aristotle's *Metaphysics*, for instance, is to be admired a sketch of the development of Greek philosophy, of the various naturalistic interpretations which have been in turn proposed for the explanation of the cosmos, and so on, up to the new orientation of the mind, when, "compelled by truth itself," it turned toward a different order of principles—that is to say, till the time of Anaxagoras, "who seems to be a sober man among the intoxicated," thus continuing up to the time of Socrates, who founded ethic and discovered the universal and the definition. A sketch of the history of civilization is to be found at the beginning of the *History* of Thucydides, and Polybius will be found discoursing of the progress that had been made in all the arts, while Cicero, Quintilian, and several others trace the progress of rights and of literature. There are also touches of human value in conflict with one another in the narratives of the struggles between Greeks and barbarians, between the truly civil and active life of the former and the proud, lazy habits of the latter. Other similar conceptions of human values will be found in many comparisons of peoples, and above all in the way that Tacitus describes the Germans as a new moral power rising up against that of ancient Rome, and perhaps also in the repugnance which the same historian experiences at seeing before him the Jews, who follow rites *contrarios ceteris mortalibus*. Finally, Rome, mistress of the world, will sometimes assume in our eyes the aspect of a transparent symbol of the human ideal, analogous to Roman law, gradually idealized in the form of natural law. But here it is rather a question of symbols than of conceptions, of our own conclusions than of the thoughts proper to the ancients. When, for instance, we examine the history of philosophy of Aristotle as outlined by him, we find that it consists above all in a rapid critical account to serve as propædeutic to his system ; and literary and artistic histories and histories of civilization seem often to be weakened by the prejudice that these are not really necessary mental forms, but luxuries and refinements. At the utmost we can speak of exceptions, incidents, tentatives; which does not in any way alter the comprehensive impression and general conclusion to the effect that the ancients never possessed explicit histories of civilization, philosophy, religions, literature, art, or rights: none, in fact, of the many possessed by ourselves. Nor did they possess 'biography' in the sense that we do, as the history of the ideal function of an individual in his own time and in the life of humanity, nor the sense of development, and when they speak of primitive times they rarely feel that they are primitive, but are rather disposed to transfigure them poetically, in the same way that Dante did by the mouth of Cacciaguida that Fiorenza which "stood soberly and modestly at peace" within the circle of the ancient days. It was one of the "severe labours" of our Vico to recover the crude reality of history beneath these poetic idylls. In this work he was assisted, not by the ancient historiographers, but by documents and mostly by languages.

The physiognomy of the histories of the ancients as described very accurately reflects the character of their philosophy, which never attained to the conception of the spirit, and therefore also failed to attain to that of humanity, liberty, and progress, which are aspects or synonyms of the former. It certainly passed from physiology or cosmology to ethic, logic, and rhetoric; but it schematized and materialized these spiritual disciplines because it treated them empirically. Thus their ethic did not rise above the custom of Greece and Rome, nor their logic above abstract forms of reasoning and discussing, nor their poetic above classes of literature. For this reason all assume the form of precepts. 'Anti-historical philosophy' has been universally recognized and described, but it is anti-historical because anti-spiritual, anti-historical because naturalistic.

The ancients also failed to notice the deficiency observed by us, for they were entirely occupied with the joy of the effort of passing from myth to science and thus to the collection and classification of the facts of reality. That is to say, they were engrossed upon the sole problem which they set themselves to solve, and solved so successfully that they supplied naturalism with the instruments which it still employs: formal logic, grammar, the doctrine of the virtues, the doctrine of literary classes, categories of civil rights, and so forth. These were all Græco-Roman creations.

But that ancient historians and philosophers were not explicitly aware of the above defect in its proper terms, or rather in our modern terms, does not mean that they were not to some extent exercised by it. In every historical period exist problems theoretically formulated and for that very reason solved, while others have not yet arrived at complete theoretical maturity, but are seen, intuited, though not yet adequately thought. If the former are the positive contribution of that time to the chain whose links form the human spirit, the latter represent an unsatisfied demand, which binds that time in another way to the coming time. The great attention paid to the negative aspect of every epoch sometimes leads to the forgetting of the other aspect, and to the consequent imagining of a humanity that passes not from satisfaction to satisfaction through dissatisfaction, but from dissatisfaction to dissatisfaction and from error to error. But obscurities and discordances are possible in so far as light and concord have been previously attained. Thus they represent in their way progress, as is to be seen from the history that we are recounting, where we find them very numerous for the very reason that the age of mythologies and of prodigies has been left behind. If Greece and Rome had not been both more than Greece and more than Rome, if they had not been the human spirit, which is infinitely greater than any Greece and any Rome—its transitory individuations—they would have been satisfied with the human portraits of their historians and would not have sought beyond. But they did seek beyond—that is to say, those very historians and philosophers sought; and since they had before them so many episodes and dramas of human life, reconstructed by their thought, they asked themselves what was the cause of those events, reasonably concluding that such a cause might be one fact or another, a particular fact; and for this reason they began to distinguish between facts and causes, and, in the order of causes themselves, between cause and occasion, as does Thucydides, or between beginning, cause, and occasion (ἀρχή, αἰτία, πρόφασις), like Polybius. They thus became involved in disputes as to the true cause of this or that event, and ever since antiquity attempts have been made to solve the enigma of the 'greatness' of Rome, assuming in modern times the guise of a solemn *experimentum* of historical thought and thus forming the diversion of those historians who linger behind. The question was often generalized in the other question as to the motive power behind all history; and here too appear doctrines, afterward drawn out to great length, such as that the form of the political constitution was the cause of all the rest, and that other doctrine relating to climate and to the temperaments of peoples. The doctrine principally proposed and accepted was that of the natural law of the circle in human affairs, the perpetual alternation of good and evil, or the passage through political forms, which always returns to the form from which it has taken its start, or as growth from infancy to manhood, declining into old age and decrepitude and ending in death. But a law of this sort, which satisfied and still satisfies the Oriental mind, did not satisfy the classical mind, which had a lively sense of human effort and of the stimulus received from obstacles encountered and conflicts endured. Hence therefore the further questions: Does fate or immutable necessity oppress man, or is he not rather the plaything of capricious fortune, or is he ruled by a wise and sagacious providence? It was also asked whether the gods are interested in human affairs or not. These questions met with answers that are sometimes pious, advocating submission to the divine will and wisdom, sometimes, again, inspired with the notion that the gods are not concerned with human affairs themselves, but solely with vengeance and punishment. All these conceptions lack firmness, and are for the most part confused, since a general uncertainty and confession of ignorance prevails in them: *in incerto judicium est*, said Tacitus, almost summing up the ancient argument on the subject in this epigram, or rather finding non-thought, failure to understand, to be the result of the argument.

What we do not understand we do not dominate; on the contrary, it dominates us, or at least menaces us, taking the form of evil; hence the psychological attitude of the ancients toward history must be described as pessimistic. They saw much greatness fall, but they never discovered the greatness that does not fall and that rises up greater after every fall. For this reason a flood of bitterness inundates their histories. Happiness, beauty of human life, always seemed to be something that had been and was no longer, and were it present would have soon been lost. For the Romans and those professing the cult of Rome, it was primitive, austere, victorious Rome ; and all the Roman historians, big and little, Livy, Sallust, and Tacitus, Paterculus and Florus, fix their gaze upon that image, as they lament the corruption of later days. Once it was Rome that trampled the world underfoot; but they knew that the triumphant queen must some day become slave from queen that once she was. This thought manifests itself in the most various forms, from the melancholy meditations of Scipio upon the ruins of Carthage to the fearful expectation of the lordship which—as Persia to Babylonia and Macedonia to Persia—must succeed to that of the Romans (the theory of the 'four monarchies' has its origin in the Græco-Roman world, whence it filtered into Palestine and into the Book of Daniel). Sometimes repressed, sometimes outspoken, we hear the anxious question : Who will be the successor and the gravedigger ? Will it be the menacing Parthian ? Will it be the Germans, so rich in new and mysterious energy ?—all this, despite the proud consciousness of ancient times that had uttered the words "Rome, the eternal city." Certainly, that general pessimism is not altogether coherent, for no pessimism can be so altogether, and here and there appear fugitive hints of a perception of human progress in this or that part of life. We find, for instance, Tacitus, bitterest of men, remarking that *nec omnia apud priores meliora, sed nostra quoque ætas multa laudis et artium imitanda tulit*, and one of the speakers in the *De oratoribus* observes that literary forms change with the times and that it is owing to the *vitio malignitatis humanæ* that we hear the perpetual praise of ancient things and the perpetual abuse of things modern.

Another interlocutor in the same dialogue draws attention to the dialectic connexion between the turbulence of life and the greatness of art, whence Rome *donec erravit, donec se partibus et dissensionibus confecit*, precisely at that time *tulit valentiorem eloquentiam*. This linking together of good and evil is not altogether absent in ancient philosophy, and is also to be found here and there in ancient historiography. Sallust, for example, is of opinion that Rome remained in good health so long as she had Carthage opposed to her and giving her trouble. Readers of Cicero and of Seneca will be aware that the idea of humanity also made considerable progress during the last days of the Republic and the first days of the Empire, owing to the influence of Stoicism. Divine providence too is courted, as was not formerly the case, and we also find Diodorus Siculus undertaking to treat the affairs of all nations as those of a single city (καθάπερ μιᾶς πολέως). But these promises remain still weak, vague, and inert (the *promissor* Diodorus, for example, carried out none of his grandiose prologue), and in any case they foretell the dissolution of the classical world. During this epoch the problem as to the signification of history remains unsolved, because the contradictory conceptions above mentioned of fortune or of the gods, the belief in a universal worsening of things, in a fall or a regression, which had already been expressed in many ancient myths, were not by any means solutions.

Owing to their failure to realize spiritual value as the immanent progressive force in history, even the loftiest of the ancient historians were not able to maintain the unity and autonomy of historiographical work, which in other respects they had discovered and asserted. Although they had penetrated the deception exercised by those histories that are really poetry, or lies and partisanship, or collections of material and unintelligent piling up of erudition, or instruments of pleasure, affording marvel for simple folk, yet they were on the other hand incapable of ever setting themselves free of the preconception of history as directed to an end of edification and chiefly of instruction. This real heteronomy then appeared to be autonomy. They are all agreed as to this: Thucydides proposed to narrate past events in order to predict from them future events, identical or similar, the perpetual return of human fortunes; Polybius sought out the causes of facts in order that he might apply them to analogous cases, and held those unexpected events to be of inferior importance whose irregularities place them outside rules; Tacitus, in conformity with his chief interest, which was rather moralistic than social or political, held his chief end to be the collection of facts notable for the vice or virtue which they contained, *ne virtutes sileantur utque pravis dictis factisque ex posteritate et infamia metus sit.* Behind them came all the minor historians, all the hypocrites, who repeated by imitation or involuntary echo or false unction and in a superficial way what in the greater writers was the result of profound thought, as, for instance, the Sallusts, the Diogenes, the Diodori, the Plutarchs, and those that resemble them. Then there were all the extractors of historical quintessences, of memorable deeds and words of statesmen, captains, and philosophers, and even of women (the γυναικῶν ἀρεταί). Ancient historiography has been called 'pragmatical,' and such it is, in the double sense of the word, ancient and modern: in so far as it limits itself to the earthly side of things and especially to the political (the 'pragmatic' of Polybius), and in so far as it adorns them with reflections and advice (the 'apodictic' of the same historian-theorist).

This heteronomous theory of history does not always remain merely theory, prologue, or frame, but sometimes operates so as to lead to the mingling of elements that are not historiographical with history, such as, for instance, is the case with the 'speeches' or 'orations' of historical personages, not delivered or not in agreement with what was really said, but invented or arranged by the historian and put into the mouths of the personages. This, in my opinion, has been wrongly looked upon as a survival of the 'epic spirit' in ancient historiography, or as a simple proof of the rhetorical ability of the narrators, because, if the first explanation hold as to some of the popular writers and the second as to certain rhetoricians, the origin of those falsifications was with the greater historians nothing but the fulfilment of the obligation of teaching and counselling accepted by them. But when such ends had been assigned to history, its intrinsic quality of truth and the line of demarcation which it drew between real and imaginary could not but vacillate to some extent, since the imaginary sometimes served excellently well and even better than the real for those ends. And setting aside Plato, who despised all knowledge save that of the transcendental ideas, did not Aristotle himself ask whether the greater truth belonged to history or to poetry? Had he not indeed said that history is 'less philosophical' than poetry? And if so why should not history have availed itself of the aid of poetry and of imagination? In any case, resistance could be opposed to this ulterior perversion by seeking the truth with vigilant eye, and also by reducing the share of the imaginary speeches and other parerga to the smallest dimensions. But it was impossible to dispense with belief in the end of instruction, because it was in any case necessary that history should have some end, and a true end had not been discovered, and the end of instruction performed almost the function of a metaphor of the truth, since it was to some extent the nearest to the truth. In Polybius critical vigilance, scientific austerity, a keen desire for ample and severe history, attain to so high a level that one would feel disposed to treat the historian of Megalopolis like one of those great pagans that medieval imagination admitted to Paradise, or at least to Purgatory, as worthy of having known the true God by extraordinary means and as a reward for their intense moral conscience. But if we envisage the matter with greater calmness we shall have to consign Polybius also to the Limbo where those who "were before Christianity" and "did not duly adore God" are received. They were men of great value and reached the boundary, even touching it, but they never passed beyond.

III
MEDIEVAL HISTORIOGRAPHY

FOR the same reason that we must not look upon the beginning of any history as an absolute beginning, or conceive of epochs in a simplicistic manner, as though they were strictly limited to the determinations represented by their general character, we must be careful not to identify the humanistic conception of history with the ancient epoch of historiography which it characterizes or symbolizes—in fact, we must not make historical the ideal categories, which are eternal. Græco-Roman historiography was without doubt humanistic, but it was a Græco-Roman humanism—that is to say, it not only had all the limitations that we have been pointing out, but also the special physiognomy which such humanism assumes in the ancient historians and thinkers, varying more or less in each one of them. Not only was it thus humanistic, but other formations of the same sort probably preceded, as they certainly followed, it in the course of the centuries. It is perhaps attractive, but it is also artificial (and contrary to the true concept of progress), to conceive of the history of philosophy and of historiography as of a series of ideal phases, which are traversed once only, and to transform philosophers into categories and categories into philosophers, making synonymous Democritus and the atom, Plato and the transcendental idea, Descartes and dualism, Spinoza and pantheism, Leibnitz and monadism, whittling down history to the dimensions of a *Dynastengeschichte*, as a German critic has satirically described it, or treating it according to a sort of 'line of buckets' theory, as an Englishman has humorously described it. Hence, too, the view that history has not yet appeared in the world, or that it has appeared for the first time and by flashes, in response to the invocations made by the historian and the critic of the present day. But every thinking of history is always adequate to the moment at which it appears and always inadequate to the moment that follows.

The opportuneness of this warning is confirmed by the astonishment of those who consider the passage from ancient to Christian or medieval historiography; for what can be the meaning of this passage, in which we find ourselves faced with a miraculous and mythological world all over again, identical as it seems, in its general characteristics, with that of the ancient historians, which has disappeared? It is certainly not progress, but rather falling into a ditch, into which also fall all the dearest illusions relating to the perpetual advance of humanity. And the Middle Ages did seem to be a ditch or a declivity, sometimes during the period itself and most clearly at the Renaissance, and this image is still represented in common belief. Restricting ourselves solely to the domain of historiography, and following up the impression of astonishment at first caused by it, we end by representing events at the beginning of the Middle Ages somewhat in the way they appeared to our writer Adolfo Bartoli, in his introductory volume to the *History of Italian Literature*, which is all broken up with cries of horror and with the gesture of covering the face lest he should see so much ugliness. "We are in a world," writes Bartoli, when speaking of Gregory of Tours, "where thought has descended so low as to cause pity, in a world where a conception of history no longer exists," and history also becomes "a humble handmaid to theology—that is to say, an aberration of the spirit." And after Gregory of Tours (continues Bartoli) there is a further fall: "Behold Fredigarius, in whom credulity, ignorance, and confusion surpass every limit . . . there survives in him nothing of a previous civilization." After Fredigarius, with the monastic chronicle, we take another step downward toward nothingness, though this would seem to be impossible. Here "we seem to see the lean monk putting his trembling head out of the narrow window of his cell every five or eleven years, to make sure that men are not all dead, and then shutting himself up again in the prison, where he lives only in the expectation of death." We must protest against such shrinking back (which makes the critic of to-day look like the "lean monk" whose appearance he has so vividly portrayed); we must assert that mythology and miracle and transcendency certainly returned in the Middle Ages—that is to say, that these ideal categories again acted with almost equal force and that they almost reassumed their ancient bulk, but they did not return *historically identical* with those of the pre-Hellenic world. We must seek in the heart of their new manifestations for the effective progress which is certainly accomplished by Gregory of Tours and Fredigarius, and even by the monkish chroniclers.

The divinity descends again to mingle anthropomorphically with the affairs of men, as a most powerful or ultra-powerful personage among the less powerful; the gods are now the saints, and Peter and Paul intervene in favour of this or that people; St Mark, St Gregory, St Andrew, or St January lead the array of the combatants, the one vying with the other, and sometimes against the other, playing malicious tricks upon one another; and in the performance or the non-performance of an act of worship is again placed the loss or gain of a battle: medieval poems and chronicles are full of such stories. These conceptions are analogous to the antique, and indeed they are their historical continuation. This is not only so (as has so often been pointed out) owing to the attachment of this or that particular of ancient faith to popular religion and to the transformation of gods into saints and demons, but also, and above all, to a more substantial reason. Ancient thought had left fortune, the divinity, the inscrutable, at the edge of its humanism, with the result that the prodigious was never completely eliminated even from the most severe historians—the door at any rate was left open by which it could return. All are aware with how many 'superstitions' philosophy, science, history, and customs were impregnated during late antiquity, which in this respect was not intellectually superior, but indeed inferior, to the new Christian religion. In the latter the fables gradually formed and miracles which were believed became spiritualized and ceased to be 'superstitions'—that is to say, something extraneous or discordant to the general humanistic conception—and set themselves in harmony with the new supernaturalistic and transcendental conception, of which they were the accompaniment. Thus myth and miracle, becoming intensified in Christianity, became at the same time different from ancient myths and miracles.

They were different and more lofty, because they contained a more lofty thought: the thought of spiritual worth, which was not peculiar to this or to that people, but common to the whole of humanity. The ancients had indeed touched upon this thought in speculation, but they had never possessed it, and their philosophers had sought it in vain or attained to it only in abstract speculation not capable of investing the whole soul, as is the case with thoughts that are profoundly thought, and as was the case with Christianity. Paulus Orosius expresses this in his *Historiæ adversus paganos*, in such accents as no Græco-Roman historian had been able to utter: *Ubique patria, ubique lex et religio mea est. . . . Latitudo orientis, septentrionis copiositas, meridiana diffusio, magnarum insularum largissimæ tutissimæque sedes mei juris et nominis sunt, quia ad Christianos et Romanos Romanus et Christianus accedo.* To the virtue of the citizen is added that of man, of spiritual man, who puts himself on a level with the truth by means of his religious faith and by his work, which is humanly good. To the illustrious men among the pagans are opposed illustrious men among the Christians who are better than illustrious, being saints; and the new Plutarch is found in the *Vitæ patrum* or *eremitarum*, in the lives of the confessors of Christ, of the martyrs, of the propagators of the true faith; the new epics describe the conflicts of the faithful against unbelievers, of Christians against heretics and Islamites. There is here a greater consciousness of conflict than the Greeks had of the conflict between Greeks and barbarians, or freedmen and slaves, which were usually looked upon rather as representing differences of nature than of spiritual values. *Ecclesiastical history* now appears, no longer that of Athens or of Rome, but of religion and of the Church which represented it in its strifes and in its triumphs—that is to say, the strifes and triumphs of the truth. This was a thing without precedent in the ancient world, whose histories of culture, of art or philosophy, did not go beyond the empirical stage, as we have seen, whereas ecclesiastical history has a spiritual value as its subject, by means of which it illuminates and judges facts. To censure ecclesiastical history because it overrules and oppresses profane history will perhaps be justified, as we shall see, from certain points of view and in a certain sense; but it is not justifiable as a general criticism of the idea of that history, and, indeed, when we formulate the censure in these terms we are unconsciously pronouncing a warm eulogy of it. The *historia spiritalis* (as we may also call it, employing the title of Avito's poem) could not and in truth would not consent to be a mere part, or to suffer rivals at its side: it must dominate and affirm itself as the whole. And since history becomes history of the truth with Christianity, it abandons at the same time the fortuitous and chance, to which the ancients had often abandoned it, and recognizes its own proper law, which is no longer a natural law, blind fate, or even the influence of the stars (St Augustine confutes this doctrine of the pagans), but rationality, intelligence, *providence*. This conception was not unknown to ancient philosophy, but is now set free from the frost of intellectualism and abstractionism and becomes warm and fruitful. Providence guides and disposes the course of events, directing them to an end, permitting evils as punishments and as instruments of education, determining the greatness and the catastrophes of empires, in order to prepare the kingdom of God. This means that for the first time is really broken the idea of the *circle*, of the perpetual return of human affairs to their starting-point, of the vain labour of the Danaids (St Augustine also combats the *circuitus*); history for the first time is here understood as *progress*: a progress that the ancient historians did not succeed in discovering, save in rare glimpses, thus falling into unconsolable pessimism, whereas Christian pessimism is irradiated with hope. Hence the importance to be attributed to the *succession of empires* and to the function fulfilled by each of them, and especially with regard to the Roman Empire, which politically unified the world that Christ came to unify spiritually, to the position of Judaism as opposed to Christianity, and the like. These questions have been answered in various ways, but on the common assumption that divine intelligence had willed those events, that greatness and that decadence, those joys and afflictions, and therefore that all had been necessary means of the divine work, and that all had competed in and were competing in the final end of history, linked one with the other, not as effects following from a blind cause, but as stages of a process. Hence, too, history understood as *universal* history, no longer in the sense of Polybius, who narrates the transactions of those states which enter into relations with one another, but in the profounder sense of a history of the universal, of the universal by excellence, which is history in labour with God and toward God. By means of this spirit which invests them, even the most neglected of the chronicles become surrounded with a halo, which is wanting to the classical histories of Greece and Rome, and which, however distant they be from our particular view-points, yet in their general aspect makes them very near to our heart and mind.

Such are the new problems and the new solutions which Christianity brought to historical thought, and it may be said of them, as of the political and humanistic thought of the ancients, that they constitute a solid possession of perpetual efficacy for the human spirit. Eusebius of Cæsarea is to be placed beside Herodotus as 'father' of modern historiography, however little disposed it may be to recognize its parents in that barbaric author and in the others who were called 'fathers of the Church,' to whom, and particularly to St Augustine, it yet owes so great a part of itself. What are our histories of culture, of civilization, of progress, of humanity, of truth, save the form of ecclesiastical history in harmony with our times—that is to say, of the triumph and propagation of the faith, of the strife against the powers of darkness, of the successive treatments of the new evangel, or good news, made afresh with each succeeding epoch? Do not the modern histories, which narrate the function performed or the pre-eminence assumed by this or that nation in the work of civilization, correspond to the *Gesta Dei per Francos* and to other like formulas of medieval historiography? And our universal histories are such not only in the sense of Polybius, but also of the universal as ideal, purified and elevated in the Christian sense; hence the religious sentiment which we experience on approaching the solemnity of history.

It will be observed that in presenting it in this way we to some extent idealize the Christian conception; and this is true, but in the same way and in the same measure as we have idealized ancient humanism, which was not only humanism, but also transcendency and mystery. Christian historiography, like ancient historiography, solved the problems that were set to it, but it did not solve other problems that were only formed afterward, because they were not set to it. A proof of this is to be found in the caprices and the myths that accompanied its fundamental conception. The prodigious and the miraculous, which, as already observed, surrounded Christian historiography, bore witness precisely to the incomplete ideality of the new and loftier God, the thought of whom became converted into a myth, his action into fabulous anecdotes. Yet when it was not a question of miracles, or when these were reduced to small compass, attenuated and held back, if not refuted, there nevertheless remained the miracle of the divinity and of the truth, conceived as transcendent, separated from and opposed to human affairs. This too was an attestation of the Christian spirit, in so far as it surpassed the ancient spirit, not with the calmness and security of thought, but with the violence of sentiment and with the enthusiasm of the imagination. Transcendency led to a consideration of worldly things as external and rebellious to divine things: hence the dualism of God and the world, of a *civitas cælestis* and of another that was *terrena*, of a *civitas Dei* and of a *civitas diaboli* which revived most ancient Oriental conceptions, such as Parseeism, and was tempered, if not internally corrected, by means of the providential course of history, internally compromised by that unconquered dualism. The city of God destroyed the earthly city and took its place, but did not justify it, although it tried to do so here and there, in accordance with the logic of its providential and progressive principle. St Augustine, obliged to explain the reasons of the fortune of Rome, escaped from the difficulty with the sophism that God conceded that greatness to the Romans as a reward for their virtues, earthly though they were and not such as to lead to the attainment of heavenly glories, but yet worthy the fleeting reward of earthly glory. Thus the Romans remained always reprobate, but less reprehensible than other reprobates; there could not have been true virtue where there had not been true religion. The contests of ideas did not appear as conflicting forms of the true in its becoming, but simply diabolical suggestions, which disturbed the truth, which was complete and possessed by the Church. Eusebius of Cæsarea treated heresies as the work of the devil, because it was the devil who prompted Simon Magus, and then Menander, and the two currents of gnosis represented by Saturninus and Basil. Otto of Frisia contemplated the Roman Empire succeeding to the Babylonian as son to father, and the kings of the Persians and the Greeks almost as its tutors and pedagogues. In the political unity of Rome he discovers a prelude to Christian unity, in order that the minds of men should form themselves *ad majora intelligenda promptiores et capaciores*, be disciplined to the cult of a single man, the emperor, and to the fear of a single dominant city, that they should learn *unam quoque fidem tenendam*. But the same Otto imagines the whole world *a primo homine ad Christum . . . exceptis de Israelitico populo paucis, errore deceptus, vanis superstitionibus deditus, dæmonum ludicris captus, mundi illecebris irretitus*, fighting *sub principe mundi diabolo*, until *venit plenitudo temporis* and God sent His son to earth. The doctrine of salvation as a grace due to the good pleasure of God, *indebita Dei gratia*, is not at all an accidental excrescence upon this conception, but is its foundation or logical complement. Christian humanity was destined to make itself unhuman, and St Augustine, however much reverence he excites by the energy of his temperament, by his gaze ever fixed above, offends us to an equal degree by his lack of human sympathy, his harshness and cruelty; and the 'grace' of which he speaks assumes in our eyes the aspect of odious favouritism and undue exercise of power. It is nevertheless well to remember that by means of these oscillations and deviations of sentiment and imagination Christian historiography prepared the problem of the surpassing of dualism. For if the search for the Christianity of the non-Christians, for grace due to all men from their very character of men, the truth of heresies, the goodness of pagan virtue, was a historical task that has matured slowly in modern times, the division and opposition of the two histories and the two cities, introduced by Christianity, was a fundamental necessity, as their unity thought in the providential divine Unity was a good preparation for it.

Another well-known aspect of this dualism is *dogmatism*, the incapacity to understand the concrete particularization of itself by the spirit in its various activities and forms. This explains the accusation levelled against ecclesiastical history of overriding and tyrannically oppressing the whole of the rest of history. This did in fact take place, because ecclesiastical history, instead of developing itself in the concrete universal of the spirit, remained rooted in a particular determination of it. All human values were reduced to a single value—that is to say, to firmness of Christian faith and to service of the Church. This value, thus abstractly conceived, became deprived of its natural virtue and declined to the level of a material and immobile fact, and indeed the vivid, fluid Christian consciousness after some centuries of development became solidified in dogmas. That materialized and motionless dogma necessarily prevailed as a universal measure, and men of all times were judged according to whether they had or had not been touched with the divine grace, were pious or impious, and the lives of the holy fathers and of believers were a Plutarch, who excluded every other profane Plutarch. This was the dogmatism of transcendency, which therefore resolved itself into *asceticism*, in the name of which the whole actual history of mankind is covered with contempt, with horror, and with lamentation. This is particularly noticeable in Augustine, in Orosius, and in Otto of Frisia, but is to be perceived at least in germ as a tendency among all the historians or chroniclers of the early Middle Ages. What thoughts are suggested by the battle of Thermopylæ to Otto of Frisia? *Tædet hic inextricabilem malorum texere cratem; tamen ad ostendendam mortalium miseriam, summatim ea attingere volo.* And what by the deeds of Alexander? *Regni Macedonum monarchia, quæ ab ipso cœpit, ipso mortuo cum ipso finitur. . . . Civitas autem Christi firmata supra firmam petram. . . .* With asceticism is linked the often noted and often ridiculed *credulity* of the medieval historians (not to be confounded with the belief in miracles, originating from religion): this credulity is generally attributed to the prevalence of imagination, or to social conditions, which rendered books rare and critical capacity difficult to find—that is to say, to things which required to be explained in their turn.

Indifference is, indeed, one of the principal sources of credulity, because no one is ever credulous in the things that touch him closely and of which he treats, while on the other hand all (as is proved in daily life) are ready to lend an ear to more or less indifferent talk. Asceticism, diminishing the interest for things of the world and for history, assisted in the neglect and dispersion of books and documents, promoted credulity toward everything heard or read, unbridling the imagination, ever desirous of the wonderful and curious, to the disadvantage of discernment. It did this not only in history properly so called, but also in the science of nature or natural history, which was also indifferent to one who possessed the ultimate truth of religion. The weak capacity for *individualization* noticeable in medieval historiography must be attributed to ascetism, which is usually satisfied with the general character of goodness or badness (the 'portrait' is very rare in it, as in the figurative arts of the same age), and it has even less consciousness of the historical differences of place and time, travestying persons and events in contemporary costume. It even goes so far as to compose imaginary histories and false documents, which portray the supposed type. This extends from Agnello of Ravenna, who declared that he wrote also the lives of those bishops of Ravenna about whom he possessed no information, *et credo* (he said) *non mentitum esse*, because, if they filled so high a past, they must of necessity have been good, charitable, zealous, and so forth, down to the false decretals of the pseudo-Isidore. We also owe to asceticism the *form of chronicle* as its intimate cause, because, when the meaning of particular facts was neglected, it only remained to note them as they were observed or related, without any ideological connexion and with only the chronological connexion. Thus we frequently find among the historians of the Middle Ages the union (at first sight strange, yet not without logical coherence) of a grandiose history, beginning with the creation of the world and the dispersion of the races, and an arid chronicle, following the other principle and becoming ever more particular and more contingent as approach is gradually made to the times of the authors.

When on the one hand the two cities, the heavenly and the earthly, and on the other the transcendency of the principle of explanation had been conceived, the composition of dualism could not be sought for in intelligence, but in myth, which put an end to the strife with the triumph of one of the two adversaries:

the myth of the fall, of the redemption, of the expected reign of Christ, of the Last Judgment, and of the final separation of the two cities, one ascending to Paradise with the elect, the other driven back into hell with the wicked. This mythology had its precedent in the Judaic expectations of a Messiah, and also, from some points of view, in Orphism, and continued to develop through gnosis, millenarism, and other heretical tentatives and heresies, until it took a definite or almost a definite form in St Augustine. It has been remarked that in this conception metaphysic became identified with history, as an entirely new thought, altogether opposed to Greek thought, and that it is a philosophical contribution altogether novel and proper to Christianity. But we must add here that, as mythology, it did not unite, but indeed confounded, metaphysic and history, making the finite infinite, avoiding the fallacy of the circle as perpetual return of things, but falling into the other fallacy of a progress beginning and ending in time. History was therefore arranged in spiritual *epochs* or phases, through which humanity was born, grew up, and attained completion : there were six, seven, or eight epochs, according to the various ways of dividing and calculating, which sometimes corresponded to the ages of human life, sometimes to the days of the creation, sometimes to both these schemes combined ; or where the hermeneutic of St Jerome upon the Book of Daniel was accepted, the succession of events was distributed among the four *monarchies*, of which the last was the Roman, not only in order of time, but also in that of the idea, because after the Roman Empire (the Middle Ages, as we know, long nourished the illusion that that empire persisted in the form of the Holy Roman Empire) there would be nothing else, and the reign of Christ or of the

Church and then of Antichrist and the universal judgment were expected to follow without any intermission. The end which history had not yet reached chronologically, being also intrinsic to the system, was ideally constructible, as the Apocalypses had already ideally constructed it, pervading theological works and even histories, which in their last section (see the works of Otto of Frisia for all of them) described the coming of Antichrist and the end of the world: hence the idea of a *history of things future*, continued by the paradoxical Francesco Patrizzi, who gave utterance to his theory in the sixteenth century in his dialogues *Upon History* (1560). This general historical picture might be here and there varied in its particulars, but never shattered and confuted; it varied in orthodoxy up to the time of Augustine, and afterward among the dissentients and the heretics: most noteworthy of these variations was the *Eternal Evangel* of the followers of Gioacchino di Flora, who divided history into three epochs, corresponding to the three persons of the Trinity: the first that of the Old Testament or of the Father, the second that of the New Testament or of the Son, the third and last, that of the Spirit. These are but artificial combinations and transactions, by means of which life always seeks to find a passage between the preconceived schemes which compress and threaten to suffocate it.

But such transactions did not avail to get the better of the discord between reality and plan which everywhere revealed itself. Hence the necessity of the *allegorical interpretation*, so dear to the Middle Ages. This consisted substantially in placing an imaginary figure between the plan and the historical reality, a mixture of both, like a bridge, but a bridge which could be crossed only in imagination. Thus personages and events of sacred and profane history were allegorized, and subtle numerical calculations made and continually reinforced with new imaginary contributions, in order to discover correspondences and parallelisms; and not only were the ages of life and the days of creation placed on a parallel line with historical epochs, but so also were the virtues and other conceptions. Such notions are still to be found in books of devotion and in the preaching of the less acute and less modernized of sacred orators. The 'reign of nature' was also included in allegorical interpretation; and since history and metaphysic had been set at variance with one another, so in like manner was natural science set at variance with both of them, and all appeared together in allegorical forms in the medieval encyclopædias, the *Pantheons* and *Mirrors of the World*.

Notwithstanding these inevitable strayings, the new idea of history as the spiritual drama of humanity, although it inclined toward myth, yet acted with such energy as to weaken the ancient heteronomous conception of history as directed toward the administration of abstract instruction, useful in actual practice. History itself was now the teaching, the knowledge of the life of the human race from its creation upon the earth, through its struggles, up to its final state, which was indicated in the near or remote horizon. History thus became the work of God, teaching by His direct word and presence, which is to be seen and heard in every part of it. Declarations are certainly not wanting, indeed they abound, that the reading of histories is useful as counselling, and particularly as inculcating, good behaviour and abstention from evil. Sometimes it is a question of traditional and conventional declarations, at others of particular designs: but medieval historiography was not conceived, because it could not be conceived, heteronomously.

If asceticism mortified minds, and if the miraculous clouded them, it is not necessary to believe, on the other hand, that either had the power to depress reality altogether and for a long period. Indeed, precisely because asceticism was arbitrary, and mythology imaginary, they remained more or less abstract, in the same way as allegorical interpretation, which was impotent to suppress the real determinations of fact. It was all very well to despise and condemn the earthly city in words, but it forced itself upon the attention, and if it did not speak to the intellect it spoke to the souls and to the passions of men. In its period of youthful vigour, also, Christianity was obliged to tolerate profane history, dictated by economic, political, and military interests, side by side with sacred history. And as in the course of the Middle Ages, in addition to the religious poetry of the sacred hymns and poems, there also existed an epic of territorial conquests, of the shock of peoples and of feudal strife, so there continued to exist a worldly history, more or less mingled and tempered with religious history. We find even fervent Christians and the most pious of priests yielding to the desire of collecting and handing down the memory of their race: thus Gregory of Tours told of the Franks, Paulus Diaconus of the Lombards, Bede of the Angles, Widekind of the Saxons. Their gentle hearts of political partisans do not cease to beat. Not only do they lament the misery and wickedness of humanity in general, but also give vent to their particular feelings, as we observe, for instance, in the monk Erchempertus, who, *ex intimo corde ducens alta suspiria*, resumes the thread of Paul's history to narrate the deeds of his glorious Lombards (now hunted back into the southern part of Italy alone and assaulted and ambushed on every side), *non regnum sed excidium, non felicitatem sed miseriam, non triumphum sed perniciem.* And Liutprand of Cremona, although he makes the deity intervene as ruler and punisher on every occasion, and even the saints in person do battle, does not fail, for instance, to note that when Berengarius proceeded to take possession of the kingdom after the death of Guido, the followers of the latter called for King Lambert, *quia semper Itali geminis uti dominis volunt, quatinus alterum alterius terrore coherceant*: which is also the definition of feudal society. They were most credulous in many things, far from profound and abandoned to their imagination, but they were not credulous, indeed they were clear-sighted, shrewd and diffident in what concerned the possessions and privileges of the churches and monasteries, of families, and of the feudal group and the order of citizenship to which each belonged. It is to these interests that we owe the formation of archives, registers, chronologies, and the exercise of criticism as to the authenticity and genuineness of documents. The conception of the new Christian virtue oppressed, but did not quench, admiration (though held sinful by the most severe) for the great name of ancient Rome, and the many works of pagan civilization, its eloquence, its poetry, its civil wisdom. Nor did it forbid admiration for Arabic or Judaic-Arabic wisdom, of which the works were well received, notwithstanding religious strife. Hence we may say that in the same way as Græco-Roman humanism did not altogether exclude the supernatural, so the Christian supernatural did not prevent human consideration of worldly passions and earthly transactions.

This becomes more and more evident as we pass from the early to the late Middle Ages, when profane historiography progresses, as the result of the struggles between Church and State, of the communal movement, of the more frequent commercial communications between Europe and the East, and the like. These are themselves the result of the development, the maturing, and the modernization of thought, which grows with life and makes life grow. Neither life nor thought remained attached to the conceptions of the fathers of the Church, of Augustine, of Orosius, to whom history offered nothing but the proof of the infinite evils that afflict humanity, of the unceasing punishments of God, and of the "deaths of the persecutors." In Otto of Frisia himself, who holds more firmly than the others to the doctrines of Augustine, we find the asperity of doctrine tempered by grace; and when he afterward proceeds to narrate the struggle between the Church and the Empire, if it cannot be said that he takes the side of the Empire, it also cannot be said that he resolutely defends that of the Church, for the eschatological visions that form so great a part of his work do not blind his practical sense and political judgment. The party of the faith against the faithless remained, however, always the 'great party,' the great 'struggle of classes' (elect and reprobate) and of 'states' (celestial and earthly cities). But within this large framework we perceive other figures more closely particularized, other parties and interests, which gradually come to occupy the first, second, and third planes, so that the struggle between God and the devil is forced ever more and more into the background and becomes somewhat vague, something always assumed to be present, but not felt to be active and urgent in the soul, as something which is still talked of, but is not deeply felt, or at least felt with the energy that the words would wish us to believe, the words themselves often sounding like a refrain, as pious as it is conventional. The miraculous gradually fills less and less space and appears more rarely: God acts more willingly by means of secondary causes, and respects natural laws; He rarely intervenes directly in a revolutionary manner. The form of the chronicles, too, becomes also less accidental and arid, the better among the chroniclers here and there seeking a different 'order'—that is to say, really, a better understanding—and we find (particularly from the thirteenth century onward) the *ordo artificialis* or internal opposed to the *ordo naturalis* or external chronological order. There are also to be found those who distinguish between the *sub singulis annis describere* and the *sub stilo historico conglutinare*—that is to say, the grouping together according to things described. The general aspect of historiography changes not a little. Limiting ourselves to Italian historiography alone, there are no longer little books upon the miracles and the translations of the bodies of saints and bishops, but chronicles of communes, all of them full of affection for the feudal superiors or for the archbishop, for the imperial or the anti-imperial side, for Milan or for Bergamo, or for Lodi. The sense of tragedy, which weighed so heavily upon Erchempertus, returns with new and stronger accents in the narrative of the deeds of Barbarossa at Milan, entitled *Libellus tristitiæ et doloris, angustiæ et tribulationis, passionum et tormentorum.* Love for one's city usurps much of the space previously devoted to things celestial, and praises of Milan, of Bergamo, of Venice, of Amalfi, of Naples, resound in the pages of their chroniclers. Thus those vast chronicles are reached which, although they begin with the Tower of Babel, yet lead to the history of that city or of that event which makes the strongest appeal to the feelings and best stimulates the industry of the writer, and become mingled with the persons and things of the present or future life. Giovanni Villani, a pilgrim to Rome to celebrate the papal jubilee, is not inspired with the ascetic spirit or raised to heaven by that solemn spectacle; but, on the contrary, "since he finds himself in the *holy* city of Rome on that blessed pilgrimage, inspecting its *great* and *ancient possessions*, and reading the *histories and the great deeds* of the Romans," he is inspired to compose the history of his native Fiorenza, "daughter and creation of Rome" (of ancient Rome prior to Christianity). His Fiorenza resembled Rome in its rise to greatness and its following after great things, and was like Rome in its fall. Thus the 'holy' and the 'blessed' do not lead him to holy and blessed thoughts, but to thoughts of worldly greatness. To the historiography of the communes answers the more seriously worldly, the more formally and historically elaborated historiography of the Norman and Suabian kingdom of Sicily. In the proem to its *Constitutiones* sovereigns are declared to be instituted *ipsa rerum necessitate cogente, nec minus divinæ provisionis instinctu*; with its Romualdo Guarna, its Abbot Telesino, its Malaterra, its Hugo Falcando and Pietro da Eboli, its Riccardo da San Germano, with the pseudo-Jamsilla, and Saba Malaspina. All of these have their heroes, Roger and William the Normans, Frederick and Manfred the Suabians, and what they praise in them is the sound political basis which they knew how to establish and to maintain with a firm hand. *Eo tempore*, says Falcando of Roger, *Regnum Siciliæ, strenuis et præclaris viris abundans, cum terra marique plurimum posset, vicinis circumquoque gentibus terrorem incusserat, summaque pace ac tranquillitate maxima fruebatur.* And the so-called Jamsilla, of Frederick II : *Vir fuit magni cordis, sed magnanitatem suam multa, quæ in eo fuit, sapientia superavit, ut nequaquam impetus eum ad aliquid faciendum impelleret, sed ad omnia cum rationis maturitate procederet; . . . utpote qui philosophiæ studiosus erat quam et ipse in se coluit, et in regno suo propagare ordinavit. Tunc quidem ipsius felici tempore in regno Siciliæ erant litterati pauci vel nulli; ipse vero imperator liberalium artium et omnis approbatæ scientiæ scholas in regno ipso constituit . . . ut omnis conditionis et fortunæ homines nullius occasione indigentiæ a philosophiæ studio retraherentur.* The state, profane culture, 'philosophy,' impersonated in the heresiarch Frederick, are thus set in clear relief. And while on the one hand more and more laical theories of the state become joined to these political and cultural currents (from Dante, indeed from Thomas Aquinas, to Marsilio of Padua), and the first outlines of literary history (lives of the poets and of men famous for their knowledge, and the rise of vernacular literatures) and histories of manners (as in certain passages in Ricobaldo of Ferrara), on the other hand scholasticism found its way to such problems and conceptions by means of the works of Aristotle, which represented as it were a first brief summary of ancient knowledge. It is unnecessary to say that Dante's poem is the chief monument of this condition of spirit, where the ideas of the Middle Ages are maintained, but the political, poetical, and philosophical affections, the love of fame and of glory, prove their vigour, although subordinated to those ideas and restrained, as far as possible, by them.

But those ideas are nevertheless maintained, even among the imperialists and adversaries of the Church, and it is only in rare spirits that we find a partly sceptical and partly mocking negation of them. Transcendency, the prescience of God, Who ordains, directs, and disposes of everything according to His will, bestows rewards and punishments, and intervenes mysteriously, always maintains its place in the distant background, in Dante as in Giovanni Villani, as in all the historians and chroniclers. Toward the close of the fifteenth century the theological conception makes a curious appearance in the French historian Comines, arm in arm with the most alert and unprejudiced policy of success at all costs. Worldliness, so rich, so various, and so complex, was yet without an ideal standard of comparison, and for this reason it was rather lived than thought, showing itself rather in richness of detail than systematically. The ancient elements of culture, which had passed from Aristotelianism into scholasticism, failed to act powerfully, because that part of Aristotelianism was particularly selected which was in harmony with Christian thought already translated into Platonic terms and dogmatized in a transcendental form by the fathers of the Church. Hence it has even been possible to note a pause in historiographical interest, where scholasticism has prevailed, a compendium of the type of that of Martin Polonus being held sufficient to serve the end of quotations for demonstration or for legal purposes. What was required upon entering a new period of progress (there is always progress, but 'periods of progress' are those in which the motion of the spirit seems to become accelerated and the fruit that has been growing ripe for centuries is rapidly plucked) was a direct conscious negation of transcendency and of

Christian miracle, of ascesis and of eschatology, both in life and in thought ; a negation whose terms (heavenly and earthly life) had certainly been noted by medieval historiography, but had been allowed to endure and to progress, the one beside the other, without true and proper contact and conflict arising between them.

IV
THE HISTORIOGRAPHY OF THE RENAISSANCE

THE negation of Christian transcendency was the work of the age of the Renaissance, when, to employ the expression used by Fueter, historiography became 'secularized.' In the histories of Leonardo Bruni and of Bracciolini, who gave the first conspicuous examples of the new attitude of historiographical thought, and in all others of the same sort which followed them—among them those of Machiavelli and of Guicciardini shine forth conspicuously—we find hardly any trace of 'miracles.' These are recorded solely with the intention of mocking at them and of explaining them in an altogether human manner. An acute analysis of individual characters and interests is substituted for the intervention of divine providence and the actions of the popes, and religious strifes themselves are apt to be interpreted according to utilitarian passions and solely with an eye to their political bearing. The scheme of the four monarchies with the advent of Antichrist connected with it is allowed to disappear; histories are now narrated *ab inclinatione imperii*, and even universal histories, like the *Enneads* of Sabellicus, do not adhere to traditional ecclesiastical tradition. Chronicles of the world, universal miraculous histories, both theological and apocalyptic, become the literature of the people and of those with little culture, or persist in countries of backward culture, such as Germany at that time, or finally are limited to the circle of Catholic or Protestant confessional historiography, both of which retain so much of the Middle Ages, the Protestant perhaps more than the Catholic (at least at a first glance), for the latter contrived at least here and there to temporize and to accommodate itself to the times. All this is shown very clearly and minutely by Fueter, and I shall now proceed to take certain observations and some information from his book, which I shall rearrange and complete with some more of my own. In the political historiography of the late Middle Ages, the theological conception had been, as we have said, thrown into the background; but henceforward it is not to be found even there, and if at times we hear its formulas, they are just like those of the Crusade against the Turks, preaching the liberation of the tomb of Christ. These were still repeated by preachers, writers of verse, and rhetoricians (and continued to be repeated for three centuries), but they found no response in political reality and in the conscience of the people, because they were but empty sound. Nor was the negation of theologism and the secularization of history accomplished only in practice, unaccompanied with complete consciousness; for, although many minds really did turn in the direction indicated by fate, or in other words by the new mental necessity, and although the polemic was not always open, but on the contrary often surrounded with many precautions, evidence abounds of the agreement of the practice with the theory of historiography. The criticism of so grave a theorist of history as Bodin is opposed to the scheme of the four monarchies. He makes it his object to combat the *inveteratum errorem de quattuor imperiis*, proving that the notion was capriciously taken from the dream of Daniel, and that it in no way corresponded with the real course of events. It would be superfluous to record here the celebrated epigrams of Machiavelli and of Guicciardini, who satirized theology and miracles. Guicciardini noted that all religions have boasted of miracles, and therefore they are not proofs of any one of them, and are perhaps nothing but "secrets of nature." He advised his readers never to say that God had aided so-and-so because he was good and had made so-and-so suffer because he was wicked, for we "often see the opposite," and the counsels of divine providence are in fact an abyss. Paolo Sarpi, although he admits that "it is a pious and religious thought to attribute the disposition of every event to divine providence," yet holds it "presumption" to determine "to what end events are directed by that highest wisdom"; for men, being emotionally attached to their opinions, "are persuaded that they are as much loved and favoured by God as by themselves." Hence, for example, they argued that God had caused Zwingli and Hecolampadius to die almost at the same time, in order that he might punish and remove the ministers of discord, whereas it is certain that "after the death of these two, the evangelical cantons have made greater progress in the doctrine that they received from both of them." Such a disposition of religious and cautious spirits is yet more significant than that of the radical and impetuous, openly irreverent, in the same way as the new importance attributed to history is notable in the increase of historiographical labour that is then everywhere noticeable, and in the formation of a true and proper philological school, not only for antiquity, but for the Middle Ages (Valla, Flavio Biondo, Calchi, Sigonio, Beato Renano, etc.), which publishes and restores texts, criticizes the authenticity and the value of sources, is occupied with the establishment of a technical method of examining witnesses, and composes learned histories.

Nothing is more natural than that the new form of historiography should seem to be a return to Græco-Roman antiquity, as Christianity had seemed to be a return to the story of Eden (the interlude of paganism having been brought to an end by the redemption), or that the Middle Ages should still seem to some to-day to be a falling back into barbarous pre-Hellenic times. The illusion of the return was expressed in the cult of classical antiquity, and in all those manifestations, literary, artistic, moral, and customary, familiar to those who know the Renaissance. In the special field with which we are at present occupied, we find a curious document in support of the difficulty that philologists and critics experienced in persuading themselves that the Greek and Roman writers had perhaps been able to deceive themselves, to lie, to falsify, to be led astray by passions and blinded by ignorance, in the same way as those of the Middle Ages. Thus the latter were severely criticized while the former were reverenced and accepted, for it needed much time and labour to attain to an equal mental freedom regarding the ancients, and the criticism of texts and of sources was developed in respect to medieval history long before it attained to a like freedom in respect to ancient history. But the greatest proof and monument of the illusion of the return was the formation of the *humanistic* type of historiography, opposed to the medieval. This had been chiefly confined to the form of chronicle and humanistic historiography, although it accepted the arrangement by years and seasons according to the examples set by the Greeks and Romans, cancelled as far as possible numerical indications, and exerted itself to run on unbrokenly, without chronological cuts and cross-cuts. Latin had become barbarous in the Middle Ages and had accepted the vocabularies of vulgar tongues, or those which designated new things in a new way, whereas the humanistic historiographers translated and disguised every thought and every narrative in Ciceronian Latin, or at least Latin of the Golden Age. We frequently find picturesque anecdotes in the medieval chronicles, and humanism, while it restored its dignity to history, deprived it of that picturesque element, or attenuated and polished it as it had done the things and customs of the barbaric centuries. This humanistic type of historiography, like the new philological erudition and criticism and the whole movement of the Renaissance, was Italian work, and in Italy histories in the vulgar tongue were soon modelled upon it, which found in the latinized prose of Boccaccio an instrument well suited to their ends. From Italy it was diffused among other countries, and as always happens when an industry is transplanted into virgin soil, and workmen and technical experts are invited to come from the country of its origin, so the first humanistic historians of the other parts of Europe were Italians. Paolo Emilio the Veronese, who *Gallis condidit historias*, gave the French the humanistic history of France in his *De rebus gestis Francorum*, and Polydore Virgil did the like for England, Lucio Marineo for Spain, and many others for other countries, until indigenous experts appeared and the aid of Italians became unnecessary. Later on it became necessary to throw off this cloak, which was too loose or too tight—indeed, was not cut to the model of modern thought. What there was in it of artificial, of swollen, of false, was blamed—these defects being indeed clearly indicated in the constructive principle of this literary form, which was that of imitation. But anyone with a feeling for the past will enjoy that historical humanistic prose as the expression of love for antiquity and of the desire to rise to its level. This love and this desire were so keen that they had no hesitation in reproducing things external and indifferent in addition to what was better and sometimes in default of it. Giambattista Vico, sometimes so sublimely puerile, is still found lamenting, three centuries after the creation of humanistic historiography, that "no sovereign has been found into whose mind has entered the thought of preserving for ever in the best Latin style a record of the famous War of the Spanish Succession, than which a greater has never happened in the world since the Second Carthaginian War, that of Cæsar with Pompey, and of Alexander with Darius." But what of this? Quite recently, during the war in Tripoli, came the proposal from the depths of one of the meridional provinces of Italy, one of those little countrysides where the shadow of a humanist still exists, that a Latin commentary should be composed upon that war entitled *De bello libico*. This proposal was received with much laughter and made even me smile, yet the smile was accompanied with a sort of tender emotion, when I recalled how long and devotedly our fathers and forefathers had pursued the ideal of a beautiful antiquity and of a decorous historiography.

Nevertheless, the belief in the effectivity or possibility of such a return was, as we have said, an illusion; nothing of what has been returns, nothing of what has been can be abolished; even when we return to an old thought the new adversary makes the defence new and the thought itself new. I read some time ago the work of a learned French Catholic. While clearing the Middle Ages of certain absurd accusations and confuting errors commonly circulated about them, he maintained that the Middle Ages are the truly modern time, modern with the eternal modernity of the true, and that therefore they should not be called the Middle Ages, which term should be applied to the period that has elapsed between the fifteenth century and our own day, between the Reformation and positivism. As I read, I reflected that such a theory is the worthy pendant to that other theory, which places the Middle Ages beneath antiquity, and that both had some time ago shown themselves false to historical thought, which knows nothing of returns, but knows that the Middle Ages preserved antiquity deep in its heart as the Renaissance preserved the Middle Ages. And what is 'humanism' but a renewed formula of that 'humanity' of which the ancient world knew little or nothing, and which Christianity and the Middle Ages had so profoundly felt? What is the word 'renaissance' or 'renewal' but a metaphor taken from the language of religion? And setting aside the word, is not the conception of humanism perhaps the affirmation of a spiritual and universal value, and in so far as it is that, altogether foreign, as we know, to the mind of antiquity, and an intrinsic continuation of the 'ecclesiastical' and 'spiritual' history which appeared with Christianity? The conception of spiritual value had without doubt become changed or enriched, for it contained within itself more than a thousand years of mental experiences, thoughts, and actions. But while it thus grew more rich, it preserved its original character, and constituted the religion of the new times, with its priests and martyrs, its polemic and its apologetic, its intolerance (it destroyed or allowed to perish the monuments of the Middle Ages and condemned its writers to oblivion), and sometimes even imitated the forms of its worship (Navagaro used to burn a copy of Martial every year as a holocaust to pure Latinity). And since humanity, philosophy, science, literature, and especially art, politics, activity in all its forms, now fill that conception of value which the Middle Ages had placed in Christian religious faith alone, histories or outlines of histories continue to appear as the outcome of these determinations, which were certainly new in respect to medieval literature, but were not less new in respect to Græco-Roman literature, where there was nothing to compare to them, or only treatises composed in an empirical and extrinsic manner. The new histories of values presented themselves timidly, imitating in certain respects the few ancient examples, but they gave evidence of a fervour, an intelligence, an afflatus, which led to a hope for that increase and development wanting to their predecessors, which, instead of developing, had gradually become more superficial and finally disappeared again into vagueness. Suffice it to mention as representative of them all Vasari's *Lives of the Painters*, which are connected with the meditations and the researches upon art contained in so many treatises, dialogues, and letters of Italians, and are here and there shot through with flashes such as never shone in antiquity. The same may be said of treatises on poetry and rhetoric, and of the judgments which they contain as to poetry and of the new history of poetry, then being attempted with more or less successful results. The 'state' too, which forms the object of the meditations of Machiavelli, is not the simple state of antiquity, city or empire, but is almost the national state felt as something divine, to which even the salvation of the soul must be sacrificed—that is to say, as the institution in which the true salvation of the soul is to be found. Even the pagan virtue which he and others opposed to Christian virtue is very different from the pure Græco-Roman disposition of mind. At that time a start was also made in the direction of investigating the theory of rights, of political forms, of myths and beliefs, of philosophical systems, to-day in full flower. And since that same consciousness which had produced humanism had also widened the boundaries of the known world, and had sought for and found people of whom the Bible preserved no record and of whom the Græco-Roman writers knew nothing, there appeared at that time a literature relating to savages and to the indigenous civilizations of America (and also of distant Asia, which had been better explored), from which arose the first notions as to the primitive forms of human life. Thus were widened the spiritual boundaries of humanity at the same time as the material.

We are not alone in perceiving the illusion of the 'return to antiquity,' for the men of the Renaissance were not slow in doing this. Not every one was content to suit himself to the humanistic literary type. Some, like Machiavelli, threw away that cloak, too ample in its folds and in its train, preferring to it the shorter modern dress. Protests against pedantry and imitation are indeed frequently to be heard during the course of the century. Philosophers rebelled against Aristotle (first against the medieval and then against the ancient Aristotle), and appeals were made to truth, which is superior both to Plato and to Aristotle; men of letters advocated the new 'classes,' and artists repeated that the great masters were 'nature' and the 'idea.' One feels in the air that the time is not far distant when the question, "Who are the true ancients?" —that is to say, "Who are the intellectually expert and mature?"—will be answered with, "We are"; the symbol of antiquity will be broken and there will be found within it the reality which is human thought, ever new in its manifestations. Such an answer may possibly be slow in becoming clear and certain as an object of common conviction, though it will eventually become so, and now suffices to explain the true quality of that return to antiquity, by preventing the taking of the symbol for the thing symbolized.

This symbolical covering, cause of prejudices and misunderstandings, which enfolded the whole of humanism, was not the sole vice from which the historiography of the Renaissance suffered. We do not, of course, speak here of the bias with which all histories were variously affected, according as they were written by men of letters who were also courtiers and supported the interests of their masters, or official historians of aristocratic and conservative states like Venice, or men taking one or the other side in the conflicts within the same state, such as the *ottimani* (or aristocratic) and the popular party of Florence, or upholders of opposed religious beliefs, such as the group of reformed divines of Magdeburg and Baronio. We do not speak here of the historians who became story-writers (they sometimes take to history, like Bandello), or of those who collected information with a view to exciting curiosity and creating scandal. These are things that belong to all periods, and are not sufficient to qualify a particular historiographical age. But if we examine only that which is or wished to be historical thought, the historiography of the Renaissance suffered from two other defects, each of which it had inherited from one of its progenitors, antiquity and the Middle Ages. And above all there came to it from antiquity the humanistic-abstract or pragmatical conception, as it is called, which inclines to explain facts by the individual in his singularity and in his atomism, or by means of abstract political forms, and the like. For Machiavelli, the prince is not only the ideal but the criterion that he adopts for the explanation of events. He does not only appear in his treatises and political opuscules, but in the *Florentine Histories*, where we meet with him at the very beginning —after the terrible imaginative description of the condition of Italy in the fifth century—in the great figure of Theodoric, by whose 'virtue' and 'goodness' not only Rome and Italy, but all the other parts of the Western empire, "arose free from the continual scourgings which they had supported for so many years from so many invasions, and became again happy and well-ordered communities." The same figure reappears in many different forms in the course of the centuries described in those histories. Finally, at the end of the description of the social struggles of Florence, we read that "this city had reached such a point that it could be easily adapted to *any form of government* by *a wise law-giver*." In like manner, the *History of Italy* by Guicciardini begins with the description of the happiness of Italy at the end of the fifteenth century, "acquired at various times and preserved for many reasons," not the least of which was "the industry and genius of Lorenzo de' Medici," who "strove in every way so to balance Italian affairs that they should not incline more in one direction than another." He had allies in Ferdinand of Aragon and Ludovic the Moor, "partly for the same and partly for other reasons," and the Venetians were held in check by all three of them.

This perfect system of equilibrium was broken by the deaths of Lorenzo, of Ferdinand, and of the Pope. All historians of this period express themselves in the same way, and although a lively consciousness of the spiritual values of humanity was in process of formation, as has been seen, yet these were spoken of as though they depended upon the will and the intelligence of individuals who were their masters, not the contrary. In the history of painting, for example, the 'prince' for Vasari is Giotto, "who, although born among inexpert artisans, alone revived painting and reduced it to such a form as might be described as good." Biographies are also constantly individualistic, for they never succeed in perfectly uniting the individual with the work which he creates and which in turn creates him.

The idea of chance or fortune persisted alongside the pragmatic conception, its ancient companion. Machiavelli assigns the course of events half to fortune and half to human prudence, and although the accent falls here upon prudence, the acknowledgment of the one does not abolish the force of the other, so mysterious and transcendent. Guicciardini attacks those who, while attributing everything to prudence and virtue, exclude "the power of fortune," because we see that human affairs "receive at all times great impulsions from fortuitous events, which it is not within the power of man either to foresee or to escape, and although the care and understanding of man may moderate many things, nevertheless that alone does not suffice, but good fortune is also necessary." It is true that here and there there seems to appear another conception in Machiavelli, that of the strength and logic of things, but it is only a fleeting shadow. It is also a shadow for

Guicciardini, when he adds that even if we wish to attribute everything to prudence and virtue, "we must at least admit that it is necessary to fall upon or be born in times when the virtues or qualities for which you value yourself are esteemed." Guicciardini remains perplexed as to one point only, as though he had caught a glimpse of something that is neither caprice of the individual nor contingency of fortune: "When I consider to what accidents and dangers of illness, of chance, of violence, of infinite sorts, is exposed the life of man, the concurrence of how many things is needful that the harvest of the year should be good, nothing surprises me more than to see an old man or a good harvest." But even here we do not get beyond uncertainty, which in this case manifests itself as astonishment. With the renewal of the idea of fortune, even to a partial extent, with the restitution of the cult of this pagan divinity, not only does the God of Christianity disappear, but also the idea of rationality, of finality, of development, affirmed during the medieval period. The ancient Oriental idea of the circle in human affairs returns; it dominated all the historians of the Renaissance, and above all Machiavelli. History is an alternation of lives and deaths, of goods and ills, of happiness and misery, of splendour and decadence. Vasari understands the history of painting in the same way as that of all the arts, which, "like human bodies, have their birth, their growth, their old age, and their death." He is solicitous of preserving in his book the memory of the artistic capacity of his time, lest the art of painting, "either owing to the neglect of men or to the malignity of the ages or to decree of heaven (which does not appear to wish to maintain things here below for long in the same state), should encounter the same disorder and ruin" as befell it in the Middle Ages. Bodin, while criticizing and rejecting the scheme of the four monarchies, and demonstrating the fallaciousness of the assertion that gold deteriorates into copper, or even into clay, and celebrating the splendour of letters, of commerce, of the geographical discoveries of his age, does not, however, conclude in favour of progress, but of the circle, blaming those who find everything inferior in antiquity, *cum, æterna quadam lege naturæ, conversio omnium rerum velut in orbem redire videatur, ut æqua vitia virtutibus, ignoratio scientiæ, turpe honesto consequens sit, ac tenebræ luci.* The sad, bitter, pessimistic tone which we observe among ancient historians, which sometimes bursts forth into the tragic, is also often to be met with among the historians of the Renaissance, for they saw perish many things that were very dear to them, and were constrained to tremble for those which they still enjoyed, or at least to fear for them by anticipation, certain that sooner or later they would yield their place to their contraries.

And since history thus conceived does not represent progress but a circle, and is not directed by the historical law of development, but by the natural law of the circle, which gives it regularity and uniformity, it follows that the historiography of the Renaissance, like the Græco-Roman, has its end outside itself, and affords nothing but material suitable for exhortations toward the useful and the good, for various forms of pleasure or as ornament for abstract truths. Historians and theorists of history are all in agreement as to this, with the exception of such eccentrics as Patrizzi, who expressed doubts as to the utility of knowing what had happened and as to the truth itself of narratives, but ended by contradicting himself and also laying down an extrinsic end. "Each one of us can find, both on his own account and on that of the public weal, many useful documents in the knowledge of these so different and so important examples," writes Guicciardini in the proem to his *History of Italy*. "Hence will clearly appear, as the result of innumerable examples, the instability of things human, how harmful they are often wont to be to themselves, but ever to the people, the ill-conceived counsels of those who rule, when, having only before their eyes either vain errors or present cupidities, they are not mindful of the frequent variations of fortune, and converting the power that has been granted them for the common weal into an injury to others, they become the authors of new perturbations, either as the result of lack of prudence or of too much ambition." And Bodin holds that *non solum præsentia commode explicantur, sed etiam futura colliguntur, certissimaque rerum expetendarum ac fugiendarum præcepta constantur*, from historical narratives. Campanella thinks that history should be composed *ut sit scientiarum fundamentum sufficiens*; Vossius formulates the definition that was destined to appear for centuries in treatises: *cognitio singularium, quorum memoriam conservari utile sit ad bene beateque vivendum*. Historical knowledge therefore seemed at that time to be the lowest and easiest form of knowledge (and this view has been held down to our own days); to such an extent that Bodin, in addition to the *utilitas* and the *oblectatio*, also recognized to history *facilitas*, so great a facility *ut, sine ullius artis adjumento, ipsa per sese ab omnibus intelligatur*. When truth had been placed outside historical narrative, all the historians of the Renaissance, like their Greek and Roman predecessors, practised, and all the theorists (from Pontanus in the *Actius* to Vossius in the *Ars historica*) defended, the use of more or less imaginary orations and exhortations, not only as the result of bowing to ancient example, but through their own convictions Eventually M. de la Popelinière, in his *Histoire des histoires, avec l'idée de l'histoire accomplie* (1599), where he inculcates in turn historical exactitude and sincerity with such warm eloquence, suddenly turns round to defend imaginary *harangues et concions*, for this fine reason, that what is necessary is 'truth' and not 'the words' in which it is expressed! The truth of history was thus not history, but oratory and political science; and if the historians of the Renaissance were hardly ever able to exercise oratory (for which the political constitution of the time allowed little scope), all or nearly all were authors of treatises upon political science, differently inspired as compared with those of the Middle Ages, which had ethical and religious thought behind them, resuming and advancing the speculations of Aristotle and of ancient political writers. In like manner, treatises on historical art, unknown to the Middle Ages, but which rapidly multiplied in the Renaissance (see a great number of them in the *Penus artis historicæ* of 1579), resumed and fertilized the researches of Græco-Roman theorists.

It is to be expected that the historiography of this period should represent some of the defects of medieval historiography in another form, owing to its character of reaction already mentioned and to the new divinity that it had raised up upon the altars in place of the ancient divinity, humanity. The Renaissance everywhere reveals its effort to oppose the one term to the other, and since scholasticism had sought the things of God and of the soul, it wished to restrict itself to the things of nature. We find Guicciardini and a chorus of others describing the investigations of philosophers and theologians and "of all those who write things above nature or such as are not seen" as 'madnesses'; and because scholasticism had defined science in the Aristotelian manner as *de universalibus*, Campanella opposed to this definition his *Scientia est de singularibus*. In like manner its men of letters, prejudiced in favour of Latin, at first refused to recognize the new languages that had been formed during the Middle Ages, as well as medieval literature and poetry; its jurists rejected the feudal in favour of the Roman legal code, its politicians representative forms in favour of absolute lordship and monarchy. It was then that first appeared the conception of the Middle Ages as a whole, opposed to another whole, formed of the ancient and the ancient-modern, into which the Middle Ages were inserted like an irksome and painful wedge. The word 'medieval' was certainly late in appearing as an official designation, employed in the divisions and titles of histories (toward the end of the seventeenth century, as it would seem, in the manuals of Cellario); previously it had only just occurred here and there; but the thought contained in it had been in the air for some time—that is to say, in the soul of everybody—eked out with other words, such as 'barbarous' or 'Gothic' ages, and Vasari expresses it by means of the distinction between ancient and 'old,' calling those things ancient which occurred before the existence of Constantine, of Corinth, of Athens, of Rome, and of other very famous cities built up to the time of Nero, of the Vespasians, of Trajan, Hadrian, and Antoninus, and 'old' those "which had their origin from St Silvester onward." In any case, the distinction was clear: on the one hand most brilliant light, on the other dense darkness. After Constantine, writes the same Vasari, "every sort of virtue" was lost, "beautiful" souls and "lofty" intellects became corrupted into "most ugly" and "basest," and the fervent zeal of the new religion did infinite damage to the arts. This means neither more nor less than that *dualism*, one of the capital traits of the Middle Ages, was retained, although differently determined, for now the god was (although not openly acknowledged) antiquity, art, science, Greek and Roman life, and its adversary, the reprobate and rebel, was the Middle Age, 'Gothic' temples, theology and philosophy bristling with difficulties, the clumsy and cruel customs of that age. But just because the respective functions of the two terms were merely inverted, their opposition remained, and if Christianity did not succeed in understanding Paganism and in recognizing its father, so the Renaissance failed to recognize itself as the son of the Middle Ages, and did not understand the positive and durable value of the period that was closing. For this reason, both ages destroyed or allowed to disappear the monuments of the previous age. This was certainly far less the case with the Renaissance, which expressed itself less violently and was deeply imbued with the thought of the Middle Ages, and, owing to the idea of humanity, had an obscure feeling of the importance of its predecessor. So much was this the case that the school of learned men and philologists already mentioned was formed at that time, with the view of investigating medieval antiquities. But the learned are the learned—that is to say, they do not take an active part in the struggles of their time, though busied with the collection and arrangement of its chronicles and remains, which they often judge in accordance with the vulgar opinion of their own time, so that it is quite customary to find them despising the subject of their labours, declaring that the poet whom they are studying has no value, or that the period to which they are consecrating their entire life is ugly and displeasing. It needed much to free the flame of intelligence from the heaps of medieval antiquities accumulated for centuries by the learned, and the Middle Ages were abhorred during the Renaissance, even when they were investigated. The drama of love and hatred was not dissimilar in its forms, nor less bitterly dualistic, although vastly more interesting, than that which was then being played out between Catholics and Protestants. The latter called the Pope Antichrist, and the primacy of the Roman Church *mysterium iniquitatis*, and compiled a catalogue *testium veritatis* of those who had opposed that iniquity even while it prevailed. The Catholics returned the compliment with remarks about Luther and the Reformation, and composed catalogues of heretics, Satan's witnesses. But this strife was a relic of the past, and would have ended by becoming gradually attenuated and dispersed; whereas the other was an element of the future, and could only be conquered by long effort and a new conception of the loftiest character.

V

THE HISTORIOGRAPHY OF THE ENLIGHTENMENT

MEANWHILE the historiography which immediately followed pushed the double *aporia* of antiquity and of the Middle Ages to the extreme; and it was owing to this radical unprejudiced procedure that it acquired its definite physiognomy and the right of being considered a particular historiographical period. The symbolical vesture, woven of memories of the Græco-Roman world, with which the modern spirit had first clothed itself, is now torn and thrown away. The thought that the ancients had not been the oldest and wisest among the peoples, but the youngest and the least expert, and that the true ancients, that is to say, the most expert and mature in mind, are to be found in the men of the modern world, had little by little made its way and become universally accepted. Reason in its nudity, henceforth saluted by its proper name, succeeds the example and the authority of the Græco-Romans, which represented reason opposed to barbaric culture and customs. Humanitarianism, the cult of humanity, also idolized by the name of 'nature,' that is to say, ingenuous general human nature, succeeds to humanism, with its one-sided admirations for certain peoples and for certain forms of life. Histories written in Latin become scarce or are confined to the learned, and those written in national languages are multiplied; criticism is exercised not only upon medieval falsifications and fables, upon the writings of credulous and ignorant monks in monasteries, but upon the pages of ancient historians, and the first doubts appear as to the truth of the historical Roman tradition. A feeling of sympathy, however, toward the ancients still persists, whereas repugnance and abhorrence for the Middle Ages continue to increase. All feel and say that they have emerged, not only from darkness, but from the twilight before dawn, that the sun of reason is high on the horizon, illuminating the intellect and irradiating it with most vivid light. 'Light,' 'illumination,' and the like are words pronounced on every occasion and with ever increasing conviction and energy ; hence the title 'age of light,' of 'enlightenment' or of 'illumination,' given to the period extending from Descartes to Kant. Another term began to circulate, at first used rarely and in a restricted sense—'progress.' It gradually becomes more insistent and familiar, and finally succeeds in supplying a criterion for the judgment of facts, for the conduct of life, for the construction of history, becomes the subject of special investigations, and of a new kind of history, the history of the *progresses* of the human spirit.

But here we observe the persistence and the potency of Christian and theological thought. The progress so much discussed was, so to speak, a progress without *development*, manifesting itself chiefly in a sigh of satisfaction and security, as of one, favoured by fortune, who has successfully encountered many obstacles and now looks serenely upon the present, secure as to the future, with mind averted from the past, or returning to it now and then for a brief moment only, in order to lament its ugliness, to despise and to smile at it. Take as an example of all the most intelligent and at the same time the best of the historical representatives of enlightenment M. de Voltaire, who wrote his *Essai sur les mœurs* in order to aid his friend the Marquise du Châtelet to *surmonter le dégoût* caused her by *l'histoire moderne depuis la décadence de l'Empire romain*, treating the subject in a satirical vein. Or take Condorcet's work, *l'Esquisse d'un tableau historique des progrès de l'esprit humain*, which appears at its end like a last will and testament (and also as the testament of the man who wrote it), and where we find the whole century in compendium. It is as happy in the present, even in the midst of the slaughters of the Revolution, as rosy in its views as to the future, as it is full of contempt and sarcasm for the past, which had generated that present. The felicity of the period upon which they were entering was clearly stated. Voltaire says that at this time *les hommes ont acquis plus de lumières d'un bout de l'Europe à l'autre que dans tous les âges précédents*. Man now brandishes the arm which none can resist : *la seule arme contre le monstre, c'est la Raison : la seule manière d'empêcher les hommes d'être absurdes et méchants, c'est de les éclairer ; pour rendre le fanatisme exécrable, il ne faut que le peindre*. Certainly it was not denied that there had been something of good and beautiful in the past. They must have existed, if they suffered from superstition and oppression. *On voit dans l'histoire les erreurs et les préjugés se succéder tour à tour, et chasser la vérité et la raison : on voit les habiles et les heureux enchaîner les imbéciles et écraser les infortunés ; et encore ces habiles et ces heureux sont eux-mêmes les jouets de la fortune, ainsi que les esclaves qu'ils gouvernent*. And not only had the good existed, though oppressed, but it had also been efficient in a certain measure : *au milieu de ces saccagements et de ces destructions nous voyons un amour de l'ordre qui anime en secret le genre humain et qui a prévenu sa ruine totale : c'est un des ressorts de la nature, qui reprend toujours sa force. . . .* And then the 'great epochs' must not be forgotten, the 'centuries' in which the arts flourished as the result of the work of wise men and monarchs, *les quatre âges heureux* of history. But between this sporadic good, weak or acting covertly, or appearing only for a time and then disappearing, and that of the new era, the quantitative and energetic difference is such that it is turned into a qualitative difference : a moment comes when men learn to think, to rectify their ideas, and past history seems like a tempestuous sea to one who has landed upon solid earth. Certainly everything is not to be praised in the new times ; indeed, there is much to blame : *les abus servent de lois dans presque toute la terre ; et si les plus sages des hommes s'assemblaient pour faire des lois, où est l'État dont la forme subsistât entière ?* The distance from the ideal of reason was still great and the new century had still to consider itself as a simple step toward complete rationality and felicity. We find the fancy of a social form limit even in Kant, who dragged after him so much old intellectualistic and scholastic philosophy. Sometimes indeed its final form was not discovered, and its place was taken by a vertiginous succession of more and more radiant social forms. But the series of these radiant forms, the progress toward the final form and the destruction of abuses, really began in the age of enlightenment, after some episodic attempts in that direction during previous ages, for this age alone had entered upon the just, the wide, the sure path, the path illumined with the light of *reason.* It sometimes even happened in the course of that period that a doctrine leading to Rousseau's inverted the usual view and placed *reason*, not in modern times or in the near or distant future, but in the past, and not in the medieval, Græco-Roman, or Oriental past, but in the prehistoric past, in the 'state of nature,' from which history represented the deviation. But this theory, though differing in its mode of expression, was altogether identical in substance with that generally accepted, because a prehistoric 'state of nature' never had any existence in the reality which is history, but expressed an ideal to be attained in a near or distant future, which had first been perceived in modern times and was therefore really capable of moving in that direction, whether in the sense of realization or return. The religious character of all this new conception of the world cannot be obscure to anyone, for it repeats the Christian conceptions of God as truth and justice (the lay God), of the earthly paradise, the redemption, the millennium, and so on, in laical terms, and in like manner with Christianity sets the whole of previous history in opposition to itself, to condemn it, while hardly admiring here and there some consoling ray of itself. What does it matter that religion, and especially Christianity, was then the target for fiercest blows and shame and mockery, that all reticence was abandoned, and people were no longer satisfied with the discreet smile that had once blossomed on the lips of the Italian humanists, but broke out into open and fanatical warfare? Even lay fanaticism is the result of dogmatism. What does it matter that pious folk were shocked and saw the ancient Satan in the lay God, as the enlightened discovered the capricious, domineering, cruel tribal deity in the old God represented by the priest? The possibility of reciprocal accusations confirms the *dualism*, active in the new as in the old conception, and rendering it unsuitable for the understanding of development and of history.

The historiographical *aporia* of antiquity was also being increased by abstract individualism or the 'pragmatic' conception. So true was this that it was precisely at that time that the formula was resumed, and pragmatism, as history of human ideas, sentiments, calculations, and actions, as a narrative embellished with reflections, was opposed to theological or medieval history and to the old ingenuous chronicles or erudite collections of information and documents. Voltaire, who combats and mocks at belief in divine designs and punishments and in the leadership of a small barbarous population called upon to act as an elect people and to be the axle of universal history (so that he may substitute for it the lay theology which has been described), is the same Voltaire who praises in Guicciardini and in Machiavelli the first appearance of an *histoire bien faite*. The pragmatic mode of treatment was extended even to the narrative of events relating to religion and the Church and was applied by Mosheim and others in Germany. Owing to this penetration of rationalism into ecclesiastical historiography and into Protestant philosophy, it afterward seemed that the Reformation had caused thought to progress, whereas, as regards this matter, the Reformation simply received humanistic thought in the new form, to which it had previously been opposed. If, in other respects, it aided the advance of the historical conception in an original manner, this was brought about, as we shall see, by means of another element seething within it, mysticism. But meanwhile not even Catholicism remained immune from the pragmatic, of which we find traces in the *Discours* of Bossuet, who represents the Augustinian conception, shorn of its accessories, reduced and modernized, lacking the irreconcilable dualism of the two cities and the Roman Empire as the ultimate and everlasting empire, allowing natural causes preordained by God and regulated by the laws to operate side by side with divine intervention, and conceding a large share to the social and political conditions of the various peoples. We do not speak of the last step taken by the same author in his *Histoire des variations des églises*, when he conceived the history of the Reformation objectively and in its internal motives, presenting it as a rebellious movement directed against authority. Even his adversary Voltaire recognized that Bossuet had not omitted *d'autres causes* in addition to the divine will favouring the elect people, because he had several times taken count *de l'esprit des nations*. Such was the strength of *l'esprit du siècle*. The pragmatic conceptions of that time are still so well known and so near to us, so persistent in so many of our narratives and historical manuals, that it would be useless to describe them. When we direct our thoughts to the historical works of the eighteenth century, there immediately rises to the memory the general outline of a history in which priests deceive, courtiers intrigue, wise monarchs conceive and realize good institutions, combated and rendered almost vain through the malignity of others and the ignorance of the people, though they remain nevertheless a perpetual object of admiration for enlightened spirits. The image of chance or caprice appears with the evocation of that image, and mingling with the histories of these conflicts makes them yet more complicated, their results yet stranger and more astonishing. And what was the use, that is to say, the end, of historical narrative in the view of those historians? Here also the reading of a few lines of Voltaire affords the explanation : *Cet avantage consiste surtout dans la comparaison qu'un homme d'état, un citoyen, peut faire des lois et des mœurs étrangères avec celles de son pays : c'est ce qui excite l'émulation des nations modernes dans les arts, dans l'agriculture, dans le commerce. Les grandes fautes passées servent beaucoup à tout genre. On ne saurait trop remettre devant les yeux les crimes et les malheurs : on peut, quoi qu'on en dise, prévenir les uns et les autres.* This thought is repeated with many verbal variations and is to be found in nearly all the books of historiographic theory of the time, continuing the Italian mode of the Renaissance in an easier and more popular style. The words 'philosophy of history,' which had later so much success, at first served to describe the assistance obtainable from history in the shape of advice and useful precepts, when investigated without prejudice—that is to say, with the one 'assumption' of *reason*.

The external end assigned to history led to the same results as in antiquity, when history became oratorical and even historico-pedagogic romances were composed, and as in the Renaissance, when 'declamatory orations' were preserved, and history was treated as material more or less well adapted to certain ends, whence arose a certain amount of indifference toward its truth, so that Machiavelli, for instance, deduced laws and precepts from the decades of Livy, not only assuming them to be true, but accepting them in those parts which he must have recognized to be demonstrably fabulous. Orations began to disappear, but their disappearance was due to good literary taste rather than to anything else, which recognized how out of harmony were those expedients with the new popular, prosaic, polemical tone that narrative assumed in the eighteenth century. In exchange they got something worse: lack of esteem for history, which was considered to be an inferior reality, unworthy of the philosopher, who seeks for laws, for what is constant, for the uniform, the general, and can find it in himself and in the direct observation of external and internal nature, natural and human, without making that long, useless, and dangerous tour of facts narrated in the histories. Descartes, Malebranche, and the long list of their successors do not need especial mention here, for it is well known how mathematics and naturalism dominated and depressed history at this period. But was historical truth at least an inferior truth? After fuller reflection, it did not seem possible to grant even this. In history, said Voltaire, the word 'certain,' which is used to designate such knowledge as that "two and two make four," "I think," "I suffer," "I exist," should be used very rarely, and in the sole sense of "very probable." Others held that even this was saying too much, for they altogether denied the truth of history and declared that it was a collection of fables, of inventions and equivocations, or of undemonstrable affirmations. Hence the scepticism or Pyrrhonism of the eighteenth century, which showed itself on several occasions and has left us a series of curious little books as a document of itself. Such is, indeed, the inevitable result when historical knowledge is looked upon as a mass of individual testimonies, dictated or altered by the passions, or misunderstood through ignorance, good at the best for supplying edifying and terrible examples in confirmation of the eternal truths of reason, which, for the rest, shine with their own light.

It would nevertheless be altogether erroneous to found upon the exaggeration to which the theological and pragmatical views attained in the historiography of the enlightenment, and see in it a decadence or regression similar to that of the Renaissance and of other predecessors. Not only were germs of error evolved at that time, not only did the difficulties that had appeared in the previous period become more acute, but there was also developed, and elevated to a high degree of efficiency, that historiography of spiritual values which Christian historiography had intensified and almost created, and which the Renaissance had begun to transfer to the earth. Voltaire as historiographer deserves to be defended (and this has recently been done by several writers, admirably by Fueter), because he has a lively perception of the need of bringing history back from the treatment of the external to that of the internal and strives to satisfy this need. For this reason, books that gave accounts of wars, treaties, ceremonies, and solemnities seemed to him to be nothing but 'archives' or 'historical dictionaries,' useful for consultation on certain occasions, but history, true history, he held to be something altogether different. The duty of true history could not be to weight the memory with external or material facts, or as he called them *events* (*événements*), but to discover what was the society of men in the past, *la société des hommes*, *comment on vivait dans l'intérieur des familles*, *quels arts étaient cultivés*, and to paint 'manners' (*les mœurs*); not to lose itself in the multitude of insignificant particulars (*petits faits*), but to collect only those that were of importance (*considérables*) and to explain the spirit (*l'esprit*) that had produced them. Owing to this preference that Voltaire accords to manners over battles we find in him the conception (although it remains without adequate treatment and gets lost in the ardour of polemic) that it is not for history to trace the portrait of human splendours and miseries (*les détails de la splendeur et de la misère humaine*) but only of manners and of the arts, that is, of the positive work; in his *Siècle de Louis XIV* he says that he wishes to illustrate the government of that monarch, not in so far as *il a fait du bien aux français*, but in so far as *il a fait du bien aux hommes*. What Voltaire undertook, and to no small extent achieved, forms the principal object of all historians' labours at this period. Whoever wishes to do so can see in Fueter's book how the great pictures to be found in Voltaire's *Essai sur les mœurs* and *Siècle* were imitated in the pages both of French writers and in those of other European countries—for instance, in the celebrated introduction by Robertson to his history of Charles V. It will also be noticed how the special histories of this or that aspect of culture are multiplied and perfected, as though several of the *desiderata* mentioned by Bacon in his classification of history had been thus supplied. The history of philosophy abandons more and more the type of collections of anecdotes and utterances of philosophers, to become the history of systems, from Brucker to Buhle and to Tiedemann. The history of art takes the shape of a special problem in Winckelmann's work and in the works of his successors. In Voltaire's own books and in those of his school it assumes that of literature; in those of Dubos and of Montesquieu that of rights and of institutions; in Germany it leads to the production of a work as original and realistic as the history of Osnabruck by Möser. In the specialist work of Heeren, the history of industry and commerce separates itself from the historical divisions or digressions of economic treatises and takes a form of its own. The history of social customs investigates (as in Sainte-Palaye's book on *Ancienne chevalerie*) even the minutest aspects of social and moral life. Had not Voltaire remarked about tournaments that *il se fait des révolutions dans les plaisirs comme dans tout le reste ?* And to limit ourselves to Italy, which at that time was also acting on the initiative, though she soon afterward withdrew and received her impulse from the other countries of Europe, it is well to remember that in the eighteenth century Pietro Giannone, expressing the desires and the attempts at their realization of a multitude of Neapolitan compatriots and contemporaries, traced the *civil* history of the Kingdom of Naples, giving much space to the relations between Church and State and to the incidents of legislation. Many followed this example in Italy and outside it (among the many were Montesquieu and Gibbon). In Italy, too, Ludovico Antonio Muratori illustrated medieval life in his *Antiquitates Italiæ*, and Tiraboschi composed a great history of Italian literature (understood as that of the whole culture of Italy), notable not less for its erudition than for its clearness of design, while other lesser writers, like Napoli Signorelli, in his *Vicende della cultura delle due Sicilie*, particularized in certain regions, sprinkling their history with the philosophy current at the time. The Jesuit Bettinelli, too, imitated the historical books of Voltaire for the history of letters, arts, and customs in Italy, Bonafede the work of Brucker for the history of philosophy, and Lanzi, in a manner far superior to those just mentioned, continued the path followed by Winckelmann in his *History of Painting*.

Not only did the historiography of the enlightenment render history more 'interior' and develop it in its interiority, but it also broadened it in space and time. Here too Voltaire represents in an eminent degree the needs of his age, with his continual accusations of narrowness and meanness levelled at the traditional image of universal history, as composed of Hebrew or sacred history and Græco-Roman or profane history, or, as he says, *histoires prétendues universelles, fabriquées dans notre Occident.* A beginning was made with the use of the material discovered, transported, and accumulated by explorers and travellers from the Renaissance onward, of which a considerable part had been contributed by the Jesuits and by missionaries. India and China attracted attention, both on account of their antiquity and of the high grade of civilization to which they had attained. Translations of religious and literary Oriental texts were soon added to this, and it became possible to discuss that civilization, not merely at second-hand and according to the narratives of travellers. This increase of knowledge relating to the East is paralleled by increase of knowledge not only in relation to antiquity (these studies were never dropped, but changed their centre, first from Italy to France and Holland, then to England, and then to Germany), but also in regard to the Middle Ages, in the works of the Benedictines, of Leibnitz, Muratori, and very many others, who here also specialized both as regards the objects of their researches and as to the regions or cities in which they conducted them, as for instance De Meo in his *Annali critici del Regno di Napoli.*

With the increase of erudition, of the variety of documents and information available, went hand in hand a more refined criticism as to the authenticity of the one and of the value as evidence of the other. Fueter does well to note the progress in method accomplished by the Benedictines and by Leibnitz (who did not surpass those excellent and learned monks in this respect, although he was a philosopher) up to Muratori, who did not restrict himself to testing the genuineness of tradition, but initiated criticism of the tendencies of individual witnesses, of the interests and passions which colour and give their shape to narratives. The enlightened, with Voltaire at their head, initiated another kind of criticism of a more intrinsic sort, directed to things and to the knowledge of things (to literary, moral, political, and military experience), recognizing the impossibility that things should have happened in the way that they are said to have happened by superficial, credulous, or prejudiced historians, and attempting to reconstruct them in the only way that they could have happened. We shall admire in Voltaire (especially in the *Siècle*) his lack of confidence in the reports of courtiers and servants, accustomed to forge calumnies and to interpret maliciously and anecdotically the external actions of sovereigns and statesmen.

This happened because the historiography of the enlightenment, while it preserved and even exaggerated pragmatism, yet on the other hand refined and spiritualized it, as will have been observed in the expressions preferred by Voltaire and even in the theologizing Bossuet : *l'esprit des nations*, *l'esprit du temps*. What that *esprit* was naturally remained vague, because the support of philosophy, in which at that time those newly imported concepts introduced an unexpected element of conflict, was lacking to refer it to the ideal determinations of the spirit in its development and to conceive the various epochs and the various nations as each playing its own part in the spiritual drama. Thus it often happened that *esprit* was perverted into a fixed quality, such as *race*, if it were a question of nations, and into a current or mode, if periods were spoken of, and was thus naturalized and pragmatized. *Trois choses*, wrote Voltaire, *influent sans cesse sur l'esprit des hommes, le climat, le gouvernement, et la religion: c'est la seule manière d'expliquer l'énigme du monde*: where the 'spirit' is lowered to the position of a product of natural and social circumstances. The suggestive word had, however, been pronounced, and a clear consciousness of the terms themselves of the social, political, and cultural struggle that was being carried on would have little by little emerged. For the time being, climate, government, religion, genius of the peoples, genius of the time, were all more or less happy attempts to go beyond pragmatism and to place causality in a universal order. This effort, and at the same time its limit—that is to say, the falling back into the abstract and pragmatic form of explanation—is also shown in the doctrine of the 'single event,' which was believed to determine at a stroke the new epoch of barbarism or of civilization. Thus at this time it was customary to assign enormous importance to the Crusades or to the Turkish occupation of Constantinople, as Fueter records, with special reference to Richardson's history. Another consequence of the same embarrassment was the slight degree of fusion attained in the various histories of culture, of customs, and of the arts that were composed at this time. The various manifestations of life were set down one after the other without any success, or even any attempt at developing them organically.

Doubtless the new and vigorous historiographical tendencies of the enlightenment were then attacking other barriers opposed to them by the already mentioned lay-theological dualism, in addition to those of pragmatism and of naturalism. This lay-theology ended by negating the principle of development itself, because the judgment of the past as consisting of darkness and errors precluded any serious conception of religion, poetry, philosophy, or of primitive and bygone institutions. What did an institution of the great importance of 'divination' in primitive civilizations amount to for Voltaire in the formative process of observation and scientific deduction? The invention *du premier fripon qui rencontra un imbécile.* Or oracles, also of such importance in the life of antiquity? *Des fourberies.* To what amounted the theological struggles between Catholics, Lutherans, and Calvinists in connexion with the Eucharist? To the ridiculous spectacle of the Papists who *mangeaient Dieu pour pain*, *les luthériens du pain et Dieu*, *les calvinistes mangèrent le pain et ne mangèrent point Dieu.* What was the only end that could be attained by the Jansenists? Boredom: a sequence of tiresome *querelles théologiques* and of petty *querelles de plume*, so that nothing remains of the writers of that time who took part in them but geometry, reasoned grammar, logic—that is to say, only what *appartient à la raison*; the *querelles théologiques* were *une maladie de plus dans l'esprit humain.* Nor does the philosophy of earlier times receive better treatment. That of Plato was nothing but *une mauvaise métaphysique*, a tissue of arguments so bad that it seems impossible they could have been admired and added to by others yet more extravagant from century to century, until Locke was reached: *Locke, qui seul a développé l'entendement humain dans un livre où il n'y a que des vérités, et, ce qui rend l'ouvrage parfait, toutes les vérités sont claires.* In poetry, modern work was placed above ancient, the *Gerusalemme* above the *Iliad*, the *Orlando* above the *Odyssey*, Dante seems obscure and awkward, Shakespeare a barbarian not without talent. Medieval literature was beneath consideration : *On a recueilli quelques malheureuses compositions de ce temps : c'est faire un amas de cailloux tirés d'antiques masures quand on est entouré de palais.* Frederick of Prussia, who here showed himself a consistent Voltairean, did not receive the new edition of the *Nibelungenlied* and the other epic monuments of Germany graciously. In a word, the whole of the past lost its value, or preserved only the negative value of evil : *Que les citoyens d'une ville immense, où les arts, les plaisirs, et la paix règnent aujourd'hui, où la raison même commence à s'introduire, comparent les temps, et qu'ils se plaignent, s'ils osent. C'est une réflexion qu'il faut faire presque à chaque page de cette histoire.*

The lack of the conception of development rendered sterile the very acquisition of knowledge of distant things and people ; and although there was in certain respects merit in introducing India and China into universal history, and although the criticism and satire of the 'four monarchies' and of 'sacred' history was to a certain extent justified, it is well to remember that in the notion mocked at was satisfied the legitimate need for understanding history in its relations with Christian and European civilized life ; and that if it had not been found possible (and it never was at that time) to form a more complete chain, in which were Arabia, India and China, and the American civilizations, and all the other newly discovered things, these additional contributions to knowledge would have remained a mere object for curiosity or imagination. India, China, and the East in general were therefore of little more use in the eighteenth century than to manifest an affection for tolerance, indeed for religious indifferentism. Those distant countries, in which there was no proselytizing frenzy, and which did not send missionaries to weary

Europe—though Europe did not spare them such visitations—were not treated as historical realities, nor did they obtain their place in the reality of spiritual development, but became longed-for ideals, countries of dream. Those who in our day renew praises of Asiatic toleration, contrasting it with European intolerance, and wax tender over such wisdom and meekness, are not aware that in so doing they are repeating uselessly and inopportunely what Voltaire has already done; and if in this matter he did not aid the better understanding of history, he at any rate fulfilled a practical and moral function which was necessary for the conditions of his own time. The defective conception of development, and not accidental circumstances, such as the publicistic, journalistic, and literary tendencies of the original among those historians, is also the profound reason for the failure of contact and of union between the immense mass of erudition accumulated by the sixteenth-century philologists, and the historiography of the enlightenment. How were those documents and collections to be employed in the slow and laborious development of the spirit, if, according to the new conception, instead of developing, the spirit was to leap, and had indeed already made a great leap and left the past far behind? It was sufficient to rummage from time to time among them and extract some curious detail, which should fit in with the polemic of the moment. *C'est un vaste magasin, où vous prendrez ce qui est à votre usage*, said Voltaire. Thus the learned and the enlightened, both of them children of their time, remained divided among themselves, the former incapable of rising to the level of history owing to their slight vivacity of spirit, the latter overrunning it owing to their too great vivacity, and reducing it to a form of journalism.

All these limits, just because they are limits, assign its proper sphere to the historiography of the enlightenment, but they must not be taken as meaning that it had not made any progress. That historiography, plunged in the work at the moment most urgent, surrounded with the splendour of the truths that it was in the act of revealing around it, failed to see those limits and its own deficiencies, or saw them rarely and with difficulty. It was aware only that it progressed and progressed rapidly, nor was it wrong in this belief. Nor are those critics (among whom is Fueter) wrong who now defend it from the bad reputation that has befallen it and celebrate its many virtues, which we also have set in a clear light and have added to, and whose connexion and unity we have proved. Yet we must not leave that bad reputation unexplained, for it sounds far more serious than the usual depreciation by every historical period of the one that has preceded it, with the view of showing its inferiority to the present. Here, on the contrary, we find a particular judgment of depreciation, pronounced even by comparison with the periods that preceded the enlightenment, so that this period, and not, for example, the Renaissance, has especially received the epithet of 'anti-historical' ("the anti-historical eighteenth century"). We find the explanation of this when we think of the dissipation then taking place of all symbolical veils, received from *venerable antiquity*, and of the *crude dualism and conflict* which were being instigated at that time between history and religion. The Renaissance was also itself an affirmation of human reason, but at the moment of its breaking with medieval tradition it was felt to be all the same tied to classical tradition, which gave it an appearance of historical consciousness (an appearance and not the reality). The philosophers of the Renaissance often invoked and placed themselves under the protection of the ancient philosophers, Plato against Aristotle, or the Greek Aristotle against the Aristotle of the commentators. The lettered men of the period sought to justify the new works of art and the new judgments upon them by appealing to the precepts of antiquity, although they sophisticated and subtilized what they found there. Philosophers, artists, and critics turned their shoulders upon antiquity only when and where no sort of conciliation was possible, and it was only the boldest among them who ventured to do even this. The ancient republics were taken as an example by the politicians, with Livy as their text, as the Bible was by the Christians. Religion, which was exhausted or had been extinguished in the souls of the cultured, was of necessity preserved for the people as an instrument of government, a vulgar form of philosophy : almost all are agreed as to this, from Machiavelli to Bruno. The sage legislator or the 'prince' of Machiavelli and the enlightened despot of Voltaire, who were both of them idealizations of the absolute monarchies that had moulded Europe politically to their will, have substantial affinities; but the sixteenth-century politician, expert in human weaknesses and charged with all the experience of the rich history of Greece and of Rome, studied finesse and transactions, where the enlightened man of the eighteenth century, encouraged by the ever renewed victories of the *Reason*, raised Reason's banner, and for her took his sword from the scabbard, without feeling the smallest necessity for covering his face with a mask. King Numa created a religion in order to deceive the people, and was praised for it by Machiavelli ; but Voltaire would have abused him for doing so, as he abused all inventors of dogmas and promoters of fanaticism. What more is to be said? The rationalism of the Renaissance was especially the work of the Italian genius, so well balanced, so careful to avoid excesses, so accommodating, so artistic; enlightenment, which was especially the work of the French genius, was radical, consequent, apt to run into extremes, logistical.

When the genius of the two countries and the two epochs is compared, the enlightenment is bound to appear anti-historical with respect to the Renaissance, which, owing to the comparison thus drawn and instituted with such an object, becomes endowed with a historical sense and with a sense of development which it did not possess, having also been essentially rationalistic and anti-historical, and, in a certain sense, more so than the enlightenment. I say more than the enlightenment, not only because the latter, as I have shown, greatly increased historical knowledge and ideas, but also precisely because it caused all the contradictions latent in the Renaissance to break out. This was an apparent regression in historical knowledge, but in reality it was an addition to life, and therefore to historical consciousness itself, as we clearly see immediately afterward. The triumph and the catastrophe of the enlightenment was the French Revolution; and this was at the same time the triumph and the catastrophe of its historiography.

VI

THE HISTORIOGRAPHY OF ROMANTICISM

THE reaction manifested itself with the sentimental return to the past, and with the defence undertaken by the politicians of old institutions worthy of being preserved or accorded new life. Hence arose two forms of historical representation, which certainly belong in a measure to all periods, but which were very vigorous at the romantic period: *nostalgic* historiography and historiography which *restored.* And since the past of their desires, which supplied the material for practical recommendations, was just that which the enlightenment and the Revolution had combated and overthrown—the Middle Ages and everything that resembled or seemed to resemble the Middle Ages—both kinds of history were, so to say, medievalized. Just as a watercourse which has been forcibly diverted from its natural bed noisily returns to it as soon as obstructions are removed, so a great sigh of joy and satisfaction, a warm emotion of tenderness, welled up in and reanimated all breasts as, after so long a rationalistic ascesis, they again took to themselves the old religion, the old national customs, regional and local, again entered the old houses and castles and cathedrals, sang again the old songs, dreamed again the old legends. In this tumult of sentiment we do not at first observe the profound and irremediable change that has taken place in the souls of all, borne witness to by the anxiety, the emotion, the pathos of that apparent return.

It would be to belittle the nostalgic historiography

of the romantic movement to make it consist of certain special literary works, for in reality it penetrated all or almost all the writings of that time, like an irresistible current, to be found not only in lesser and poorer spirits, such as De Barante, nor only in the more poetically disposed, such as Chateaubriand, but in historians who present some of the most important or purely scientific thoughts, for example Niebuhr. The life of chivalry, the life of the cloister, the Crusades, the Hohenstaufen, the Lombard and Flemish communes, the Christian kings of Spain at strife with the Arabs, the Arabs themselves, England divided between Saxons and Normans, the Switzerland of William Tell, the *chansons de geste*, the songs of the troubadours, *Gothic* architecture (characteristic vicissitude of a name, applied in contempt and then turned into a symbol of affection), became at this time the object of universal and national sympathy, as did the rough, ingenuous popular literature, poetry, and art : translations or abbreviations of the medieval chronicles were even reprinted for the enjoyment of a large and eager circle of readers ; the first medieval museums were formed ; an attempt was made to restore and complete ancient churches, castles, and city palaces. Historiography entered into close relations and exchange of ideas with the new literary form of historical romance, which expressed the same nostalgia, first with Walter Scott and then with his innumerable followers in all countries. (This literary form was therefore quite different from the historical fiction of Manzoni, which is free from such sentiment and whose historical element has a moral foundation.) I have already remarked that this nostalgia was far more modern of content than at first supposed ; so much so that every one was attracted to it by the motive that most appealed to himself, whether religious or political, Old Catholic, mystical, monarchical, constitutional, communal-republican, national-independent, liberal-democratic, or aristocratic. Nevertheless, when the past was taken as a poetic theme, there was a risk that the idealizing tendency of the images would be at strife with critical reflection: hence the cult of the Middle Ages, which had become a superstition, came to a ridiculous end. Fueter quotes an acute remark of Ranke, relating to one of the last worthy representatives of the romantic school, Giesebrecht, author of the *History of the German Empire*, admirer and extoller of the 'Christian-Germanic virtues,' of the power and excellence of the medieval heroes. Ranke described all this as "at once too virile and too puerile." But the puerility discernible at the sources of this ideal current, before it falls into the comic, is rather the sublime puerility of the poet's dream.

The actual modern motives, which present themselves as sentiments in nostalgic historiography, acquired a reflex form with the same or other writers, as tendencies to the service of which their narratives were bent. Here, too, it would be superfluous to give an account of all the various forms and specifications of these tendencies (which Fueter has already done admirably), from the persistent Rousseauism of Giovanni Müller to Sismondi, or from the ideal of a free peasantry of Niebuhr, the ultramontane ideal of Leo, the imperialistic-medieval ideal of the already mentioned Giesebrecht and Ficker, the old liberal of Raumer, the neo-liberal of Rotteck and Gervinus, the anglicizing of Guizot and Dahlmann, or the democratic ideal of Michelet, to the neo-Guelfish ideal of Troya and Balbo and Father Tosti, to the Prussian hegemony of Droysen and of Treitschke, and so on. But all of these, and other historians with a particular bias, lean, with rare exceptions, on the past, and find the justification of their bias in the dialectic of tradition or in tradition itself. Nobody any longer cared to compose by the light of abstract reason alone. The extreme typical instance is afforded by the socialistic school, which took the romantic form in the person of its chief representative, Marx, who endowed it with historiographical and scientific value. His work was in complete opposition to the socialistic ideals that had appeared in the eighteenth century, and he therefore boasted that they had passed from the state of being a *Utopia* to that of a *science*. His science was nothing less than historical necessity attributed to the new era that he prophesied, and materialism itself no longer wished to be the naturalistic materialism of a d'Holbach or a Helvétius, but presented itself as 'historical materialism.'

If nostalgic historiography is poetry and that with a purpose is practical and political, the historiography, the true historiography, of romanticism is not to be placed in either of the two, in so far as it is considered an epoch in the history of thought. Certainly, poetry and practice arose from a thought and led to a thought as its material or problem: the French Revolution was certainly not the cause or the effect of a philosophy, but both the cause and the effect, a philosophy in the act, born from and generating the life that was then developed. But thought in the form of thought, and not in the form of sentimental love of the past or effort to revive a false past, is what determines the scientific character of that historiography, which we desire to set in a clear light. And it reacted in the form of thought against the thought of the enlightenment, so crudely dualistic, by opposing to it the conception of development.

Not indeed that this concept was something entirely new, which had then burst forth in bud for the first time : no speculative conception that is really such can be absent at one time and appear at another. The difference lies in this, that at a given period scientific problems seem to apply to one rather than to another aspect of thought, which is always present in its totality. So that when we say that the conception of development was absent from antiquity and from the eighteenth century, we utter a hyperbole. There are good reasons for this hyperbole, but it remains a hyperbole and should not be taken literally and understood materially. Nor are we to believe that there was no suspicion or anticipation of the important scientific conception of development prior to the romantic period. Traces of it may be found in the pantheism of the great philosophers of the Renaissance, and especially in Bruno, and in mysticism itself, in so far as it included pantheism, and yet more distinctly in the reconstruction of the bare bones of the theological conception with the conception of the course of historical events as a gradual education of the human race, in which the successive revelations should be the communication of books of a gradually less and less elementary nature, from the first Hebrew scriptures to the Gospels and to the revisions of the Gospels. Lessing offers an example of this. Nor were the theorists of the enlightenment always so terribly dualistic as those that I have mentioned, but here and there one of them, such as Turgot, although he did not altogether abandon the presupposition as to epochs of decadence, yet recognized the progress of Christianity over antiquity and of modern times over Christianity, and attempted even to trace the line of development passing through the three ages, the mythological, the metaphysical, and the scientific. Other thinkers, like Montesquieu, noticed the relativity of institutions to customs and to periods; others, like Rousseau, attached great importance to the strength of sentiment. Enlightenment had also its adversaries during its own period, not only as represented by political abstraction and fatuous optimism (such as that of Galiani, for instance), but also in more important respects, destined later to form the special subject of criticism, such as contempt for tradition, for religion, and for poetry and arid naturalism. Hence the smile of Hamann at the blind faith of Voltaire and of Hume in the Newtonian astronomical doctrines and at their lack of sense for moral doctrines. He held that a revival of poetry and a linking of it with history were necessary, and considered history to be (here he was just the opposite of Bodin) not the easiest but the most difficult of all mental labours. But in the *Scienza nuova* of Vico (1725) was to be found a very rich and organic anticipation of romantic thought (as should now be universally recognized and known). Vico criticized the enlightenment only in its beginnings (when it was still only natural jurisprudence and Cartesianism), yet he nevertheless penetrated more deeply than others who came after him into its hidden motives and measured more accurately its logical and practical consequences. Thus he opposed to the superficial contempt for the past in the name of abstract reason the unfolding of the human mind in history, as sense, imagination, and intellect, as the divine or animal age, the heroic age, and the human age. He held further that no human age was in the wrong, for each had its own strength and beauty, and each was the effect of its predecessor and the necessary preparation for the one to follow, aristocracy for democracy, democracy for monarchy, each one appearing at the right moment, or as the justice of that moment.

The conception of development did not, however, in the romantic period, remain the thought of a solitary thinker without an audience, but broadened until it became a general conviction ; it did not appear timidly shadowed forth, or contradictorily affirmed, but took on body, coherence, and vigour, and dominated spirits. It is the formative principle of the idealist philosophy, which culminated in the system of Hegel. Few there were who resisted its strength, and these, like Herbart, were still shut up in pre-Kantian dogmatism, or tried to resist it and are more or less tinged with it, as is the case with Schopenhauer and yet more with Comte and later with positivistic evolutionism. It gives its intellectual backbone to the whole of historiography (with the exception here too of lingerers and reactionaries), and that historiography corrects for it, in greater or less measure, the same one-sided tendencies which came to it from the sentimental and political causes already described, from tenderness for the near past or for "the good old times," and for the Middle Ages. The whole of history is now understood as necessary development, and is therefore implicitly, and more or less explicitly, all redeemed ; it is all learned with the feeling that it is sacred, a feeling reserved in the Middle Ages for those parts of it only which represented the opposition of God to the power of the devil. Thus the conception of development was extended to classical antiquity, and then, with the increase of knowledge and of attention, to Oriental civilizations. Thus the Romans, the Ionians, the Dorians, the Egyptians, and the Indians got back their life and were justified and loved in their turn almost as much as the world of chivalry and the Christian world had been loved. But the logical extension of the conception did not find any obstacle among the philosophers and historians, even in the repugnance that was felt for the times to which modern times were opposed, such as the eighteenth century. The spectacle was witnessed of the consecration of Jacobinism and of the French Revolution in the very books of their adversaries, Hegel, for instance, finding in those events both the triumph and the death, the one not less than the other, the 'triumphant death' of the modern abstract subjectivity, inaugurated by Descartes. Not only did the adversaries, but also the executioners and their victims, make peace, and Socrates, the martyr of free thought and the victim of intolerance, such as he was understood to be by the intellectualists of the eighteenth century and those who superstitiously repeat them in our own day, was condemned to the death that he had well deserved, in the name of History, which does not admit of spiritual revolutions without tragedies. The drafter, too, of the *Manifesto of the Communists*, as he was hastening on the business of putting an end to the burgess class, both with his prayers and with his works, gave vent to a warm and grandiose eulogium of the work achieved by the burgess class, and in so doing showed himself to be the faithful child of romantic thought; because, for anyone who held to the ideology of the eighteenth century, capitalism and the burgess class should have appeared to be nothing but distortions due to ignorance, stupidity, and egoism, unworthy of any praise beyond a funeral oration. The passions of the greater part of those historians were most inflammable, not less than those of the enlightened, yet satire, sarcasm, invective, at least among the superior intellects, vividly encircled the historical understanding of the time, but did not oppress or negate it. The general impression experienced from those narratives is that of a serious effort to render justice to all, and we owe it to the discipline thus imparted to the minds and souls of the thinkers and historians of romanticism that it is only the least cultivated or most fanatical among the priests and Catholics in general who continue to curse Voltaire and the eighteenth century as the work of the devil. In the same way, it is only vulgar democrats and anti-clericals, akin to the former in their anachronism and the rest, who treat the reaction, the restoration, and the Middle Ages with equal grossness. Enlightenment and the Jacobinism connected with it was a religion, as we have shown, and when it died it left behind it survivals or superstitions.

To conceive history as development is to conceive it as history of ideal values, the only ones that have value, and it was for this reason that in the romantic period there was an ever increasing multiplication of those histories which had already increased to so considerable an extent in the preceding period. But their novelty did not consist in their external multiplication, but in their internal maturation, which corrected those previously composed, consisting either of learned collections of disconnected items of information, or judgments indeed, but judgments based upon an external model, which claimed to be constructed by pure reason and was in reality constructed by arbitrary and capricious abstraction and imagination. And now the history of poetry and of literature is no longer measured according to the standard of the Roman-humanistic ideal, or according to the classical ideal of the age of Louis XIV, or of the ratiocinative and prosaic ideal of the eighteenth century, but discovers by degrees its own measure in itself, and beginning with the first attempts of Herder, of the Schlegels, and then of Villemain, of Sainte-Beuve, and of Gervinus, and for antiquity of Wolf and Muller, finally reaches the high standard represented by the *History of Italian Literature* of de Sanctis. Suddenly the history of art feels itself embarrassed by the too narrow ideal of Lessing and of Winckelmann, and there is a movement toward colour, toward landscape, toward pre-Hellenic and post-Hellenic art, toward the romantic, the Gothic, the Renaissance, and the baroque, a movement that extends from Meyer and Hirth to Rumohr, Kluger, Schnaase, till it reaches Burckhardt and Ruskin. It also tries here and there to break down the barriers of the schools and to attain the really artistic personality of the artists. The history of philosophy has its great crisis with Hegel, who leads it from the abstract subjectivism of the followers of Kant to objectivity, and recognizes the only true existence of philosophy to consist of the history of thought, considered in its entirety, without neglecting any one of its forms. Zeller, Fischer, and Erdmann in Germany, Cousin and his school in France, Spaventa in Italy, follow Hegel in such objective research. The like takes place in the history of religion, which tries to adopt intrinsic criteria of judgment, after Spittler and Planck, the last representatives of the rationalistic school, with Marheinecke, Neander, Hase, and finds a peculiarly scientific form with Strauss, Baur, and the Tubingen school; and from Eichhorn to Savigny, Gans, and Lassalle in the history of rights. The conception of the State always yields the leadership more and more to that of the nation in the history called political, and 'nationality' substitutes the names of 'humanity,' 'liberty,' and 'equality,' and all the other ideas of the preceding age that once were full of radiance, but are now dimmed. This nationalism has wrongly been looked upon as a regression in respect of that universalism and cosmopolitanism, because (notwithstanding its well-known sentimental exaggerations) it notably assists the concrete conception of the universal living only in its historical creations, such as nations, which are both products and factors of its development. And the value of *Europeanism* is revived as the result of this acquisition of consciousness of the value of nations. It had been too much trampled upon during the period of the enlightenment, owing to the naturalistic spirit which dominated at that time, and to the reaction taking place against the historical schemes of antiquity and Christianity, although it was surely evident that history written by Europeans could not but be 'Europocentric,' and that it is only in relation to the course of Græco-Roman civilization, which was Christian and Occidental, that the civilizations developed along other lines become actual and comprehensible to us, provided always that we do not wish to change history into an exhibition of the different types of civilization, with a prize for the best of them! The difference is also made clear for the same reason between history and pre-history, between the history of man and the history of nature, which had been illegitimately linked by the materialists and the naturalists. This is to be found even in the works of Herder, who retains a good many of the elements of the century of his birth mingled with those of the new period. But it is above all in romantic historiography that we observe the search for and very often the happy realization of an organic linking together of all particular histories of spiritual values, by relating religious, philosophical, poetical, artistic, juridical, and moral facts as a function of a single motive of development. It then becomes a commonplace that a literature cannot be understood without understanding ideas and customs, or politics without philosophy, or (as was realized rather later) rights and customs and ideas without economy. And it is worth while recording as we pass by that there is hardly one of these histories of values which has not been previously presented or sketched by Vico, together with the indication of their intrinsic unity. Histories of poetry, histories of myth, of rights, of languages, of constitutions, of explicative or philosophical reason, all are in Vico, although sometimes wrapped up in the historical or sociological epoch with which each one of them was particularly connected. Even modern biography (which illustrates what the individual does and suffers in relation to the mission which he fulfils and to the aspect of the Idea which becomes actual in him) has its first or one of its first notable monuments in the autobiography of Vico—that is to say, in the history of the works which Providence commanded and guided him to accomplish "in diverse ways that seemed to be obstacles, but were opportunities."

This transformation of biography does not imply failure to recognize individuality, but is, on the contrary, its elevation, for it finds its true meaning in its relation with the universal, as the universal its concreteness in the individual. And indeed individualizing power, perception of physiognomies, of states of the soul, of the various forms of the ideas, sense of the differences of times and places, may be said to show themselves for the first time in romantic historiography. That is to say, they do not show themselves rarely or as by accident, nor any longer in the negative and summary form of opposition between new and old, civil and barbarous, patriotic and extraneous. It does not mean anything that some of those historians lost themselves (though this happened rarely) in an abstract dialectic of ideas, and that others more frequently allowed ideas to be submerged in the external picturesqueness of customs and anecdotes, because we find exaggerations, one-sidedness, lack of balance, at all periods and in all progress of thought. Nor is the accusation of great importance that the colouring of times and places preferred by the romantics was false, because the important thing was precisely this attempt to colour, whether the result were happy or the reverse (if the latter, the picture had to be coloured again, but always coloured). A further reason for this is that, as has been already admitted, there were fancies and tendencies at work in romanticism beyond true and proper historiography, which bestowed upon the times and places illustrated that imaginary and exaggerated colouring suggested by the various sentiments and interests. History, which is thought, was sometimes idealized at this period as an imaginary living again in the past, and people asked of history to be carried back into the old castles and market-places of the Middle Ages ; for their enjoyment they asked to see the personages of the time in their own proper clothes and as they moved about, to hear them speak the language, with the accent of the time, to be made contemporary with the facts and to acquire them with the ingenuous spirit of a contemporary. But to do this is not only impossible for thought, but also for art, because art too surpasses life, and it would be something useless, because it is not desired, for what man really desires is to reproduce in imagination and to rethink the past *from the present*, not to tear himself away from the present and fall back into the dead past. Certainly this last was an illusion, proper to several romantics (who for that matter have their successors in our own day), and in so far as it was an illusion either remained a sterile effort or diffused itself in a lyrical sigh ; but an illusion of that kind was one of many aspects and did not form an essential part of romantic historiography.

We also owe it to romanticism that a relation was established for the first time and a fusion effected between the learned and the historians, between those who sought out material and thinkers. This, as we have said, had not happened in the eighteenth century, nor, to tell the truth, before it, in the great epochs of erudition of Italian or Alexandrian humanism, for then antiquaries and politicians each followed their own path, indifferent to one another, and the only political ideal that sometimes gleamed from the bookshelves of the antiquary (as Fueter acutely observes of Flavius Blondus) was that of a government which by ensuring calm should permit the learned to follow their peaceful avocations ! But the watchword of romantic historiography was anticipated in respect to this matter also by Vico, in his formula of the *union* of *philosophy* with *philology*, and of the reciprocal *conversion* of the *true* with the *certain*, of the idea with the fact. This formula proves (we give it passing mention) that the historical saying of Manzoni, to the effect that Vico should be united with Muratori, was not altogether historically exact—that is to say, philosophy with erudition, for Vico had already united these two things, and their union constitutes the chief value of his work. Nevertheless, notwithstanding its inaccuracy, the saying of Manzoni also proves how romantic historiography had noted the intimate connexion that prevails between erudition and thought in history, which is the living and thinking again of the document that has been preserved or restored by erudition, and indeed demands erudition that it may be sought out and prepared. Neither did romanticism limit itself to stating this claim in the abstract, but really created the type of the philologist-thinker (who was sometimes also a poet), from Niebuhr to Mommsen, from Thierry to Fustel de Coulanges, from Troya to Balbo or Tosti. Then for the first time were the great collections and repertories of the erudition of the seventeenth and eighteenth centuries valued at their true worth; then were new collections promoted, supplementary to or correcting them according to criteria that were ever more rigorous in relation to the subject and to the greater knowledge and means at disposal. Thus arose the work known as the *Monumenta Germaniæ historica* and the German philological school (which was once the last and became the first), the one a model of undertakings of this sort, the other of the disciplines relating to them, for the rest of Europe. The philological claim of the new historiography, aided by the sentiment of nationality, also gave life in our Italy to those historical societies, to those collections of chronicles, of laws, of charters, of 'historical archives' or reviews, institutions with which historiographical work is concerned in our day. A notable example of the power to promote the most patient philology inspired with purely historical needs is to be found, among others, in the *Corpus inscriptionum latinarum*, conceived and carried out by a historian endowed with the passionate energy and the synthetic mind of a Mommsen. In the eighteenth century (with one or two very rare and partial exceptions) historians disdained parchment and in-folios, or opened them impatiently, *bibentes et fugientes*; but in the nineteenth century no serious spirit dared to affirm any longer that it was possible to compose history without accurate, scrupulous, meticulous study of the documents upon which it is to be founded.

The pragmatic histories of the last centuries, therefore, melted away at the simple touch of these new historiographical convictions, rather than owing to direct and open criticism or polemic. The word 'pragmatic,' which used to be a title of honour, began to be pronounced with a tinge of contempt, to designate an inadequate form of historical thought, and the historians of the enlightenment fell into discredit, not only Voltaire and the French, but the Humes, the Robertsons, and other English historians. They appeared now to be quite without colour, lacking in historical sense, their minds fixed only on the political aspect of things, superficial, vainly attempting to explain great events by the intentions of individuals and by means of little things or single details. The theory, too, of history as the orator and teacher of virtue and prudential maxims also disappeared. This theory had enjoyed a long and vigorous life during Græco-Roman antiquity and again from the Renaissance onward (when I say that all these things disappeared, the exception of the fossils is always to be understood, for these persisted at that time and persist in our own day, with the air of being alive). The attitude of the Christian spirit toward history was resumed. This spirit contemplates it as a single process, which does not repeat itself, as the work of God, which teaches directly by means of His presence, not as matter that exemplifies abstract teaching, extraneous to itself. The word 'pragmatic' was indeed pronounced with a smile from that time onward, as were the formulas of *historia magister vitæ* or that directed *ad bene beateque vivendum*: let him who will believe these formulas—that is to say, he who echoes traditional thoughts without rethinking them and is satisfied with traditional and vulgar conceptions. What is the use of history? "History itself," was the answer, and truly that is not a little thing.

The new century glorified itself with the title of 'the century of history,' owing to its new departures, which were born or converged in one. It had deified and at the same time humanized history, as had never been done before, and had made of it a centre of reality and of thought. That title of honour should be confirmed, if not to the whole of the nineteenth century, then to its romantic or idealistic period. But this confirmation should not prevent our observing, with equal clearness, the *limit* of that historicity, without which it would not be possible to understand its later and further advance. History was then at once deified and humanized; but did the divinity and humanity truly flow together in one, or was there not at bottom some separation between the two of them? Was the disagreement between ancient worldly thought and ultramundane Christian thought really healed, or did it not present itself again in a new form, though this form was attenuated and more critical intellectually? And which of the two elements prevailed in this disagreement in its abstractness, the human or rather the divine?

These questions suggest the answer, which is further

suggested by a memory familiar to all, namely, that the romantic period was not only the splendid age of the great evolutionary histories, but also the fatal age of the *philosophies of history*, the transcendental histories. And indeed, although the thought of immanence had grown gradually more and more rich and profound during the Renaissance and the enlightenment, and that of transcendency ever more evanescent, the first had not for that reason absorbed the second in itself, but had merely purified and rationalized it, as Hellenic philosophy and Christian theology had tried to do in their own ways in their own times. In the romantic period, purification and rationalization continue, and here was the mistake as well as the merit of romanticism, for it was no longer a question of setting right that ancient opinion, but of radically inverting and remaking it. The transcendental conception of history was no longer at that time called revelation and apocalypse, but *philosophy of history*, a title taken from the enlightenment (principally from Voltaire), although it no longer had the meaning formerly attributed to it of history examined with an unprejudiced or philosophical spirit adorned with moral and political reflections, but the meaning, altogether different, of a philosophical search of the sphere above or below that of history—in fact, of a theological search, which remained theological, however lay or speculative it may have been. And since a search of this sort always leads to a rationalized mythology, there is no reason why the name of 'mythology' should not be extended to the philosophy of history, or the name of 'philosophy of history' to mythology, as I have extended it, calling all transcendental conceptions of history 'philosophy of history,' for they all separate the fact and the idea, the event and its explication, action and end, the world and God. And since the philosophy of history is transcendental in its internal structure, it is not surprising that it showed itself to be such in all the very varied forms that it assumed in the romantic period, even among philosophers as avid of immanence as Hegel, a great destroyer of Platonism, who yet remained to a considerable extent engaged in it, so tenacious is that enemy which every thinker carries in himself and which he should tear from his heart, yet cannot resist.

But without entering into a particular account of the assumptions made by the romantics and idealists in the construction of their 'philosophies of history,' it will be sufficient to observe the consequences, in order to point out the transcendental tendency of their constructions. These were such as to compromise romantic histories in the method and to damage them in the execution, though they were at first so vigorously conceived as a unity of philosophy and philology. One of the consequences was precisely the falling again into contempt of erudition among those very people who adopted and promoted it, and on other occasions a recommendation of it in words and a contempt of it in deeds. This contradictory attitude was troubled with an evil conscience, so much so that its recommendations sound but little sincere, the contempt timid, when it shows itself, though it is more often concealed. Nevertheless one discovers fleeting words of revelation among these tortuosities and pretences, such as that of an *a priori history* (Fichte, Schelling, Krause, and, to a certain extent at least, Hegel), which should be true history, deduced from the pure concepts, or rendered divine in some vision of the seer of Patmos, a history which should be more or less different from the confusion of human events and facts, as philosophical history, leaving outside it as refuse a merely *narrative* history, which should serve as raw material or as text for the sermons and precepts of the moralists and politicians. And we see rising from the bosom of a philosophy, which had tried to make history of itself, by making philosophy also history (proof that the design had not been really translated into act), the distinction between philosophy and history, between the historical and the philosophical way of thinking, and the mutual antipathy and mutual unfriendliness of the two orders of researchers. The 'professional' historians were obliged to defend themselves against their progenitors (the philosophers), and they ended by losing all pity for them, by denying that they were philosophers and treating them as intruders and charlatans.

Unpleasantness and ill-will were all the more inevitable in that the 'philosophers of history'—that is to say, the historians obsessed with transcendency—did not always remain content (nor could they do so, speaking strictly) with the distinction between philosophical and narrative history, and, as was natural, attempted to harmonize the two histories, to make the facts harmonize with the schemes which they had imagined or deduced. With this purpose in view, they found themselves led to use violence toward facts, in favour of their system, and this resulted in certain most important parts being cut out, in a Procrustean manner, and in others that were accepted being perverted to suit a meaning that was not genuine but imposed upon them. Even the chronological divisions, which formed a merely practical aid to narratives, were tortured (as was the custom in the Middle Ages) that they might be elevated to the rank of ideal divisions. And not only was the light of truth extinguished in the pursuit of these caprices, not only were individual sympathies and antipathies introduced (take as an instance typical of all of them the idealization of Hellas and of this or that one of the Hellenic races), but there appeared a thing yet more personally offensive to the victims—that is to say, there penetrated into history, under the guise of lofty philosophy, the personal loves and hates of the historian, in so far as he was a party man, a churchman, or belonged to this or that people, state, or race. This ended in the invention of Germanism, the crown and perfection of the human race, a Germanism which, claiming to be the purest expression of Arianism, would have restored the idea of the elect people, and have one day undertaken the journey to the East. Thus were in turn celebrated semi-absolute monarchy as the absolute form of states, speculative Lutheranism as the absolute form of religion, and other suchlike vainglorious vaunts, with which the pride of Germany oppressed the European peoples and indeed the whole world, and thus exacted payment in a certain way for the new philosophy with which Germany had endowed the world. But it must not be imagined that the pride of Germany was not combated with its own arms, for if the English speculated but little and the French were too firm in their belief in the *Gesta Dei per Francos* (become the *gestes* of reason and civilization), yet the peoples who found themselves in less happy conditions, and felt more keenly the censure of inferiority or of senility thus inflicted upon them, reacted: Gioberti wrote a *Primato d'Italia*, and Ciezkowski a *Paternostro*, which foretold the future primacy of the Slavonic people and more especially of the Poles.

Yet another consequence of the 'philosophies of history' was the reflourishing of 'universal histories,' in the fallacious signification of complete histories of humanity, indeed of the cosmos, which the Middle Ages had narrated in the chronicles *ab origine mundi* and *de duabus civitatibus* and *de quattuor imperiis*, and the Renaissance and enlightenment had reduced to mere vulgar compilations, finding the centre for its own interest elsewhere. The *imagines mundi* returned with the philosophies of history, and such they were themselves, transcendental universal histories, with the 'philosophy of nature' belonging to them. The succession of the nations there took the place of the series of empires : to each nation, as formerly to each empire, was assigned a special function, which once fulfilled, it disappeared or fell to pieces, having passed on the lamp of life, which must not pass through the hands of any nation more than once. The German nation was to play there the part of the Roman Empire, which should never die, but exist perpetually, or until the consummation of the ages and the Kingdom of God.

To develop the various forms of the philosophy of history would aid in making clear the internal contradictions of the doctrine and in ascribing the reasons for the introduction of certain corrections for the purpose of doing away with the contradictions in question, but which in so doing introduced others. And in making an examination of this kind a special place should be reserved for Vico, who offers a 'philosophy of history' of a very complex sort, which on the one side does not negate, but passes by in silence the Christian and medieval conception (as it does not deny St Augustine's conception of the two cities or of the elect and Gentile people, but only seriously examines the history of the latter), while on the other side it resumes the ancient Oriental motive of the circles (courses and recourses), but understands the course as growth and development, and the recourse as a dialectical return, which on the other hand does not seem to give rise to progress, although it does not seem to exclude it, and also does not exclude the autonomy of the free will or the exception of contingency. In this conception the Middle Ages and antiquity ferment, producing romantic and modern thought.[1] But in the romantic period the idea of the circle (which yet contained a great mental claim that demanded satisfaction) gave place to the idea of a linear course, taken from Christianity and from progress to an end, which concludes with a certain state as limit or with entrance into a paradise of indefinite progress, of incessant joy without sorrow. In a conception of this kind there is at one time a mixture of theology and of illuminism, as in Herder, at another an attempt at a history according to the ages of life and the forms of the spirit, as with Fichte and his school ; then again the idea realizes its logical ideal in time, as in Hegel, or the shadow of a God reappears, as in the deism of Laurent and of several others, or the God is that of the old religion, but modernized, noble, judicious, liberal, as in moderate Catholicism and Protestantism. And since the course has necessarily an end in all these schemes, announced and described and therefore already lived and passed by, attempts to prolong, to prorogue, or to vary that end have not been wanting, such personages as the Abbots Gioacchini arising and calling themselves the 'Slav apocalyptics' or by some other name, and adding

[1] The exposition and criticism of Vico's thought are copiously dealt with in the second volume of my *Saggi filosofici* *I La filosofia di Giambattista Vico* (Bari, 1911).

new eras to those described. But this did not change anything in the general conception. And there was no change effected in it by the philosophies of history of the second Schelling, for example, which are usually called irrationalistic, or of the pessimists, because it is clear that the decadence which they describe is a progress in the opposite sense, a progress in evil and in suffering, having its end in the acme of evil and pain, or leading indeed to a redemption and then becoming a progress toward the good. But if the idea of circles, which repeat themselves identically, oppresses historical consciousness, which is the consciousness of perennial individuality and diversity, this idea of progress to an end oppresses it in another way, because it declares that all the creations of history are imperfect, save the last, in which history comes to a standstill and which therefore alone has absolute value, and which thus takes away from the value of reality in favour of an abstraction, from existence in favour of the inexistent. And both of these—that is to say, all the philosophies of history, in whatever way determined—lay in ambush to overwhelm the conceptions of development and the increase in historiographical value obtained through it by romanticism; and when this injury did not occur (as in several notable historians, who narrated history admirably, although they professed to obey the rules of the abstract philosophy of history, which they saluted from near or far, but took care not to introduce into their narratives), it was a proof that the contradiction had not been perceived, or at least perceived as we now perceive it, in its profound dissonance. It was a sign that romanticism too had problems upon which it laboured long and probed deeply, and others upon which it did not work at all or only worked a little and kept waiting, satisfying them more or less. History too, like the individual who works, does 'one thing at a time,' neglecting or allowing to run on with the help of slight provisional improvements the problems to which it cannot for the time being attend, but ready to direct full attention to them when its hands are free.

VII

THE HISTORIOGRAPHY OF POSITIVISM

THE philosophies of history offended the historical consciousness in three points, as to which it has every right to be jealous: the integrity of historical events, the unity of the narration with the document, and the immanence of development. And the opposition to the 'philosophy of history,' and to the historiography of romanticism in general, broke out precisely at these three points, and was often violent. This opposition had at bottom a common motive, as has been shown clearly by the frequent sympathy and fraternizing among those who represent it, though dissensions as to details are common among them. It is, however, best to consider it in its triplicity for reasons of clearness, and to describe it as that of the *historians*, the *philologists*, and the *philosophers*.

To the historians, by whom we mean those who had a special disposition for the investigation of particular facts rather than theories, and a greater acquaintance with and practice of historical than speculative literature, is due the saying that history *should be history and not philosophy*. Not that they ventured to deny philosophy, for on the contrary they protested their reverence for it and even for religion and theology, and condescended to make an occasional rapid and cautious excursion into those waters; but they generally desired to steer their way through the placid gulfs of historical truth, avoiding the tempestuous oceans of the other discipline: philosophy was relegated to the horizon of their works. Nor did they even contest, at least in principle, the right of existence of those grandiose constructions of 'universal history,' but they recommended and preferred national or otherwise monographical histories, which can be sufficiently studied in their particulars, substituting for universal histories collections of histories of states and of peoples. And since romanticism had introduced into those universal histories and into the national histories themselves its various practical tendencies (which the philosophy of history had then turned into dogmas), the historians placed abstention from national and party tendencies upon their programme, although they reserved the right of making felt their patriotic and political aspirations, but, as they said, without for that reason altering the narrative of the facts, which were supposed to move along independently of their opinions, or chime in with them spontaneously in the course of their natural development. And since passion and the philosophic judgment had been confused and mutually contaminated in romanticism, the abstention was extended also to the judgment as to the quality of the facts narrated ; the *reality* and not the *value* of the fact being held to be the province of the historian, appeal being made to what theorists and philosophers had thought about it, where a more profound consideration of the problem was demanded. History should not be either German or French, Catholic or Protestant, but it should also not pretend to apply a more ample conception to the solution of these or similar antitheses, as the philosophers of history had tried to do, but rather should neutralize them all in a wise scepticism or agnosticism, and attenuate them in a form of exposition conducted in the tone of a presidential summing-up, where careful attention is paid to the opinions of opposed parties and courtesy is observed toward all. There was diplomacy in this, and it is not astonishing that many diplomatists or disciples of diplomacy should collaborate in this form of history, and that the greatest of all the historians of this school, Leopold Ranke, in whom are to be found all the traits that we have described, should have had a special predilection for diplomatic sources. He always, indeed, combated philosophy, especially the Hegelian philosophy, and greatly contributed to discredit it with the historians, but he did this decorously, carefully avoiding the use of any word that might sound too rough or too strong, professing the firm conviction that the hand of God shows itself in history, a hand that we cannot grasp with ours, but which touches our face and informs us of its action. He completed his long and very fruitful labours in the form of monographs, avoiding universal constructions. When, at the end of his life, he set to work to compose a *Weltgeschichte*, he carefully separated it from the universe, declaring that it would have been " lost in phantasms and philosophemes " had he abandoned the safe ground of national histories and sought for any other sort of universality than that of nations, which " acting upon one another, appear one after the other and constitute a living whole." In his first book he protested with fine irony that he was not able to accept the grave charge of judging the past or of instructing the present as to the future, which had been assigned to history, but he felt himself capable only of showing " how things really had happened " (*wie es eigentlich gewesen*) ; this was his object in all his work, and he held fast to it, thus culling laurels unobtainable by others, attaining even to the writing of the history of the popes of the period of the Counter-Reformation, although he was a Lutheran and remained so all his life. This history was received with favour in all Catholic countries. His greatest achievement was to write of French history in a manner that did not displease the French. A writer of the greatest elegance, he was able to steer between the rocks, without even letting appear his own religious or philosophical convictions, and without ever finding himself under the obligation of forming a definite resolution, and in any case never pressing too hard upon the conceptions themselves to which he had recourse, such as 'historical ideas,' the perpetual struggle between Church and State, and the conception of the State. Ranke was the ideal and the master to many historians within, and to some without, his own country. But even without his direct influence, the type of history that he represented germinated everywhere, a little earlier or later according to position and to the calming down of the great political passions and philosophical fervour in the different countries. This took place, for instance, in France earlier than in Italy, where the idealistic philosophy and the national movement made their strength felt in historiography after 1848, and even up to 1860. But the type of history which I should almost be disposed to baptize with the name of 'diplomatic,' taking seriously the designation that I had at first employed jocosely, still meets with success among the moderately disposed, who are lovers of culture, but do not wish to become infected with party passions or to rack their brains with philosophical speculations: but, as may be imagined, it is not always treated with the intelligence, the balance, and the finesse of a Leopold Ranke.

The ambition of altogether rejecting the admission of thought into history, which has been lacking to the diplomatic historians (because they were without the necessary innocence for such an ambition), was, on the other hand, possessed by the philologists, a most innocent group. They were all the more disposed to abound in this sense, since their opinion of themselves, which had formerly been most modest, had been so notably increased, owing to the high degree of perfection attained by research into chronicles and documents and by the recent foundation (which indeed had not been a creation *ex nihilo*) of the critical or historical method, which was employed in a fine and close examination into the origin of sources and the reduction of these, and in the internal criticism of texts. This pride of the philologists prevailed, the method reaching its highest development in a country like Germany, where haughty pedantry flourishes better than elsewhere, and where, as a result of that most admirable thing, scientific seriousness, 'scientificism' is much idolized. This word was also ambitiously adopted for everything that concerns the surroundings and the instruments of true and proper science, such as is the case with the collection and criticism of narratives and documents. The old school of learned men, French and Italian, who did not effect less progress in 'method' than was attained during the nineteenth century in Germany, did not dream that they were thus producing 'science,' much less did they dream of vying with philosophy and theology, or that they could drive them from their positions and take their places with the documentary method. But in Germany every mean little copier of a text, or collector of variants, or examiner of the relations of texts and conjecturer as to the genuine text, raised himself to the level of a scientific man and critic, and not only dared to look upon himself as the equal of such men as Schelling, Hegel, Herder, or Schlegel, but did so with disdain and contempt, calling them 'anti-methodical.' This pseudo-scientific haughtiness diffused itself from Germany over the other European countries, and has now reached America, though in other countries than Germany it met more frequently with irreverent spirits, who laughed at it. Then for the first time there manifested itself that mode of historiography which I have termed 'philological' or 'erudite' history. That is to say, the more or less judicious compilations of sources which used to be called *Antiquitates*, *Annales*, *Penus*, *Thesauri*, presented themselves disguised as histories, which alone were dignified and scientific. The faith of these historians was reposed in a narrative of which every word could be supported by a text, and there was nothing else whatever in their work, save what was contained in the texts, torn from their contexts and repeated without being thought by the philologist narrator. Their object was that their histories should reach the rank of comprehensive compilations, starting from those relating to particular times, regions, and events, and finally attaining to the arrangement of the whole of historical knowledge in great encyclopædias, out of which articles are to be supplied, systematic or definitional, put together by groups of specialists, directed by a specialist, for classical, romantic, Germanic, Indo-European, and Semitic philology. With a view to alleviating the aridity of their labours, the philologists sometimes allowed themselves a little ornament in the shape of emotional affections and ideal view-points. With this purpose, they had recourse to memories of their student days, to the philosophical catchwords which had been the fashion at the time, and to the ordinary sentiments of the day toward politics, art, and morality. But they did all this with great moderation, that they might not lose their reputation for scientific gravity, and that they might not fail in respect toward scientific philological history, which disdains the vain ornaments in which philosophers, dilettantes, and charlatans delight. They ended by tolerating historians of the type above described, but as a lesser evil, and as a general rule inclined to pardon the sins arising out of their commerce with 'ideas' in favour of the 'new documents' which they had discovered or employed, and which they could always dig out of their books as a useful residue, while purifying them from 'subjective' admixtures—that is to say, from the elaboration of them which had been attempted. Philosophy was known to them only as 'philosophy of history,' but even thus rather by reason of its terrible ill-fame than from direct acquaintance. They remembered and were ever ready to repeat five or six anecdotes concerning errors in names and dates into which celebrated philosophers had actually fallen, easily forgetful of the innumerable errors into which they fell themselves (being more liable as more exposed to danger); they almost persuaded themselves that philosophy had been invented to alter the names and confuse the dates which had been confided to their amorous care, that it was the abyss opened by the fiend to lead to the perdition of serious 'documentary history.'

The third band of those opposed to the philosophy of history was composed of philosophers or of historian-philosophers, but of those who rejected the name and selected another less open to suspicion, or tempered it with some adjective, or accepted it indeed, but with opportune explanations: they styled themselves positivists, naturalists, sociologists, empiricists, criticists, or something of that sort. Their purpose was to do something different from what the philosophers of history had done, and since these had worked with the conception of the *end*, they all of them swore that they would work with the conception of the *cause*; they would search out the cause of every fact, thus generalizing more and more widely the causes or the cause of the entire course of history: those others had attempted a *dynamic* of history; they would work at a *mechanic* of history, a social physics. A special science arose, opposed to the philosophy of history, in which that naturalistic and positivistic tendency became exalted in its own eyes: sociology. Sociology classified facts of human origin and determined the laws of mutual dependence which regulated them, furnishing the narratives of historians with the principles of explanation, by means of these laws. Historians, on the other hand, diligently collected facts and offered them to sociology, that it might press the juice out of them—that is to say, that it might classify and deduce the laws that governed them. History and sociology, then, stood to one another in the same relation as physiology and zoology, physics and mineralogy, or in another relation of the same sort; they differed from the physical and natural sciences only by their greater complexity. The introduction of mathematical calculation seemed to be the condition of progress for history as for all the sciences, physical and natural. A new 'science' came forward to support this notion, in the shape of that humble servant of practical administration and inspired creation of bureaucracy known as statistics. And since the whole of science was being modelled upon the idea of a factory of condensation, so were 'syntheses' invoked and outlined for history—that is to say, historical frameworks, in which the laws and facts that dominate single histories should be resumed, as though in a sort of table or atlas, which should show at a glance causes and the facts which arose from them.

Need we recall the names and supporters of this school—Comte, Buckle, Taine, and so on, until we come to those recent historians who follow them, such as Lamprecht and Breysig? Need we recall the most consequent and the most paradoxical programmes of the school, as, for instance, Buckle's introduction to his history of civilization or Bourdeau's book on the *Histoire des historiens*? These and similar positivistic doctrines are present to the memory, either because they are nearest to us chronologically, or because the echo of the noise they made in the world has not yet ceased, and we see everywhere traces of their influence. Everywhere we see it, and above all in the prejudice which they have solidly established (and which we must patiently corrode and dissolve), that history, true history, is to be constructed by means of the *naturalistic* method, and that *causal* induction should be employed. Then there are the manifold naturalistic conceptions with which they have imbued modern thought: race, heredity, degeneration, imitation, influence, climate, historical factors, and so forth. And here, too, as in the case of the philosophies of history, since it suffices us to select only the essential in each fact, we shall not dwell upon the various particular forms of it—that is to say, upon the various modes in which historical causes were enunciated and enumerated, and upon the various claims that one or other of them was supreme: now the race, now the climate, now economy, now technique, and so forth. Here, too, the study of the particular forms would be of use to anyone who wished to develop in particular the dialectic and to trace the internal dissolution of that school, to demonstrate in its particular modes its intrinsic tendency to surpass itself, though it failed to do so by that path.

We have already mentioned that the three classes of opponents of the 'philosophies of history' and the three methods by which they proposed to supplant it—diplomatic, philological, and positivistic history—showed that they disagreed among themselves. Confirmation of this may now be found in the contempt of the diplomatic historians for mere erudition and in their diffidence for the constructions of positivism, the erudite, for their part, being fearful of perversions of names and dates and shaking their heads at diplomatic histories and the careless style of the men of the world who composed them. Finally, the positivists looked upon the latter as people who did not go to the bottom of things, to their general or natural causes, and reproved the erudite with their incapacity for rising to the level of laws and to the establishment of facts in accordance with these laws, sociological, physiological, or pathological. But there is further confirmation of what has been noted in respect to the common conception that animated them all and of their substantial affinity, because when the erudite wished to cloak themselves in a philosophy of some sort, they very readily strutted about draped in some shreds of positivistic thought or phraseology. They also participated in the reserve and in the agnosticism of the positivists and the diplomatic historians toward speculative problems, and in like manner it was impossible not to recognize the justice of their claim that evidence should be reliable and documents authentic. The diplomatic historians agreed with them in the formula that history should not be philosophy and that research should dispense with finality and follow the line of causality. In fact, all three sorts of opponents, at one with the transcendency of the philosophy of history, negated the unity of history with philosophy, but in various degrees and with various particular meanings, with various preliminary studies and in various ways.

And although these schools were in agreement as to what they negated, all three of them become for us exposed to a criticism which unites them beneath a single negation. For not even do the ability and the intelligence of a Ranke avail to give vigour to the moderatism and to maintain firmly the eclecticism of diplomatic history, and the transaction breaks down before the failure on the part of those who attempted it, owing to its being contrary to their own powers and intrinsically impossible. The idea of an agnostic history turns out to be fallacious —that is to say, of a history that is not philosophical but does not deny philosophy, that is not theological but is not anti-theological, limiting itself to nations and to their reciprocal influence upon one another, because Ranke himself was obliged to recognize powers or ideals that are superior to nations and that as such require to be speculatively justified in a philosophy or in a theology. In this way he laid himself open to the accusations of the positivists, who discredited his ideas as 'mystical.' For the same reason others were proceeding to reduce them little by little from the position of ideals or movements of the spirit to natural and physiological products, as was attempted by Lorenz, an ardent follower of Ranke, who, with his doctrine of generation and of heredity, fell into that physiologism and naturalism from which the master had preserved himself. And when this passage from spirituality to nature was accomplished, the dividing line between history and pre-history, between history of civilization and history of nature, was also not respected. On the other hand, a return was made to the 'philosophies of history,' when ideas were interpreted as transcendental and as answering to the designs of the divine will, which governs the world according to a law and conducts it according to a plan of travel. The boasted impartiality and objectivity, which was based upon a literary device of half-words, of innuendoes, of prudent silences, was also equally illusory, and the Jesuit who objected to Ranke and his history of the popes will always prevail from the point of view of rigorous criticism—either the Papacy is always and everywhere what it affirms itself to be, an institution of the Son of God made man, or it is a lie. Respect and caution are out of place here. *Tertium non datur.* Indeed, it was not possible to escape from taking sides by adopting that point of view; at the most a third party was thus formed, consisting of the tolerant, the tepid, and the indifferent. The slight coherence of Ranke's principles can be observed in that part of his *Universal History* where, when speaking of Tacitus he touches upon his own experience as a teacher of history, he declares that "it is impossible to speak of a tranquil and uniform progressive development of historiography either among the ancients or the moderns, because the object itself is formed in the course of time and is always different, and conceptions depend upon the circumstances among which the author lives and writes." He thus comes to perform an act of resignation before blind contingentism, and the present historical sketch shows how unjust this is, for it has traced the organic and progressive development of historical thought from the Greeks to modern times. And the whole of the *Universal History* is there to prove, on the other hand, that his slight coherence of ideas, or web of ideas that he left intentionally vague, made it difficult for him to give life to a vast historical narrative, so lacking in connexion, so heavy, and sometimes even issuing in extraneous reflections, such, for example, as those in the first pages of the first volume, where there is a comparison of Saul and Samuel with the emperors at strife with the popes, and of the policy of Rehoboam and Jeroboam with the political strife between the centralizing states and the centrifugal regions of modern times. We find in general in Ranke an inevitable tendency to subside into the pragmatic method. And what has been said of Ranke is to be repeated of his disciples and of those who cultivated the same conciliatory type of history. As for philological history, the description that has been given of the programme makes clear its nullity, for it leads by a most direct route to a double absurdity. When the most rigorous methods of examining witnesses is really applied, there is no witness that cannot be suspected and questioned, and philological history leads to the negation of the truth of that history which it wishes to construct. And if value be attributed to certain evidence arbitrarily and for external reasons, there is no extravagance that may not be accepted, because there is no extravagance that may not have honest, candid, and intelligent men on its side. It is not possible to reject even miracles by the philological method, since these repose upon the same attestations which make certain a war or a peace treaty, as Lorenz has shown by examining the miracles of St Bernard in the light of the severest philological criticism. In order to save himself from the admission of the inconceivable and of the nullification of history, which follows the nullification of witnesses, there remains nothing but appeal to thought, which reconstitutes history from the inside, and is evidence to itself, and denies what is unthinkable for the very reason that it is not to be thought. This appeal is the declaration of bankruptcy for philological history. We may certainly say that this form of history more or less sustains itself as history, to the extent that it has recourse to all the aids furnished by history proper, and contradicts itself; or it contradicts itself and yet does not sustain itself, or only for a little while and in appearance, by again adopting the methods of pragmaticism, of transcendency, and of positivism. And the last of these in its turn encounters the same experiences in a different order, because its principle of history that explains facts causally presupposes the facts, which as such are thought and therefore are in a way already explained. Hence a vicious circle, evident in the connexion between history and sociology, each one of which is to be based upon and at the same time to afford a base for the other, much in the same way as a column which should support a capital and at the same time spring from it. But if, with a view to breaking the circle, history be taken as the base and sociology as its fulfilment, then the latter will no longer be the explanation of the former, which will find its explanation elsewhere. And this will be, according to taste, either an unknown principle or some form of thought that acts in the same way as God, and in both cases a transcendental principle. Hence we have the fact of positivism leading to philosophies of history, as exemplified in the Apocalypses and the Gospels of Comte, of Buckle, and of others of like sort: they are all most reverent theologians, but chaotic, falling back into those fallacious conceptions which had been refuted by romantic historiography.

Truly, when faced with such histories as these, superficial or unintelligent or rude and fantastic, romanticism, conscious of the altitude to which it had elevated the study of the development of human affairs, might have exclaimed (and indeed it did exclaim by the mouth of its epigoni) to its adversaries and successors, in imitation of the tone of Bonaparte on the 18th of Brumaire: "What have you done with the history which I left to you so brilliant? Were these the new methods, by means of which you promised to solve the problems which I had not been able to solve? I see nothing in them but *revers et misère*!" But we who have never met with absolute regressions during the secular development of historiography shall not allow ourselves to be carried away upon the polemical waves now beating against the positivistic and naturalistic school which is our present or recent adversary, to the point of losing sight of what it possessed that was substantially its own, and owing to which it really did represent progress. We shall also refrain from drawing comparisons between romanticism and positivism, by measuring the merits of both, and concluding with the assertion of the superiority of the former; because it is well known that such examinations of degrees of merit, the field of professors, are not permissible in history, where what follows ideally after is virtually superior to that from which it is derived, notwithstanding appearances to the contrary. And in the first place, it would be erroneous, strictly speaking, to believe that what had been won by romanticism had been lost in positivism, because when the histories of this period are looked upon from other points of view and with greater attention, we see how they were all preserved. Romanticism had abolished historical dualism, for which there existed in reality positive and negative, elect and outcast, facts. Positivism repeated that *all facts are facts* and all have an equal right to enter history. Romanticism had substituted the conception of development for the abysses and the chasms that previous historiography had introduced into the ocurse of events, and positivism repeated that conception, calling it *evolution*. Romanticism had established periods in development, either in the form of a cycle of phases, like Vico, or as phases without a circle and in linear order, like the German romantics, and had exemplified the various phases as a series of the forms of the spirit or of psychological forms, and positivism renewed these conceptions (although owing to the lack of culture usual with its adherents it often believed that it had made discoveries never made before), as can be proved by a long series of examples. These range from the *three ages* of mental development of Comte to the *eight phases* of social development or *four political periods* which are respectively the 'novelties' of the contemporaries Lamprecht and Breysig. Romanticism, judging that the explanation of events by means of the caprices, the calculations, and the designs of individuals taken atomistically was frivolous, took as the subject of history the universals, the Idea, ideas, the spirit, nations and liberty, and positivism ; it also rejected individualistic atomicism, talking of *masses*, *races*, *societies*, *technique*, *economy*, *science*, *social tendencies* ; of everything, in fact, with the exception that the caprice of Tizius and Caius was now no longer admitted. Romanticism had now not only reinforced the histories of ideal values, but had conceived them as in organic connexion ; positivism in its turn insisted upon the *interdependence of social factors* and upon the *unity* of the real, and attempted to fill up the interstices of the various special histories by means of the history of *civilization* and of *culture*, and so-called *social* history, containing in itself politics, literature, philosophy, religion, and every other class of facts. Romanticism had overthrown heteronomous, instructive, moralizing, serviceable history, and positivism in its turn boasted that its history was a *science*, an end in itself, like every other science, although like every science it afforded the basis for practice, and was therefore capable of application. Romanticism had enhanced the esteem for erudition, and had given an impetus to intercourse between it and history. But whence did the erudition and philology of the positivistic period derive that pride which made them believe that they were themselves history, save from the consciousness that they had inherited from romanticism, which they had preserved and exaggerated? Whence did they inherit the substance of their method save (as Fueter well notes) from the romantic search for the primitive, the genuine, the ingenuous, which manifested itself in Wolf, who inaugurated the method? It is well to remember that Wolf was a pre-romantic, an admirer of Ossian and of popular poetry. And, finally, what is the meaning of the efforts of positivism to seek out the *causes* of history, the *series* of historical facts, the *unity* of the factors and their dependence upon a *supreme cause*, save the speculations of the romantics themselves upon the manner, the end, and the value of development? Whoever pays attention to all these and other resemblances which we could enumerate must conclude that positivism is to romanticism as was the enlightenment to the Renaissance—that is to say, it is not so much its antithesis as it is the logical prosecution and the exaggeration of its presuppositions. Even its final conversion into theology corresponds to that of romanticism. This is for the rest an obvious matter, for transcendency is always transcendency, whether it be thought of as that of a God or of reason, of nature or of matter.

But thinking of it as Matter or Nature, this naturalistic and materialistic travesty, which at first seems

And as the precise affirmation of the positivity of history represented an advance in thought, so the antithesis of materialism, pushed to an extreme, was an advance in the preparation of the new problem and in the new way of solving the relation between spirit and nature. *Oportet ut scandala eveniant*, and this means that even scandal, the scandal of the absurd, and of offensive false criticisms of human conscience, is an advance.

VIII

THE NEW HISTORIOGRAPHY
CONCLUSION

THE romantic current not only maintained itself in its excesses during the dominion of positivism, and, as we have shown, insinuated itself even into its naturalistic antithesis, but it also persisted in its genuine form. And although we have not spoken of pedantic imitators and conservatives—whose significance is slight in the history of thought, that is to say, confined to the narrow sphere in which they were compelled to think for themselves—we have nevertheless recorded the preservation of romanticism in the eclecticism of Ranke, who adhered to the theories of Humboldt (another 'diplomatist').

Idealistic and romantic motives continued to illuminate the intellect and soul among the philosophers, from Humboldt to Lotze and from Hartmann to Wundt and those who corresponded to them in other countries. The like occurred in historiography properly so called, and could not but happen, because, if the formulas of agnosticism and of positivism had been followed to the letter, all light of thought would have been extinguished in blind mechanicism—that is to say, in nothing—and no historical representation would have been possible. Thus political, social, philosophical, literary, and artistic history continued to make acquisitions, if not equally important with those of the romantic period (the surroundings were far more favourable to the natural sciences and to mathematics than to history), yet noteworthy. This is set forth in a copious volume upon historiography (I refer to the work of Fueter already several times mentioned in this connexion). There due honour will be found accorded to the great work accomplished by Ranke, which the rapidity of my course of exposition has induced me to illustrate rather in its negative aspects, causing me, for instance, to allude solely to the contradictions in the *History of the Popes*, which is notwithstanding a masterpiece. The cogent quality of the romantic spirit at its best is revealed in the typical instance of Taine, who is so ingenuously naturalistic in his propositions and in the directive principles of his work, yet so unrestrainedly romantic in particular instances, as, for example, in his characterization of the French poets or of the Dutch and Italian painters. All this led to his ending in the exaggerated anti-Jacobin romanticism of his *Origines de la France contemporaine*, in the same way that Zola and the other verists, those verbal enemies of romanticism, were lyrical in all their fiction, and the leader of the school was induced to conclude his works with the abstract lyricism of the *Quatre évangiles*. What has been observed of Taine is to be applied to Buckle and to the other naturalists and positivists, obliged to be historical against their will, and to the positivists who became followers of historical materialism, and found the dialectic established in their house without being able to explain what it was or whence it came. Not all theorists of historiography showed themselves to be so resolutely and madly naturalistic as Bourdeau and one or two others; indeed these were few in number and of inferior reputation. Eclecticism prevailed among the majority of them, a combination of necessity and of liberty, of masses and individuals, of cause and end, of nature and spirit: even the philosophy of history was admitted, if in no other form, then as a *desideratum* or a problem to be discussed at a convenient time (even though that were the Greek Kalends). Eclecticism, too, presented the greatest variety, from the low level of a trivial arranging of concepts in an artificial manner to the lofty heights of interior labour, from which it seemed at every moment that a new gospel, no longer eclectic, must issue.

This last form of eclecticism and the open attempts to renew romantic idealism more or less completely, as well as romantic methods of historiography, have become more frequent since modern consciousness has withdrawn itself from positivism and has declared its bankruptcy. But all this is of importance rather as a symptom of a real advance in thought. And the new modern philosophies of intuition and philosophy of values must be looked upon rather as symptoms than as representing progress in thought (I mean in general, and not in the particular thoughts and theories which often form a real contribution). The former of these, however, while it correctly criticizes science as an economic construction useless for true knowledge, then proceeds to shut itself up in immediate consciousness, a sort of mysticism, where historical dialectic finds itself submerged and suffocated; and the latter, placing the conception of value as guardian of the spirit in opposition to the conceptions of science like "a philosophical *cave canem*" (as our imaginative Tari would have said), leaves open a dualism, which stands in the way of the unity of history and of thought as history. When we look around us, therefore, we do not discover that *new philosophy* which shall lay the foundations and at the same time afford justification for the new historiography by solving the antithesis between imaginative romanticism and materialistic positivism.

And it is clear that we are not even able to discuss such a philosophy as a *demand*, because the demand for a particular philosophy is itself the thinking of that particular philosophy, and therefore is not a demand but an actuality. Hence the dilemma either of saying nothing about it, and in this case of not speaking even of positivism as a period that has been closed and superseded, or of speaking of the new philosophy as of something that lives and exists, precisely because it does live and exist. And since to renounce talking of it has been rendered impossible by the very criticism that we have devoted to it, nothing remains save to recognize that philosophy as something that exists, not as something to be invoked. Only we must not *look around us* in order to see where it is, but return *to ourselves* and have recourse to the thought that has animated this historical sketch of historiography and to all the historical explanations that have preceded it. In the philosophy that we have delineated, reality is affirmed to be spirit, not such that it is above the world or wanders about the world, but such as coincides with the world; and nature has been shown as a moment and a product of this spirit itself, and therefore the dualism (at least that which has troubled thought from Thales to Spencer) is superseded, and transcendency of all sorts, whether materialistic or theological in its origin, has also been superseded with it. Spirit, which is the world, is the spirit which develops, and is therefore both one and diverse, an eternal solution and an eternal problem, and its self-consciousness is philosophy, which is its history, or history, which is its philosophy, each substantially identical with the other; and consciousness is identical with self-consciousness—that is to say, distinct and one with it at the same time, as life and thought. This philosophy, which is in us and is ours, enables us to recognize it—that is to say, to recognize ourselves outside of us—in the thought of other men which is also our thought, and to discover it more or less clearly and perfectly in the other forms of contemporary philosophy, and more or less clearly in contemporary historiography. We have frequent opportunities of effecting this recognition, which is productive of much spiritual comfort. Quite lately, for instance, while I was writing these pages, the historical work of a historian, a pure historian, came into my hands (I select this instance among many) where I read words at the very beginning which seemed to be my very own: "My book is based upon the conviction that German historical inquiry must elevate itself to freer movement and contact with the great forces of political life and culture, without renouncing the precious tradition of its method, and that it must plunge into philosophy and politics, without experiencing injury in its end or essence, for thus alone can it develop its intimate essence and be both universal and national."[1] This is the philosophy of our time, which is the initiator of a new philosophical and historiographical period.

But it is not possible to write the history of this philosophy and of this historiography, which is *subject* and not *object*, not for the reason generally adopted, which we have found to be false, since it separates the fact of consciousness from the fact, but for the other reason that the history which we are constructing is a history of 'epochs' or of 'great periods,' and the new

[1] Friedrich Meinecke, *Weltburgerthum und Nationalstaat: Studien zur Genesis des deutschen Nationalstaates*, second edition, preface, p. vii (Munchen u. Berlin, Oldenburg, 1911.)

period is new, just because it is not a period—that is to say, something closed. Not only are we not able to describe its chronological and geographical outline, because we are ignorant as to what measure of time it will fill (will it develop rapidly in thirty or forty years, or will it encounter obstacles, yet nevertheless continue its course for centuries?), what extent of countries it will include (will it remain for long Italian or German, confined to certain Italian or German circles, or will it diffuse itself rapidly in all countries, both in general culture and in public instruction?), but we are unable to limit *logically* what may be its value outside these considerations. The reason for this is that in order to be able to describe its limitations, it must necessarily have developed its antitheses—that is to say, the new problems that will infallibly arise from its solutions, and this has not happened: we are ourselves on the waves and we have not furled our sails in port preparatory to a new voyage. *Bis hierher ist das Bewusstsein gekommen* (Knowledge has reached this point in its development), said Hegel, at the end of his lectures upon the philosophy of history; and yet he had not the right to say so, because his development, which went from the unconsciousness of liberty to the full consciousness of it in the German world and in the system of absolute idealism, did not admit of prosecution. But we are well able to say so, for we have overcome the abstractness of Hegelianism.

INDEX OF NAMES

Agnello of Ravenna, 212
Alcmæon of Crete, 93
Aristotle, 72, 79, 166, 188, 189, 190, 198, 221, 222, 232, 239, 240, 262
Asellio, 186
Augustine, St, 57, 178, 205, 207, 208, 209, 211, 213, 214, 218, 248–249, 285
Avito, 205

Bacon, 253
Balbo, C., 36, 45, 266, 278
Bandello, M., 233
Barante, De, 36, 265
Baronio, C., 233
Bartoli, A., 201–202
Baur, C., 273
Beato Renano, 226
Bede, 216
Benedictines, 49, 255
Bernheim, E., 70
Bettinelli, S., 254
Biondo, F., 168, 226, 277
Bodin, 225, 237, 238, 269
Bolingbroke, 30–31
Bonafede, 254
Boscoli, 43
Bossuet, 175, 248–249, 256
Bourdeau, 297, 310
Bracciolini, P., 224
Breysig, C., 297, 304
Brucker, 253, 254
Bruni, L., 224
Bruno, G., 166, 268
Buckle, 46, 297, 302, 310
Buhle, 253
Burckhardt, J., 273
Burke, E., 31

Calchi, 226
Campanella, T., 238, 240
Casanova, 81–82
Cellario, 240
Chateaubriand, 265
Châtelet, Marquise du, 245
Cicero, 47, 187, 190, 196
Ciezkowski, A., 284
Colletta, P., 45
Comines, 222
Comte, A., 175, 270, 297, 302, 304
Condorcet, 175
Cousin, 273

Dahlmann, 266
Daniel, 195, 213, 225
Dante, 221, 222, 258
Davidsohn, 175
Democritus, 200
Descartes, 79, 140, 164, 200, 244, 251, 271
Diodorus Siculus, 196, 197
Diogenes of Halicarnassus, 47, 187, 197
Droysen, 22, 36, 266
Dubos, 253

Eichhorn, 273
Erchempertus, 216, 219
Erdmann, 273
Eusebius of Cæsarea, 206, 209

Ferrari, G., 115
Fichte, 69, 282, 286
Ficker, 266
Fischer, 273
Flint, 71, 175
Florus, 195
Fredegarius, 202
Frederick II of Prussia, 221
Fueter, E., 168, 170, 171–172, 173, 176, 178–179, 224, 225, 252, 253, 255, 257, 266, 277, 305, 310
Fustel de Coulanges, 83, 278

Galiani, F., 269
Gans, E., 273
Gervinus, 266, 273
Giannone, P., 28, 176, 177, 254
Gibbon, 254
Giesebrecht, 266
Gioacchino di Flora, 214, 286
Gioberti, V., 284
Goncourts, 36
Gottl, 128
Gracian, B., 164
Gregory of Tours, 201–202, 216
Grote, 36
Guicciardini, F., 28, 178, 224, 226, 234, 235–236, 238, 248
Guizot, 266

HAMANN, 164, 269
Hartmann, E, 309
Hase, 273
Hecolampadius, 226
Heeren, 253
Hegel, 47, 57–58, 68, 71, 79, 102, 103, 105, 153, 157, 160, 166, 270, 271, 273, 282, 286, 293, 314
Helmholtz, 179
Helvétius, 267
Herbart, 270
Herder, 124, 273, 274, 286, 293
Herodotus, 35, 178, 181, 182, 183–184, 185, 206
Hesiod, 181, 184
Hirth, 273
Holbach, d', 267
Homer, 181, 184
Hugo Falcando, 220
Humboldt, 47, 309
Hume, 269, 279

JAMSILLA (pseudo), 220, 221
Jerome, St, 213

KANT, 73, 79, 133–153, 244, 246, 273, 306
Kluger, 273
Krause, 282

LABRIOLA, 45, 70
Lamprecht, 297, 304
Lanzi, 254
Lassalle, 273
Laurent, 286
Leibnitz, 166, 200, 255
Leo, 266
Lessing, 268, 273
Liutprand of Cremona, 217
Livy, 35, 167, 178, 185, 195, 250, 262
Locke, 258
Lombroso, C, 307
Lorenz, O, 115, 299, 301
Lotze, 309
Lucian, 186, 187
Luther, 242

MACHIAVELLI, 28, 31, 164, 169–170, 171, 175–176, 178, 224, 226, 231–232, 234, 235, 236, 248, 250, 262
Magdeburg group of reformed divines, 233
Malaterra, 220
Malebranche, 140, 251
Manzoni, A, 265, 277–278
Marheinecke, 273
Marineo, L, 228
Mario Vittorino, 20
Marsilio of Padua, 221
Martial, 231
Martin Polonus, 222
Marx, K, 35, 79, 267, 271
Maurini, 168
Meinecke, F, 313
Meo, A De, 255
Meyer, 273
Michelet, 175, 266
Mommsen, 36, 176, 278, 279
Montesquieu, 253, 254, 269
Moser, J, 150, 186, 253
Mosheim, 248
Muller, G, 266
Muller, K O, 273
Muratori, 254, 255, 256, 277

NAPOLI SIGNORELLI, P, 254
Navagero, A, 231
Neander, 273
Niebuhr, 175, 176, 186, 265, 266, 278

OSSIAN, 305
Otto of Frisia, 209, 211, 214, 218

PAIS, H, 176
Paolo Emilio, 228
Pascal, 164
Paterculus, 195
Patrizzi, F, 214, 237
Paulus Diaconus, 216
Paulus Orosius, 204, 211, 218
Perizonius, 182
Pietro da Eboli, 220
Planck, 273
Plato, 166, 198, 200, 222, 232, 258, 262
Plutarch, 43, 197, 204, 210
Polybius, 57, 58, 167, 178, 185, 186–187, 188, 190, 193, 197, 199, 206, 207
Polydore Virgil, 228
Pontanus, 239
Popelinière, de la, 239

QUINTILIAN, 187, 190
Quintus Curtius, 184

RANKE, 266, 291–292, 299, 300–301, 309, 310
Raumer, 266
Renan, 38
Riccardo da San Germano, 220

Rickert, 70
Ricobaldo of Ferrara, 221
Robbia, L Della, 43
Robertson, 253, 279
Rollin, 175
Romualdo Guarna, 220
Rotteck, 266
Rousseau, 32, 246, 269
Rumohr, 273
Ruskin, 273

SABA MALASPINA, 220
Sabellicus, M A, 224
Sainte-Beuve, 273
Sainte-Palaye, 254
Sallust, 195, 196, 197
Salvemini, G, 175
Sanctis, F. de, 74, 131–132, 273
Sanctis, G de, 176
Sarpi, 31, 226
Savigny, 273
Schelling, 282, 293
Schlegel, 273, 293
Schlosser, 89–90
Schnaase, 273
Schopenhauer, 103, 104, 270
Scipio, 195
Seneca, 196
Sextus Empiricus, 72
Shakespeare, 258
Sigonio, C, 226
Simmel, 70
Sismondi, 266
Socrates, 190, 271
Spaventa, B, 273
Spencer, 312
Spinoza, 164, 200
Spittler, 273
Strauss, 273

TACITUS, 35, 167, 178, 184, 185, 190, 194, 195, 197, 300
Taine, 65, 66, 68, 75–76, 297, 307, 310
Tari, A., 311
Telesino, Abbot, 220
Thales, 181, 312
Thierry, 36, 278
Thomas Aquinas, 221
Thucydides, 178, 183, 184, 185, 186, 190, 193, 197
Tiedemann, 253
Tiraboschi, 254
Tocqueville, 175
Tolstoi, 54
Tosti, L, 266, 278
Treitschke, 266
Troya, 266, 278
Turgot, 268–269

ULRICI, 167

VALLA, 226
Vasari, 231, 235, 236, 240–241
Vega, Lope de, 172
Vico, G B, 31, 79, 96, 102–103, 105, 124, 164, 171, 191, 229, 269–270, 275, 277–278, 285–286, 304
Villani, G, 220, 222
Villari, P, 175
Villemain, 273
Voltaire, 150, 175–176, 245, 248–263, 269, 272, 279, 281
Vossius, 167, 238–239

WACHLER, 168–169
Widekind, 216
Winckelmann, 124, 176–177, 253, 254, 273
Wolf, 273, 305
Wundt, 309

XENOPHON, 185

ZELLER, 71, 273
Zeno, 181
Zola, 310
Zwingli, 226

Lightning Source UK Ltd.
Milton Keynes UK
174804UK00004B/14/P

9 781177 698368